Séamus MacHugh

CYPRUS

An Island Apart
a personal experience

Rimal Publications

By the same author: *Half Way Round the World in 180 Days*

© Séamus MacHugh 1999

First published in 1999
by Rimal Publications
P.O.Box 57017
Limassol 3311- Cyprus

ISBN 9963-610-14-5

Edited by
Fox Communications and Publications
UK

Designed by EN TIPIS Voula Kokkinou
9A Avlonos str., 1075 Nicosia Cyprus
Tel.: 357-2-767291, Fax: 357-2-765438

Printed and bound in Cyprus
by Zavallis Litho Ltd

Cover from a painting by Georgios Kepola
Photographs by Sandra and Séamus MacHugh, Voula Kokkinou
and Kathy Fitzpatrick

For my wife Sandra
and our children Fionn, Siobhan and Conor
whose company is always such a pleasure
and to the children of our extended family,
Chiara, Jérôme and Mina
whose company we are unable to enjoy often enough

ACKNOWLEDGEMENTS

I would like to say 'thank you' for your company to those of my friends who shared some of the journeys of this book with me: to Kathy and Sean Fitzpatrick from Bavaria, Tony Hill from Australia, Peg and Brent Barr and Janie Ravenhurst from Canada, Amee Persaud from New York, Edith and Bill Schwartz from elsewhere in the US and Najla Srouji from the Côte d'Ivoire, the last three long-time residents of Cyprus. Their combined breadth of knowledge filled many gaps in mine. I am especially indebted to Christakis Georgiou, novelist and playwright for reading the first draft of this book, for his correction of historical inaccuracies as well as for the valuable suggestions he made; to the erudite antiquarian Aghis Philippides for reading the final draft with such meticulous care and enthusiasm that it was a pleasure to correct errors and implement his helpful comments; to Lorna Flynn for indispensable 'technical' assistance, to Najla Srouji again for her occasional (sometimes mystifying) facilitations and to my dear friend Costas who on many, many occasions joyfully disputed with me on the 'Cyprus Solution', never, he insisted, on the 'Cyprus Problem.' His first recommendation for a solution, always said smilingly and without malice, was 'we must get rid of the sultan' (meaning Denktash). Sadly Costas passed away unexpectedly on Good Friday last year. His exuberant laugh and generous personality has left an unfillable gap in many lives. I am particularly grateful to Bernadette and Peter Boylan for the loan of their summer house in Kilkee, Co. Clare, Ireland. The week I spent there, correcting the proofs of this book, was thoroughly enjoyable. Sincere thanks also to my friendly, wise and 'expeditious' editor, Leonard Harrow, and to my publisher, Nora Shawwa, for her enthusiasm and encouragement and for being the warm, generous person that she is. Finally, a very special vote of thanks to my wife, Sandra, my constant and (usually) cheerful companion on these as on so many other journeys whose constructive criticism and professional proof reading are always an additional bonus.

Séamus MacHugh
Cyprus, 1999

CONTENTS

Map
Introduction

The spelling of place names in this book is the one used by the Public Information Office in its most recent maps. The author reluctantly accepts the name changes to facilitate the tourist-readers of this book

IN AND AROUND NICOSIA

IN AND AROUND LARNAKA

NORTHERN CYPRUS

IN AND AROUND LIMASSOL

PAFOS AND AKAMAS

A DAY IN THE TROODOS MOUNTAINS

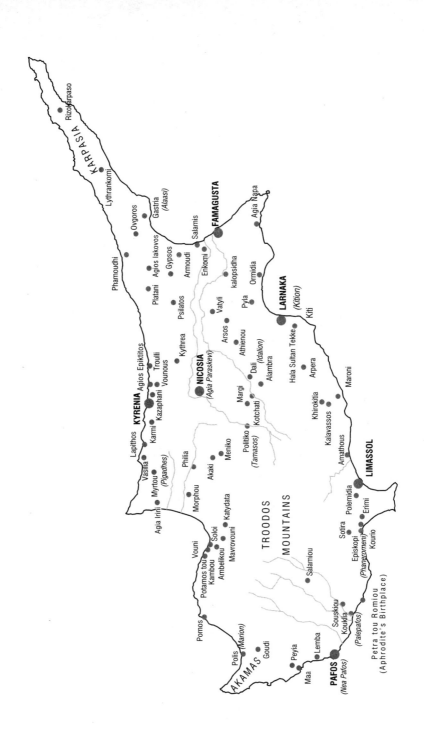

INTRODUCTION

This book was written, at least partly, in response to a review in the Cyprus Weekly (March 1995) of a previous book by the author. In the concluding paragraph of his review of *Half Way Round the World in 180 Days*, the reviewer wrote: 'It's a pity that the book was written before Mr MacHugh arrived in Cyprus but I am sure that his stay on the island will provide more than enough material for a second volume of memoirs.' I took that innocent remark as a kind of challenge.

There are at least two other reasons why the book was written. One was my own impulse to put in writing my personal experience of Cyprus over several years of living here. It is not, therefore, a fly-by-night book, neither does it claim to be an erudite disquisition on the political situation existing in Cyprus today.

It is not a book for scholars who want to study deeply the history of the island, although I hope that it will go some way towards satisfying the reasonable curiosity of intelligent people.

In Cyprus there is everywhere a wealth of archaeological remains, a history written in marble and stone that is fascinating and a perennial culture going back 5,000 years or more. The book is about some of that. It is also indirectly about a people that at times in their turbulent past lost everything but their own soul. There is in Cyprus still a village life, wild scenery, incandescent light and the omnipresence of a Christian Church as old as Christianity itself. There are on this island two peoples, both calling themselves

Cypriot, still sadly living apart, holding separate traditions but with a common bond that unites them to this historic place.

The book tells of things such as those. And much more. There is also my very personal experience of living for the second time in my life only a few minutes drive from a controversial border, the other one being that between the two parts of Ireland.

An additional reason for writing the book is that I perceived a need for it. There are guidebooks to Cyprus, some good ones, others of less interest to the ordinary reader. But, as far as I am aware, there is none that offers to the visitor a mix of history, culture and personal experience told in a lighter vein. Approximately two million people visit Cyprus each year, a great many of whom would like to balance the pleasures of beach and sun with an appreciation of the other riches the country has to offer. The island is small enough and places of interest accessible enough, to make it possible over a week or two, to combine the luxury of a mild dose of hedonism at the beach with the deeper thrill of a cultural experience. The purpose of this book is not to supplant the good guide books on Cyprus – they serve a different purpose – but to offer visitors to the island a pleasant read, in the hope also of making their visit more enjoyable and rewarding.

Nicosia
February 1999

In and Around Nicosia

1

ROLLERCOASTER RULE

I caught my first glimpse of Cyprus through a heat haze. As the Alitalia plane circled lower and lower, the wide embrace of Larnaka Bay shimmered below me and through the streaky porthole window I could see, stretching to the east, an elongated, white ribbon of hotels and apartment blocks. When the plane banked, the spread of the city north and west became apparent. Larnaka had become a tourist town. Here, as elsewhere, the romantic brochures had succeeded only too well, ultimately negating themselves in the process, for the more attractive and 'romantic' a holiday destination is advertised, the more likely it is that after a few years it becomes the victim of its own popularity. Mass advertising spawns mass tourism and mass tourism inhibits all but the cheapest forms of romance. For which we are all to blame. Why should I alone and not tens of thousands of others go to where the sun shines daily and the silver beaches beckon? Democracy is the spoiler of romance. At least 80 percent of my fellow passengers on the flight were tourists, taking sun, sand and sea for granted, possibly sex, too (was this not Aphrodite's Isle, after all?), looking forward to the anonymity of the crowd, where, strangers in a foreign land, they could be themselves, that is, as unlike themselves for the other 50 weeks of the year as possible. I was not a tourist and was to find out over the following three years that Cyprus has a lot more to offer besides sun and beaches. Meantime the plane, having made its final turn over rocks and baren land, approached the runway. A perceptible shuffle and a spattering of voices as the wheels touched the ground; then the brisk, informative bulletin from the steward: *siamo arrivati all'aereoporto internazionale di Larnaka ... sono le ore sedici, tempo locale ... la temperatura in città è 37 Celsius.* So here I was in sweltering heat at 4 pm on 31 August, 1995.

I was met by Sandra, my wife, oven brown and relaxed, who had preceded me to Cyprus by three weeks. She was, she told me triumphantly, driving a borrowed, air-conditioned car. Welcome news, indeed, but, despite the heat, I was glad to be 'home' after eight weeks on the road. Home was an apartment in Nicosia I had not yet seen but where we were to stay during our time in Cyprus. Over a long, cool drink we swapped family news and the latest gossip about friends. I had many questions about Cyprus, its climate and its people, the social environment and the political situation. Before coming here, we had, of course, read the books that were available to us in New Zealand, not many, as it turned out, and I knew some of the answers already but I wanted confirmation from my wife's three week old experience of life on the island. I little realised then that three years later, I would still be asking questions and not always be satisfied by the answers. But all that was to come. Soon, on this last day of August, we were on the road to Nicosia, the capital, driving into a burning sun through a bare, barren plain, called the Mesaoria, craggy and unprepossessing, a moonscape, bereft alike of trees and animals. The African savannah, near where I once lived in Tanzania, was more interesting. My first impression of Cyprus was that it was made of chalk.

Why, I hear you ask, did I land in the airport of a relatively small, coastal town 45 kms from the capital? Hasn't Nicosia got its own airport? Well, yes and no (a frequent enough reply in Cyprus, I was to find out, especially in answer to questions about recent Cypriot history and the current political situation). So, yes, it does have an airport and an international one at that, but no, it's not operational. It was bombed and cratered during the 1974 war with Turkey (of which more later) and, for political reasons, hasn't yet been repaired. At the time of the invasion it was guarded and held by troops of the United Nations who were prepared to defend it by any and all means, if necessary, and now lies in the buffer zone between the two areas of divided Cyprus (and divided Nicosia). The UN keeps a small helicopter base there but I have yet to hear a plane land or take off from what was once Nicosia International Airport. There's more behind all this, of course, than meets the eye and here is probably as good a place as any to tell you a little of the history of Cyprus in the hope that the present situation will become clearer to you.

For our purposes here we'll go back to the end of the 12th century, more precisely to 6 May 1190. On that day Richard 1 of

England, called the Lionheart, was leading the Third Crusade to the Holy Land when a terrible storm blew up near the coast of Cyprus and his fleet was shipwrecked off Amathous, 10 kms east from Limassol. When he got ashore he found that his beloved sister, Joanna, and his less beloved fiancée, Berengaria, who, like Desdemona, had reached the shelter of the harbour a day or two before the main fleet, had been ill-treated by the local despot and self-styled emperor, Isaac Comnenus. Richard was naturally outraged at this turn of events and responded by trading insults of such vulgarity and vigour with Comnenus that a pretext was provided him to let his men loose in Amathous, pillaging and destroying it. The soldiers of Comnenus were no match for Richard's seasoned troops so he decided to push on and take over the whole island. Within a very short time he proclaimed himself Lord of Cyprus, thereby establishing what might be called the first tenuous 'British connection' with the island. Interesting to note that just 21 years previously his father, Henry II, had become Overlord of Ireland, establishing a 'British connection' there, too. Neither 'connection' was to prove particularly felicitous.

Jolted no doubt by the ferocity of the storm, the Lionheart decided to tidy up his affairs with such alacrity that, six days after he landed, he married Berengaria in a glittering ceremony in the Byzantine citadel at Limassol, precursor to the Crusader castle which is still there and also had her crowned queen of England. But there was more to be done as he didn't really want to keep the island and, what, with the wedding and the repairs to his fleet, he was in urgent need of ready cash. Short though his remaining time on the island was – two weeks – he still managed to find a buyer for it and made a quick sale to the Knights Templar on hire purchase terms for £100,000. A lot of money in 1191! Tradition has it that he also managed to fit in a honeymoon in the castle at Kyrenia but, as he was reputedly gay, the brief time available for Berengaria would not have mattered greatly to him. So, after a busy, profitable and, we should hope, on the whole, enjoyable three weeks, Richard, on 1 June, resumed his leadership of the Third Crusade!

I thought of him and his knights as we drove up the new double-carriage highway. His troops would have taken a similar route to fight the decisive battle of 'the war' against Comnenus. From Limassol to Nicosia is a distance of 87 kms and it can occasionally be as hot in Cyprus in May as in August. Had these been the temperatures in May 1191 I don't know whether I should have had more sympathy for the horses or the foot soldiers, but in such weather it would not have been a pleasant journey for either. Even Richard himself was taken ill by the time they reached Nicosia and had to hand over command of the army to the more seasoned Guy de Lusignan.

The Templars turned out to be brutal landlords and also fell behind in their payments so, in a year's time, Richard called in his debt and, for the second time, sold the island. The buyer this time was Guy de Lusignan, ex-king of Jerusalem. Guy and his fellow Crusaders mixed in well with the local populace, as French colonials usually do and, at the same time, imparted to them their Western culture thus initiating what some (mainly Westerners) have called the 'Golden Age of Medieval Cyprus'. The Lusignans, or Franks, as they were also called, built and, over the following several centuries, continued to build cathedrals, monasteries and castles. They also made the island the chief trading centre for the whole Mediterranean region.

King succeeded king in the boisterous fashion of the late Middle Ages but the island enjoyed a period of relative peace and progress which lasted for nearly 200 years until two 'Italians', one Genovese, the other Venetian, caused an international incident by disputing which of them should hold the right hand reins of the king's horse! Of such frivolous vanities are wars made. Genoa did, indeed, go to war with Cyprus and for 90 years held on to the flourishing port of Famagusta but the Venetians didn't forget and exactly 100 years later, in a subtle piece of *Realpolitik*, betrothed one of their own, Caterina Cornaro, as wife and consort to King James II of Cyprus. When her husband died prematurely, Caterina succeeded to the throne, becoming the last queen of Cyprus. In 1489, however, under pressure from home, she was persuaded to hand over Cyprus to the Venetians who turned out to be not at all popular with the local population. They imposed heavy taxes and were really only interested in building strong, bulky, military fortifications against an anticipated invasion by the Turks. They did a good job on the walls which still grandly stand around the old city of Nicosia, as well as in Famagusta and Kyrenia. Their prescience, too, proved correct, for the Turks, in the days of the Ottoman empire, looked askance at this history of revolving-door potentates in an island just off their shores and decided that it was their turn next; so, in 1570 Sultan Selim II occupied the island bringing it under Turkish control. The Turks held on to it for the following 308 years until, at the Treaty of San Stefano in 1878, which ended hostilities between Russia and Turkey, the then sultan leased it to Britain as 'payment for favours received'. In the upheaval of 1914 Britain annexed Cyprus making it a Crown Colony in 1925.

Boulders and chalkfaced crags of rock had by now given way to fertile land. Not all was green, however, as the long rainless summer had followed a winter drought, an occurrence that would repeat itself over the following three years. Signposts indicated villages. We saw one or two on the flat plain, choked by the sun and shimmering in the early evening heat. Others, to our left, had located themselves more sensibly in the foothills of the long mountain range called the Troodos. They could expect a gentle, winnowing wind by nightfall, enough to dry sweat and make sitting outside pleasant. Nicosia, Sandra told me, used to have the enviable reputation of halving its daytime temperature at night because of a topographical gift of the gods that funnelled cool breezes down from the tall Pentadaktylos Range close by. Now, though the winds still come, there are fewer trees and more cement block high rises which retain heat. But thankfully, she said, it was still possible to get a good night's sleep in Nicosia without air-conditioning.

Soon after the Second World War while the long draught of the Cold War began settling in on Europe, India achieved independence, Ireland declared itself a republic and 'winds of change' began blowing across Africa. Cyprus, too felt the stirrings of similar aspirations for uniting Cyprus with Greece – *Enosis* – begun in the 30s, became more belligerent, resulting in the mid 50s in an underground armed struggle. There were eventually two underground movements, EOKA A and EOKA B, the pro-Greece one(s) and TMT, the pro-Turkish one whose goal was TAXIM, a partitioned island. A word of further clarification about the two EOKAs. The acronym, translated into English, means 'The National

Organization of Cypriot Fighters'. EOKA A was founded in 1955 by General George Grivas, a Cypriot who followed a career in the Greek army. He had experience of leading guerrilla groups in World War 11 and in the Greek civil war which followed. Passionate about getting rid of British colonial rule and just as enthusiastic about promoting union with Greece, he led a campaign of sabotage and armed guerrilla warfare towards achieving those ends. When the British left in 1960 his first goal was, indeed, achieved but the constitution establishing the Republic barred the second. However, when the colonels staged a successful coup in Athens in 1967, the idea of *Enosis* was revived and Cyprus was to become the first addition to a 'Greater Greece'. In order to achieve this, the Junta would first have to topple Makarios, the Archbishop-President of an independent Cyprus who now wanted to keep it that way. Grivas was again chosen to lead a subversive campaign and to do so he formed EOKA B. The end result of this sedition was the tragedy of 1974.

History ran deep through the veins of both Greek and Turkish Cypriots. Turkey had ruled Cyprus for over 300 years prior to 1878 and Turkish Cypriots (in 1960 about 18 percent of the population) were different from their Greek co-citizens in language, religion and culture. Greek Cypriots, on the other hand, were there from time immemorial and had absorbed successive, lengthy occupations by Assyrians, Phoenicians, Romans and Franks without ever sacrificing their Hellenic soul. Nevertheless, despite their different ancestries, each community had learned to live more or less amicably with the other until the political push for union with Greece. *Enosis* changed the equation. Britain knew that neither the Turkish Cypriots nor Turkey (old enemies of Greece, anyway) would ever consent to the union of Cyprus with mainland Greece, a thousand miles away, in effect presenting to the latter what was tantamount to an immovably moored fleet of potentially aggressive aircraft carriers forty miles off the Turkish coast. Under these circumstances Britain in 1960, with the concurrence of Turkey and Greece, devised a constitution for Cyprus which its leader, Archbishop Makarios III, had no option but to accept. But it was a flawed constitution whose glaring inequalities were destined to provoke future conflict between the two different ethnic communities. Turkish Cypriots, for example, though only 18 per cent of the population, were guaranteed 40 percent representation in both the police and the army and 30 percent in the civil service which had traditionally provided them with safe jobs. The Greek Cypriots, not surprisingly, could not stomach this undemocratic measure, though they were themselves more interested – and suited – to entrepreneurial activity. Their extraordinary talent for making money improved the material development of the new republic and made them prosperous. The Turkish Cypriot, on the other hand, was by temperament less interested in the country's economic expansion and also less driven in the acquisition of personal wealth.

In time the Greek Cypriots resented their Turkish co-citizens benefiting from *their* 'economic miracle' and sought to have political power commensurate with their numbers and their economic power. On their side, the Turks, followers of the Prophet, had to stomach the unpalatable pill of being ruled by a Greek Orthodox archbishop as president. And an autocratic one at that! The stage was set. There was dissension galore to capitalise on, especially the determination of the president to change the constitution to make it more representative of the numerical balance between the two ethnic peoples who make up the island. Turkish Cypriots, on the other hand, were happy with the constitution as it was and wanted the status quo to continue.The 13 points that Makarios wanted changed in the constitution were rejected, not first by the Turkish Cypriot leadership but by Ankara, whose ambassador handed over a letter to Makarios on December 16 which he rejected. Things began to boil up between the two communities. Five days later a police patrol car was fired on and in the fracas a policeman was wounded and a young Turk was killed. Next day all Turkish Cypriot Government employees left their posts and fortified themselves in their own enclaves. The following day the Armenian quarter of Nicosia was attacked by Turkish Cypriots extremists and a number of Turkish Cypriot patients at the hospital 'went missing', presumed killed. On Christmas Eve things deteriorated with both Turkish Cypriot and Greek Cypriot army contingents leaving their barracks and taking up offensive positions. Shots were fired. Tension grew. Old animosities flared and within 24 hours, on Christmas night, that festive night on which the whole

Christian community around the world was commemorating the birth of the Prince of Peace, the pro-*Enosis* dissidents in Makarios' own camp attacked the Turks and there was a bloodbath. Some would have it that hundreds were killed but whatever the truth of the matter (and much of it is still murky) those few days became a watershed in the relations between the two communities.

We had already reached the outskirts of Nicosia. There was the inevitable evidence of city sprawl with new buildings, mostly commercial, under construction. Passing us as we drove towards the city centre were the usual, cylindrical tankers, growling at their ceaseless task of ferrying petrol to the city (three years hence some would be ferrying water too), long-framed lorries bearing containers and other, stumpier ones, more numerous, with their carapaces of perpetually revolving cement mixers. Buses, too, grandiose and sleek, with darkened sun-proof windows, full of tourists up from Agia Napa, Larnaka or Limassol for a day's sight-seeing in Nicosia – and cars. I was surprised at the number of late model BMWs and Mercedes. Not for the first time I asked myself why hadn't I heard more about Cyprus before coming here? Six months ago I couldn't have said whether it was first world, or third world and did events of the Cold War, I wondered and Tanzania's own minuscule revolt in 1963, squeeze out all mention in the local press there of the greater bloodbath in Nicosia? Caught up with my own concerns in Tanzania at that time, I was totally unaware of it. I had a lot to catch up on.

As a result of the breakout of hostilities at Christmas 1963, the Turkish community pulled itself out of the constitutional administration of the island and set up their own structures in their own enclaves, much as the IRA did in the 1970s in establishing 'no go' areas in Northern Ireland. Peaceful co-existence was shattered. The unitary state was no more. In 1964 a UN peacekeeping force was stationed on the island and, after a lengthy cooling off period, intercommunal talks were set up. By the early 70s both sides were ready for an agreement. The Greeks saw that they could, like other small nations, go it alone and succeed; the Turks no longer wanted to be isolated in an economic backwater. These talks might well have succeeded in their mission of establishing an entente had not the junta, known as 'The Colonels', who had assumed power in Greece in 1967, fostered a right wing revolt against Makarios. The Cypriot National Guard staged a coup in July 1974 and in the ensuing two weeks of disorder and instability, with Britain and Greece refusing to intervene, the Turks twice invaded from the North ostensibly to protect the lives and civil rights of the Turkish minority. The upshot was that the island was divided and the Turkish minority of nearly one-fifth took over almost two-fifths of the territory of the republic. A forced and almost total exodus of the Greek Cypriot population in the North then occurred. Two hundred thousand of them, men, women and children, had to leave their homes, farms and properties, taking what movables they could in cars and trucks. A similar trek in the opposite direction was made by large numbers of Turkish Cypriots, who, understandably in the circumstances, did not feel safe in the South. Over the following years Denktash, the Turkish Cypriot leader in the north, brought over tens of thousands of Anatolian Turks who were given the lands and properties of the exiled Greek Cypriots.

Eventually, in 1983 the Turkish Cypriots, with Denktash as president, set up their own independent state which they call 'The Turkish Republic of Northern Cyprus', often referred to by its acronym TRNC. This is still the situation today though the 'Northern Republic' is recognised only by Turkey and various resolutions of the UN have instructed that it be dismantled. The border, the Green Line, as it's called here, cuts through the city of Nicosia and, in its total length, is still guarded and patrolled by over 1,200 United Nations' forces.

Since 1974 tension between the two sides has flared and simmered, simmered and flared, without any serious breach of the peace. All that changed in the autumn of 1996 when four Greek Cypriots and one Turk were killed in angry, tragic and inauspicious cross-border incidents. There remains dispute about who was responsible for the death of the young Turkish soldier (actually of Kurdish descent) but the brutal murder of two of the Greek Cypriots was graphically relayed on world wide television. Passions ran high, Greece and Turkey became more openly and aggressively involved, with the result that the international community, fearing belligerent outcomes, sent envoy after envoy to Nicosia, in the hope of bringing both sides together for peace talks. Some progress has been made but it will take great goodwill on both sides to bridge the gaps that have been allowed to widen and solidify over the past 20 odd years.

At the time of writing in 1998 negotiations for the entry of Cyprus into the European Union are about to begin. Rauf Denktash, the leader of the Turkish Cypriots and the self-styled president of the 'Northern Republic', has refused to join in the negotiations except as a separate state, something that the Greek Cypriots, under their newly re-elected president, Glafcos Clerides, will never agree to. Top US and British diplomats are urgently engaged in seeking a solution to what is rather euphemistically called 'The Cyprus Problem'. They know that it is really a powder keg that could ignite more than Cyprus. S 300 missiles, currently under construction in Russia, are due to be delivered to the Greek Cypriots in a few months time, a development that will surely turn up the heat a notch further.* All this is complicated by the decision of the European Union to put Turkey's accession talks for entry to the EU on the long finger, if on any finger at all and by America's strategic interests in the area. The Cyprus Problem is a geopolitical problem.

It always was. Peter Preston in his perceptive Guardian column of 6 May 1998 calls it 'an artificial tragedy inflicted from outside.' He rightly blames both the British and the Americans and unequivocally states that in 1974 'partition didn't just happen. It was willed, and, in substantial measure, engineered.' That engineering has now come 'home to roost'. There will be no movement on Cyprus, he believes, unless the Turks come to the party, which they are at present loathe to do, unless there is some corresponding movement on their application to join the EU. 'No EU opportunity', he correctly concludes, 'no dice.' The Americans know this too and continue to put pressure on EU members to soften their stance towards Turkey. The entry of the whole island into the European Community, with its policy of gradually raising the living standards of all member states to an equal level, would enormously help the economic re-integration of the island and facilitate a political solution. What is certain is that in today's circumstances the 'Cyprus Problem', which began through outside interference, will not be solved except through outside intervention. A solution is urgent, the time short.

Dame Ann Hercus, the newly appointed Head of the U.N. Mission in Cyprus, is a clear headed and pragmatic New Zealander. Though she has remained tight-lipped about the results of her on -going shuttle diplomacy to break the deadlock between the two sides there are, early in 1999, some indications of a positive outcome.

This then is the island that Sandra and I found ourselves in on 31 August 1995. She had secured a position teaching English literature at the International Baccalaureate level in the American International School of Cyprus. We have seen much of Cyprus over the intervening years, some of it many times and this book is an account of our experiences.

* On the 29th of December 1998 President Clerides cancelled the deployment of S 300 missiles in Cyprus. His personal decision was warmly approved abroad but at home there was some adverse political fall out.

2

PERSPECTIVES FROM A FIFTH STOREY WINDOW

Living five storeys up (out of ten) with no garden and no animals is a new experience. No dog to walk. No roses to tend. I hasten to add, however, that many flats here improvise on their balconies their own little 'hanging gardens' of boxed flowers and decorative greenery; pot-plants, too, and small shrubs claim attention in hallways and living rooms while on the flat rooftops of the larger apartment blocks there are climbers and spread-out barrel gardens. Dogs? I've seen well groomed ones in our apartment block, often quite large ones, too – German Shepherds, Huskies (in this climate!) Afghans and Labradors. One meets them in the elevators at the end of day and gives them polite, meaningless nods of the head. They are being taken by their proud owners for a walk among the trees in a nearby reserve. Well-mannered creatures, with shiny coats, they seldom growl at you. But, how on earth do they manage! I wonder if they share facilities with their owners, or have these had special stakes implanted on their balconies as conveniences?

Despite the fact that dogs look well cared for, the Cypriot attitude to animals seems to be an ambivalent one. One woman poisoned over a hundred cats on a recent Sunday morning, fifty-six of them, by adoption at least, the property of a well-known Cypriot columnist in an English language newspaper. He's been railing ever since – and rightly so – against the indifference of the various government departments responsible for the welfare of animals. According to him this was not a single, demented incident but additional proof of an attitude to animals that runs deep in Cypriot society. According to the CSPCA there is a reluctance among Cypriots, even an aversion, to having animals spayed, on what grounds I've yet to find out, though a knowledgeable friend offered an explanation, at least as far as cats are concerned. Cats, it seems, are not often kept as domestic pets in Cyprus but rather as peripatetic protectors against snakes. The story goes that St Helena, mother of the Emperor Constantine, was alarmed on a visit to the island by the large number of snakes she encountered. She thereupon suggested that the islanders keep cats (promising to send them a boatload) and suggested they let them run loose outside their houses as natural predators on the snakes. And so apparently they did and still do, even in cities, where the chance of running into a snake is remote. From my window I can see numberless cats sunning themselves in yards and garages, or on the bonnets of cars in the open air car parks beneath our apartment block. I don't know if anyone owns them (I think not) nor who feeds them, though by and large they look well enough fed. I've seen kindly old ladies, either from the flats, or from the nearby houses, all dressed in charcoal black, seemingly 'adopt' three, four or five each and give them leftovers. Sometimes, however, perhaps when the fare is lenten, they – the cats – rush out of the outside garbage containers when you open the door in the morning. But there is not a rat, or a mouse in sight. The lady who gave me the information about the snakes maintains that it's out of respect for St Helena, that Cypriots do not spay their cats. Incidentally, the advice seems to have worked only marginally well as there are still quite a few snakes in the rural areas, only one of which, however, is poisonous. And can a cat kill a snake? Apparently yes, – a friend saw one protect its litter by killing a viper. The poisonous one, the one with the thick body, broad head and blunt nose, is called the *saittaros*. Its horny tail is distinctive but it is its bite that is deadly. I guess the woman who poisoned the hundred cats must be a non-believer.

We ourselves have seen a man take his Sunday morning relaxation by 'playing' with a rabbit, cuffing it in a friendly fashion, chucking it about and frequently holding it up high by the ears for his dog to sniff at. Hilarious stuff – I'm sure they both enjoyed it. I wonder what he does for fun the rest of the week. On another occasion, however, we've seen five white, well-fed, well groomed cats walking proprietarily among the outdoor tables of a restaurant, magnificently sited on a cliff-top in the grounds of a 14th century abbey. Attentive but unobtrusive, they had excellent manners and waited patiently until one of the guests was prepared to share a morsel. I later saw a replete one walking on a narrow parapet ledge carefully and wisely as a mitred abbot processing to the altar. And once I saw an immaculately groomed dog take his place in the queue going up to Communion. It all seems hard to add up.

A compensation for living in an eyrie is that you get a bird's eye view of everything. The thing that strikes you first, especially in the early morning at this time of year – mid-autumn – is the extraordinary clarity and luminescence of the light. It isn't just bright, it's sharp, brilliant, defining. It illumines and etches buildings, trees and the distant mountains as if one were drawing a line around each with a fine-edge pencil. The white and off-white colour of so many of the buildings strengthens and enhances it. Though there is no sun yet you shade your eyes against the penetrating brightness. It may sound banal but, for the first time in my life, I understand what 'seeing things in a different light' really means. Oh, for a painter's brush to catch and put on canvas the essence of such light, surely as close as we'll ever get on earth to the imagined purity of celestial light. Standing on our balcony, cup of tea in hand, at about 6 am on a September morning, looking north towards the Pentadaktylos (and clearly picking out the Turkish gun emplacements there) is the best time to see that divinely unique light. When God commanded the dark saying 'Let there be light', this is how light must have obeyed.

A more mundane thing you notice immediately looking down from this position of vantage is that an extraordinary number of the well-built, modern houses have building irons poking up out of their flat roofs. Water tanks, too, (a gravity-flow system operates here, as it does in many former British colonies) are not embedded but rest on iron stilts and can easily be removed by crane. Looking down at them the houses seem to be unfinished, expectant, incomplete, waiting for something to happen as, indeed, they are, waiting for a wedding, for it's the custom in this patriarchal, familial, cohesive society for the daughter to receive on her marriage the gift of a flat 'upstairs'. They're called 'dowry apartments'. So the spiked roof is both an assertion and a promise. It says 'you will continue to live at home after your marriage and we promise to provide accommodation for you.' The family, according to this way of thinking, doesn't so much lose a daughter as gain a 'son' and should the marriage fail and end in divorce – about 20 percent do – the erstwhile 'son' moves out and the daughter, in whose sole name the flat has been registered, continues to have a home for herself and the children, not to mention a mother and grandmother downstairs to look after their needs. That's why alimony – a concept alien to traditional Cypriot culture – is not a big issue here. Yet what, I asked, if there are two daughters? The answer was straightforward and simple. The parents would provide another flat on top of the first one, if they could afford it, otherwise they would move out to a smaller apartment themselves and give their home to the second daughter. There are some modern variations on this theme, of course, but such was and, to a great extent, still is the traditional practice and certainly one explanation for the roof irons. Another, just as likely to be true, since in Cyprus as elsewhere a family may consist entirely of sons, is the tax deduction the owner can claim on 'unfinished buildings'. A less romantic explanation it's true but one that has its own attractions. It seems that in Cyprus what you miss in the swings you can still gain in the roundabouts.

From our windows we can see most of the inner city with its jutting high-rise, TV aerials sprouting from the roofs like ships' masts. Rectangular control boxes and penthouse attics look from a distance like masters' cabins. Ubiquitous watertanks, like metal sarcophagi awaiting resurrection, vie for space with solar panels and a pallid array of cyclop saucers. Clothes hang limply from strands of wire. The roof is full. Away in the distance the large, green cube of Universal Life dominates the skyline, especially at night. But trees are plentiful, too, the twenty-metre tall cypresses the most conspicuous. At street level olive, lemon and orange grow in – and out of – gardens. If I crane my neck I can see the copse in front of the presidential palace and the barer yards around several Orthodox churches whose red domes and parchment-coloured walls touch the scene with a softer hue. The Green Line itself, that misnomer which divides the city with its ugly stockade of dilapidated buildings, is only twenty minutes' walk away.

At the rear of our apartment looking through the kitchen window we can see, jammed in between us and the next block of high rise buildings, a farmlet. It covers about two acres and is host to six small houses with red-tiled roofs and a number of lean-to shacks and outhouses.

To the left is the open air work place of a man who makes endless, big, red-ochre plant holders. The ground is hard earth, ochre in the pot factory, dusty brown elsewhere, much like the well swept *kiwanja* (forecourt) of any African village. One old lady has made a small walkway, edged with whitewashed stones and half embedded cement blocks, also whitewashed. There, in the cool of the evening, she walks, dressed in her long black skirts, adjusting stones, plucking dried-up weeds, tending a few flowers. This small, private, precious 'garden' contrasts strongly with the rocks and other rubble that has been raked into ungainly piles under nearby trees and shrubs. Cats, and dogs on chains, lie spread-eagled in the sun. Well fed pigeons flutter from roof to ground and back again – I have serious doubts about their longevity. Hens peck under the watchful surveillance of a cocky, young rooster. Six, irregular, improvised clothes lines, stretching between trees, sway and flap in the small breezes and the whole area is unevenly spaced with cypress and olive trees and taller ones that look like eucalyptus. Large, fierce-looking, finger-pointing, grey-green cacti do duty in several places as hedges. Bougainvillaea creeps around the corner of one house. For all the world these couple of acres in the middle of a city could be a small village anywhere in Cyprus. There are many such oases of rusticity scattered through Nicosia and one always comes across them with a feeling of surprise and pleasure. They show, I think, that Cypriots are still essentially a village people, as are the Irish, and only slowly and begrudgingly are they becoming metamorphosed into city dwellers. These are the last outposts of communal living that have not yet been swallowed up by the conglomerates of high-rise. Long may they last though one could hope that their dogs refrain from night-time barking and their roosters quit crowing at false dawns. It is not without significance that in the whole island there are only six main towns and six hundred villages.

Not all vacant spaces in Nicosia are private farmlets. Some of the rubbish-strewn, fenced-off areas you come across so unexpectedly, often with a tumbled-down house on them, or a bomb of a car, belong to Turkish Cypriots who fled north in 1974 and now live 'in occupied territory'. They are a waste land waiting to be redeemed, eyesores, that betray the status (apart from the footpaths) of a modern capital. As the government of the Republic of Cyprus refuses to recognise the puppet regime in the north, legally and morally, houses, land and properties, previously owned by Turkish Cypriots in the south, are still rightfully theirs, the absence of their owners being viewed as an extended holiday, or a prolonged business trip from which they will one day return. To do anything else would be to recognise the permanence of the Green Line, which splits the island. On a similar, logical premise the government in Nicosia has instructed the banks to make loans available to persons displaced from the North – refugees, they're called here – using their houses, lands and other property in the North as collateral. Only very recently has the North begun to change this convention and it was reported in the Cypriot press last week that the Northern regime was beginning to issue title deeds to property previously owned by Greek Cypriots in the North. Invalid and not worth the paper they're written on, cry the southern Cypriots. And so the impasse continues and the interposing shabbiness.

But it *is* only interposing and the unobservant visitor, especially the one who hugs the city centre, will see little or nothing of it. Although we live in, perhaps, the tallest block of apartments in Nicosia, only 15 minutes from the city centre and despite the fact that the very next house to us is empty, dilapidated and derelict, its surrounds overgrown with weeds, the suburb through which we walk to our neighbourhood park, still in the process of construction but already with hundreds of trees ten metres tall, is full of attractively styled, detached or semi-detached, older houses. Nearly all have well kept, road-front gardens, always with two or three compulsory fruit trees, which, in also providing shade, serve a second essential purpose in this climate. Many of the houses have an upstairs veranda with an awning, nearly all have a shaded area at street level where meals can be eaten outside from May to November. Ornate railings are common and windows invariably have slatted, wooden shutters in blue, green or brown which contrast cheerfully with the off-white, pink of buff colours of the houses themselves.

Low-pitched roofs dressed with terracotta tiles alternate with flat cement ones. Ubiquitous cats lounge on doorsteps or under trees and shrubs. There are few dogs. These houses are as handsome and substantial as you'd find in a large city anywhere, and here, as well, have the additional attractive features that Greek originality gives to each. This is a country without Coronation Streets.

3

DOWN AND ABOUT IN NICOSIA

When I first came down from the eyrie and ventured out into the streets of suburban Nicosia my most dramatic impression was the absence of footpaths. You notice these things more when you're a pedestrian – and we, who've never been without a car, are now, by choice, full time pedestrians. The roads, too, in a most unmanly fashion, are shoulderless and all over the city building rods lie flat and waiting, roadside, for structures already being built, or about to be built. But I mustn't skip over the footpaths, indeed it would be impossible to skip on them at all. When they exist – and they do sometimes exist – they're quite narrow, so narrow that if two people walking side by side meet a third, one of them has to execute a nimble ballet-like movement on to the road and back again. There does, in fact, seem to be an antipathy in Cyprus to the use of footpaths as footpaths. You'll notice at once, for example, that they are invariably used as car parks, not just, mind you, a couple of wheels sneakily cresting the kerb but as much of the car, or van, or pick-up as can possibly fit across the entire metre or so of footpath. You have to be very, very slender to weave in and out through *these* parked vehicles, most of which seem to be of the larger, stockier varieties.

Cars, however, aren't the only obstacle to safe side-walking in Cyprus. In the middle of many footpaths large, square holes with direct access to Mother Earth have been provided for flowers, shrubs and small trees. A fine idea, you might think, linking city streets with country gardens, reversing the image of the concrete jungle. Excellent! But I challenge you to share a footpath with a row of robust, adolescent cacti. Utterly impossible, I assure you, unless you're a cat, or at most, no taller than the lovely, pink and tan Cypriot poodle. And the shade-providing small trees – lovely idea – have their lower branches at the level of a small donkey, so that any normal six-footer, with or without a straw stetson, has to improvise a graceful road-curve, one out, one in, out-in again every five or six metres. Now, you could be forgiven for thinking that cars and trees and shrubs show the only possible biases against footpaths in Cyprus but you'd be wrong. There are also newspaper stands and advertising boards horizontally so placed that they can – and do – block off the entire footpath in those places where somebody forgot to plant a tree. Walking can be a hazard in Cyprus and nearly 20 percent of the people killed on the roads each year are pedestrians.

Nicosian footpaths also run out on you. One minute you're on one and the next minute it has disappeared. So you cross the street and keep walking until the same caper occurs on the other side. Again you switch sides and this zigzag game of street tag – now you have it, now you don't – continues until you've almost reached the centre of the city. There, as if to compensate for suburban deficiencies, there are some very wide footpaths, as large as small malls in places. You still have to be careful, though, because there are frequent steps, some of them quite steep, suddenly dropping you on to another footpath at a lower level, or, on to an entrance-way, or even, more or less briefly, on to the road itself. Such unexpected drops are as much a hazard as the corny joke of some trickster in a bar pulling the stool from under you when you stand to hitch your trousers. The footpath makers of Cyprus prefer staccato to glissando and are a constant danger to absorbed window-shoppers like my wife. Holes are another hazard, especially if one has a back strain as I had during my first month here. Each jolt can set your recovery back a whole day at the very least. Underfoot, too, there is a great variety of surfaces, ranging from terrazzo tiles and stone slabs, to cement blocks, loose shale and what looks like grey, sandy gravel mixed with a fine, slate dust – excellent, I found out, for knocking the shine off polished shoes. So, *enfin*, despite their interesting variety, it behoves us, daily users, to include in the litany of our morning prayers the additional invocation – 'From the footpaths of Cyprus, O Lord, deliver us!'

Traffic violations have been until recently one of the main problems of Cypriot law enforcement officers, as the police are called here. This is not surprising when you consider figures released by a recent *Research Review*: two out of three Cypriot males and one out of three females confessed to having driven illegally. Seventeen is the legal driving age here but a rule so honoured in the breach surely needs a searching look at. The beeps, burps and short, shrill barks from a variety of horns are a continuous reminder of how cautiously people must drive on narrow suburban streets, made more narrow, of course, by the cars parked on either side. But there is no cacophonous horn symphony of the kind one would hear in Rome, Athens, or Cairo, except after football matches when the home team wins. On first arriving in Cyprus, I, weaving in and out, for a long time thought the horns were barking at me but careful research has long since led me to a contrary conclusion: they're barking at themselves and most of the time, I swear, don't see me at all which, whilst it's a minor relief on the one hand, on the other, does seem rather to increase the risk of personal damage. Miraculously one sees relatively few pronged cars in circulation. They would, in any case, impugning his skill and damaging his status, be unacceptable to your average Cypriot.

Whoever drives a car in a foreign country (Italy, Spain and Portugal come to mind) firmly believes that all the local drivers are insane motor-maniacs. I've heard foreign drivers here say the same thing about Cypriot drivers. Certainly they are adventurous and don't at all mind taking risks. Seldom, for example, do they wear seat belts (compulsory), or crash helmets on motor bikes (compulsory). In the city suburbs they frequently drive at 70, or 80 km/h but, to be fair, my own experience is that they will stop for you at a zebra crossing, *if* they see you time enough in advance, not always possible, of course, if they're driving at speed. Many times, too, I've had cars stop for me to cross a busy road where there was no designated crossing. This courtesy, frustrating as it must be for other drivers, compensates a little for the rashness associated with 'normal' driving here. Well, it does, if you're a pedestrian anyway.

Interestingly, the British control driving within their own extra-territorial enclaves here and, by all accounts, are much stricter in applying the rules of the road. A French friend of mine was fined CP70 (approximately US$155) for driving early in the morning on a straight stretch of road 'safely above the 100 kph limit' (his words). That was bad enough, he thought, but to rub salt into his wounded feelings, the British insisted that he pay the fine in person in the British enclave more than an hour's drive from his home! This did nothing to promote Franco-British entente.

On Cypriot roads in 1996 there were 128 fatalities. Two years previously when 133 people were killed on the island's roads the fatality rate per 100,000 of the population was 20.8, the second highest ratio in the world (after Portugal). In the UK the equivalent ratio is 6.4. Some locals blame this high ratio on the enormous influx of 'refugees' who fled south after the Turkish invasion of 1974. Almost one third of the entire Greek Cypriot population of the island left all they owned in the north and jumped in their cars, trucks, lorries, whatever had four wheels and was mobile and travelled to safety in the south. A wave of ethnic cleansing comparable at that time to none other! But the sudden appearance on the roads in the south of so many extra vehicles and the understandable leniency with which traffic violations were treated, gave rise to bad driving habits, many of which still remain. This was the explanation given me by a retired Cypriot police inspector and I've no doubt that there is a good deal of truth in it.

The principal inter-city highways between Nicosia and Larnaka and Nicosia and Limassol are excellent two lane motorways. A central line of white posts with broad white markers on either side is all that in some places separates the two lines of traffic. A flimsy enough separation, you might think, but in fact it's an ingenious innovation. Remove the posts, which is easily done, and the road can be used as an airport with mile after mile of serviceable runway. The guide lines for planes to land are already in place! Keeps the roads in good repair, too. Though I have driven on these roads in cars of all descriptions and found them excellent, my first four-wheeled outing was in an old Bedford bus.

4

TAKING THE BUS TO KAIMAKLI

'Nicosia is a city with three names,' the lively, dark-haired guide with the infectious smile explained. A small group of us–eight or nine–had pulled ourselves up and aboard a relic of a bus, a Bedford, with wooden body, low roof and hard, plastic seats, which, courtesy of the municipality, was taking us to Kaimakli, an outlying village. 'Four, if you count the very first one,' she added with an apologetic smile, 'but that goes back to Neolithic times, more than 5000 years BC. It was called Ledra then but nobody knows very much about it and nobody calls it Ledra today.' She spoke perfect English, easy to listen to and fluent. 'But the name isn't entirely forgotten because just down there,' she pointed behind the Cyprus Tourist Office, which we had just left, 'there's a street called Ledra and another called Onasagoras, who was king of the city-state of Ledra in the 7th century BC. In fact those are the two principal streets of the Old City, the city within the walls and if you can come on Thursday we'll walk around it.' Three times a week, on Mondays, Tuesdays and Thursdays, from 10 am to noon, the Cyprus Tourist Organisation, courtesy of a progressive mayor and council, provides a free, guided tour of the Old City (Thursdays), of Medieval Nicosia (Tuesdays) and of an adjacent village (Mondays). All three are well worth while. But back to the moment – the engine of our bus sprang into surprisingly smooth life, as Georgia, for that was her name (translated into English, of course, for the benefit of those, mostly elderly British, who find the simplest Greek word intimidating) explained that in Greek and Roman times the city was called Lefkosia 'the place of the white poplars'. Apparently there were stands of them stretching along the banks of the Pedieos, the part-time river that still flows after rain. Looked at from the Pentadaktylos Mountains, not far from the city, the trunks of the poplars presented a white appearance, hence the name, which is still used today as the official name of the city. Useless, for example, to look up 'Nicosia' in the telephone directory! I suppose it's a small way of showing identity with the long past, a declaration of one's Cypriotness, much as, for the same reason, several generations of people in Ireland have ceased to call Co. Offaly, King's County, or Dun Laoire, Holyhead. It's a linguistic patriotism that goes hand-in-hand with a sense of national identity, especially in times of heightened allegiance, or increased threat. The Lusignans, however, for some unknown reason (they were French) found the ancient name difficult to pronounce and changed it in the 12th century to Nicosie, or, in English, Nicosia. Subsequently, the Turks, exercising their own right of nomenclature, called it Lefkosha. And still do. Signposts in the one-third part of the city which they occupy today point southwards to Lefkosha, alias Lefkosia, alias Nicosia, all names for the remaining two-thirds of the same city! By this time we were driving through the traffic-jammed city and Georgia was explaining about the walls.

There were many pirate raids, she said, on the port cities from the 7th to the 10th centuries AD. Marauders from the Arab world, especially, came in greater numbers and virtually destroyed such cities as Salamis, Pafos and Kourio. So the Byzantines, who controlled Cyprus at the time, wisely decided to move the capital inland and Nicosia became the island's metropolis in 965 AD. When the Lusignans arrived they found the old Byzantine walls in a dilapidated state and set about building their own, including a keep, or tower, in the heart of the Old City, not far from the old municipal buildings. That was in 1211. These walls were, however, insufficient to stave off a sacking of Nicosia by the Genovese in 1373 so the Lusignans started on a major repair and reconstruction job. They heightened and strengthened them, added ramparts and round towers, especially one particularly strong one on the south side, called the Margarita Tower, not too far from the present-day Hilton. But their immense work of reconstruction was to prove all in vain. The Venetians attacked and captured the city in 1489 and then they, in their turn, set about mending and improving the fortifications but it wasn't until the mid-16th century when they feared an imminent invasion and attack by the Turks that in a final fling of arrogance they decided to make the walls impregnable. To achieve this they had Venice send them the foremost military engineer of the day, one Giulio Savorgnano. His first decision was to reduce the perimeter of the walls by half, from approximately 9 kms to 4.2 kms, which is the perimeter length today. In effecting this reduction he had the whole city outside his new perimeter razed to the ground and the stone used for the new construction, surely a serious archaeological sin if ever there was one. These walls still stand in all the massiveness of their fortress-like bravura. 'There are also 11 pentagonal-shaped bastions,' Georgia added, 'each with a perimeter of 325 m, large enough to accommodate 2,000 infantrymen and four pieces of heavy artillery. In fact,' she continued with a palpable irony in her voice, 'in one section they still fulfil their primary purpose, being part of the Green Line, that demarcates the border between North and South.' She showed us several schools which had been built in the moat extension below the walls and said that from time to time Turkish youths threw stones and other missiles into the school playgrounds. It has to be said that the Greeks, too, marshal their children for protest marches. Sad, as involving children in such animosities only perpetuates hatred, as is only too evident in places like Palestine and Northern Ireland.

These moats, 80 metres wide, were originally filled with water and were supposed to operate as an integral part of the city's defence system. It would have been relatively easy, the generals thought, for the 22,000 infantrymen on the bastions to pick off an invading army as they waded through the moat with their weapons held high over their heads. So it would but for one small factor: the water came from the River Pedieos, itself not a very reliable source, and all the Turks had to do as they began their siege of the city in 1570 was to divert the river's course! Reminds me of the story told about another great scientific theorist who, on building a kennel for his dog with an appropriately large door, provided another much smaller one alongside for the use of his cat. Not all was lost, however, and the moats are used today variously as car parks, tennis courts, public gardens and children's playgrounds. These Venetian walls certainly add character to the city, the Old City, in particular, neatly dividing it from the busy, bustling, new, commercial city 'outside the walls'.

On our way to Kaimakli village Georgia had the bus stop by the side of the road on the outskirts of the city. The view was of a wasteland of rubble and barren earth across which we looked towards Northern Cyprus. She pointed out a blue UN Jeep patrolling the buffer zone and showed us on the hillside opposite, provocatively clear-cut in tree, shrub and grass, the red crescent flag of Turkey. Near it a smaller rendition of the flag of 'The Turkish Republic of Northern Cyprus' carries its claimant message, 'HOW GOOD IT IS TO BE A TURK', yet much as a small boy might hold on to his parent's outstretched hand, complaining about the effrontery of the robust youngster across the street noisily licking an ice cream, so occupants of the TRNC look with envy at the economic prosperity of the South.

We saw villages, cosy in the warm sun, scattered this way and that across the opposing hills, villages that before 1974 had been occupied by Greek Cypriots. More than twenty years later they still nestled into the mountainside, like etchings carved in wood or stone, as if nothing at all had happened. More poignantly we saw the small topmost village from which our driver, driving this very bus, packed with his family and friends, had fled after the invasion. His brow was deeply furrowed as he looked up once, then got out of the bus, lit a cigarette and faced in the opposite direction. Everything he owned apart from the bus was up there still. Who occupied his house now? Who farmed his small garden, tended his few vines and picked his olives? Would he and his children and his grandchildren ever live in their home village again, ever again occupy the ancestral home?

The only Checkpoint Charlie along the entire Green Line is in Nicosia but from a vantage point near the border at Famagusta Georgia told us she could see her former apartment. I didn't ask her if it were her parents' apartment also – she looked far too young to have had one of her own twenty-two years ago. You could see pain and incomprehension in the eyes of these two people: why did the world do nothing besides pass ineffectual resolutions? Was it because the Greek Cypriots did not wallow in their misery? Was it because they did not take refuge in being victims but from somewhere had found the strength to build fresh lives and new homes? Survivors, not victims, but still with the same feelings and rights as the rest of us. Closer to us, much closer, across the rude emptiness of the wasteland another Turkish flag flew high, furling and unfurling in the breeze. We moved on.

Once we reached the centre of the village of Kaimakli, the bus dropped us. Walking, we saw craftsmen working at their trades in open spaces beside their homes, or in dark-looking workshops. More often than not a man pursued his work alone, hardly noticing our presence in the street. Old, run-down houses were being restored in a scheme partially funded by the European Community. The idea was not only to prolong the lives of the old houses but also to preserve the distinctive beauty and simplicity of their original architecture in both its structure and ornamental features. Columns with capitals of carved stone, wooden doors with finely chiselled, recessed panels, wrought iron grilles above the doors with the date of the building of the house as an inset centrepiece and balconies with delicate, finely curved railings are all features of these old houses which the craftsmen either repair or create anew. The solid, limestone buildings are sometimes faced and painted in light pastel colours making a street look like a painting by Manet. But other houses show the crazy patterns of uncut limestone and have balconies in bolder colours that keep guard over arched entrances. The tradition of stone carving and robust, black grillwork has been handed down through the generations from the Venetians, and before them the Lusignans, who built their palaces and public buildings here from the 12th to the 16th centuries. The same effort to restore and preserve is evident in several of the narrow streets of the Old City, Georgia said, especially in the section called Laiki Gitonia.

Georgia took particular pleasure in pointing out the various fruit and ornamental trees to us as we continued our walk. Often these spread their branches out on to the roadway and their fruit seemed a communal offering. 'Every Greek Cypriot house', she said, 'has at least two trees, an olive and a lemon, two fruits that we use a lot in our cooking.' But looking around we also saw heavily laden mandarin trees, their fruit sprinkling the ground and a loquat or two whose delicious, yellow fruit would not be ready till May. And everywhere, on streets, in gardens and parks was the ubiquitous bitter-orange tree whose fruit is used for making marmalade and jams. I tried eating one once and got a mouthful of acid. I noticed that many of the trees had already been stripped at lower branch level so perhaps the community jam-making season had begun – but how would they reach the rest? I imagined whole bright lines of aluminium step-ladders invading the parks and suburban streets on weekends, with men and women as on stilts, picking. I tried one and it tasted more like a bitter lemon. Was that, I wondered, where Lawrence Durrell got the title for his well-known book on Cyprus in the 50s, *Bitter Lemons*? Of the ornamentals Georgia pointed out the white summer jasmine already beginning to flower, out of season, the Persian lilac and a bush of large fluted, cream hibiscus, almost open. The 'last rose of summer' can have but little meaning in Cyprus as we passed several bushes still vigorously blooming in mid-winter. It was time for coffee.

Georgia took us to a small cafe opposite a church where a funeral was taking place. Mourners were going in and coming out of the church in two continuous streams, stopping only to give money to a lady seated by the door who issued each with a receipt. 'Who's for coffee, who's for tea?' Georgia's grasp of colloquial English was charming. All but one of us chose coffee and we were given a second choice: Nescafé, or Cyprus coffee? Nothing else on offer in the traditional coffee-shop, no *caffe latte*, no cappuccino, no espresso – these you can have in plenty in the Western-style cafeterias but I have the distinct impression that they would be despised in the *cafeneion*. And, since the 1974 invasion, Turkish coffee has become Cyprus coffee (and Turkish delight, Greek delight – I'm not sure about Turkish baths. Saunas?) Several of us chose it. How did we like it, bitter (without sugar), half-sweet, or sweet. Three important words, *skettos, metrios, glikos*. This was an immediate and irrevocable decision as the sugar is added to the small pot, your individual small pot, when the coffee is being boiled. *Metrios*, the half-sweetened kind, was the table's most popular choice though one brave and grandly rotund Greek lady had the courage to ask for 'very sweet'. The coffee is served in small cups with the steeped coffee grounds still inside and accompanied by a glass of water. There is a cap of brown froth, or cream, on top of the coffee and interestingly, the Greek word for this is *kaimaki*, directly derived from the name of the village we were in – Kaimakli. It seems that the village had a high reputation in the old days, and probably still has, for the rich quality of its sheep and goats' milk. For the same reason the little village is also well known for its *halloumi*, a salty cheese, quite delicious when grilled, or even fried. I usually take the precaution of first putting the *halloumi* in a pot of boiling water to reduce the salinity, with excellent results.

Though more than half our group was female, Georgia told us that these traditional coffee shops were not frequented by women. They were considered the exclusive habitat of men, their bonding place, their business office, their social centre. If the funeral service across the road represents the first great leveller in all societies, the coffee shop in Cyprus is the second. At some time during the day most of the males of a village will put in an appearance, the *mukhtar* (a Turkish word, meaning 'headman') and the priest, the teacher and the labourer. All will be known to the proprietor and each will be served according to his well-known individual taste. No sugar! Not too much froth! Boiled twice! Within its four, white-washed walls deals are struck, land is bought and sold, and comments are made on the local scene. Above all politics is talked, night, noon and morning. The Greek, mainlander or islander, Athenian or Cypriot, is a political animal. Every table had its pack of cards already waiting and a good deal of petty gambling goes on. Backgammon is also popular.

I looked around and saw several older men, wearing ancient suits and ties, their caps still on, sitting at separate tables. They had thrust their coffee cups aside, the daily paper, already read, was lying on a chair and they were concentrating on a card game that looked very much like patience. I asked Georgia what they were doing. 'Prophesying,' she said, 'and if I wanted my prophecy told they'd do it for me.' I shook my head – oracles I'd had enough of. 'They ask themselves questions,' she continued, 'mostly political ones, and to get an answer they play each game to its end. Takes a lot of games when you've just read the paper! And then, later on, today or tomorrow, they compare their answers with what really happened in the world of politics and of men – no doubt, sometimes of women, too, for wasn't the prime minister of Turkey at that time a woman – and they get great satisfaction if they've forecast correctly.' Augurers they undoubtedly are who have substituted cards for entrails! Slightly senile though a few of these pensioners sometimes may be, they can sit all day on their rush-bottomed chairs, over a single cup of coffee, playing their card games or staring into the thoughts that invariably come to the old. No one will hassle them, no one will tell them it's time to go. The institution of the *cafeneion*, the coffee shop, has a great deal to recommend it.

'Do women mind being excluded from the coffee shops?' I asked.

'Not at all,' she said, 'we have plenty of cafés we can go to in town if we want to and we have neighbourhood coffee meetings of our own where the women get together and talk about the things that interest them. Who can be bothered with prophecies and politics,' she asked, 'when we have more important things to discuss?' It was time to go. The Greek lady who had ordered the very sweet coffee smilingly paid for all our coffees. And for the lady who chose tea!

Because of the funeral we did not stay long inside this church, it was obviously not an appropriate time for tourists, but, almost immediately, Georgia took us to another much smaller and darker one and explained to us the ecclesiastical furnishings of Orthodoxy and its rituals. But first the lady with the receipt book? She was an official representative of a charitable society – in this case of an anti-cancer trust – chosen by the family of the deceased and to which mourners were asked to contribute instead of sending cards or flowers. Each person, or family, gave what he, or she, wished. A receipt was issued and the names and amounts are later acknowledged by the family and published in a local newspaper. 'This', said Georgia, 'was a meaningful and lasting tribute to the memory of the deceased.' It was certainly better than the cryptic 'no cut flowers, please', often appended to death notices in other countries. Better even than the increasingly common alternative suggestion that in lieu of flowers one might post a donation to a nominated charity. The Cypriot way immediately and publicly incorporated the grieving community of family and friends in a practical gesture of solidarity. In circumstances of more tragic, or accidental death, the collection preached its own sermon. Money, for example, collected and spent advertising the necessity for motor-cyclists to wear helmets would be a practical way of commemorating the death from head injuries of a motor cyclist who wasn't wearing a helmet. Of the 117 killed on the roads in 1995, 40 were people riding bikes of one kind or another, nearly all of whom were not wearing helmets! There is always the danger, of course, in this kind of published listing of donations that regard and sympathy for the family of the deceased could be measured by the size of the donation. It is, however, no more prone to misinterpretation than the size of a wreath, or the number of requiem masses paid for. Whatever the measure of respect shown to the deceased and his family, if it is seen in merely monetary terms, it is subject to misinterpretation. Here, at least, one-upmanship, if it does exist, is put to sound, practical use.

Meanwhile the family of the deceased stood in a semi-circle around the coffin, which rested in front of the *iconostasi*, accepting the condolences of the congregation as one by one they went up to express their sympathy. Outside, the black-robed priest, in his priest's high hat and wearing a broad stole with black crosses on a white background, was helping to extricate cars from make-do parking places, where people had parked higgledy-piggledy before going into the church. It was the first time I'd seen a priest on traffic duty and it somehow endeared him to me. He was probably also saving the mourners from the fierce verbal battles that would otherwise have ensued. Elsewhere men had gathered in little groups, talking quietly and smoking (no sudden conversions here). The sun glinted from the lacquered bonnet of the small low-slung hearse. Soon the whole congregation would proceed to the cemetery for the burial.

5

INSIDE A GREEK ORTHODOX CHURCH

Still in Kaimakli we walked to the small church of St Michael the Archangel, part of which had suffered a recent fire. Georgia spoke about her church, its icons and its rubrics, with gentle pride, reverence and conviction. She was extremely knowledgeable about all facets of the liturgy and even attempted a theological explanation of the differences between the Orthodox and Roman Catholic Churches – something, she said, to do with the provenance of the Holy Spirit from the Father alone, or from the Father and the Son. There was a strong inference that a dispute about such finer points (wasn't it a mystery anyway?) should no longer keep apart the two great arms of the Christian community in the East and in the West. When I mentioned the opposing stands in each of the Churches on divorce and a married clergy, she tuttutted and said these were mere house-keeping matters. It is certainly true that through historical circumstances the Cypriot Orthodox Church is very wealthy so that the house-keeping needs of a married clergy are easily taken care of. About one in five marriages, she said, now ends in a church adjudicated divorce, a huge increase over the last twenty or thirty years, but when the marriage had irretrievably broken down, what else was there to do? She smiled and shrugged her shoulders and took us on a tour of the church.

Georgia first took us to the *iconostasi*, a kind of partition between the body of the church and what we in the West call the sanctuary. She pointed out the 'royal door' in its centre through which only the priest could pass to the altar and the 'holy of holies' behind the curtain. Women were not allowed back there at all but a few selected men, who assisted in the church, were permitted to pass through another 'door' – an open space, really – on the extreme left of the iconostasi. She drew the curtain gently aside for us but I could make out little besides the altar, its cloths and its vessels.

The *iconostasi* itself was a permanent structure faced with icons, many either totally or partially covered in silver, or silver plate. Besides adding a baroque lushness to the *iconostasi*, and indeed, to the church as a whole, the silver also protected the icon from the devout kisses of the faithful. One kissed the silver plate instead. I wonder how frequently it has to be renewed – not often, I should think, human faces last a lifetime.

Members of the Greek Orthodox communion, on entering a church, bless themselves, without the benefit of holy water, using only the thumb, index and middle fingers of the right hand and touching the right shoulder before the left. They then go to an icon resting on a kind of easel with a thin curtain loosely covering it. Drawing the curtain aside, they kiss the icon which is either that of the saint to whom the church is dedicated, or that of the saint whose nameday is being celebrated. Namedays are more important in Cyprus than birthdays. I've been once or twice in a flower shop picking up gifts of cacti for my wife, they make an enduring change from roses, when I saw three or four attendants hard at work making and decorating elaborate bouquets. Thinking a Moonie wedding was in the offing I enquired about this frenetic activity and was told that it was St Michael's nameday, or St Anastasia's, or St Whoever's and that all the people in the office, or guardroom, or staffroom where there were Michaels, or Anastasias or Whoevers were banding together to send a bouquet of affection and remembrance to them. Lucky them! I felt sorry for the Homers and Aristotles and Socrates, of whom there are many here and whose names, as far as I know, do not appear on any hagiographical list. Later on in the evening the recipient of the bouquet is joyfully 'at home' for several hours to all his relatives and friends. Thankfully, as far as budgets are concerned, you celebrate only one name no matter how many your enthusiastic parents may have bestowed on you.

Each village also has its patron saint and some have more than one. Each year the villagers celebrate the name day of the village patron in a festival called the *panayiri*. In Cyprus the *panayiri* is a way of life. First there is the religious side of it with vespers and a holy liturgy in the village church. This is followed, in the words of one Cypriot writer, 'by a commercial open market where anything goes.' George Lanitis, in his own inimitable way, continues 'There are people whose job it is to go from *panayiri* to *panayiri* from Pafos to Paralimni, living out, or in tents without washing facilities – you can easily smell that – earning their living by selling anything from shoes to shirts to lace underwear, even wedding dresses, as well as *soujouko*, walnuts, dangerous and not so dangerous toys, doughnuts dipped in sticky syrup and laced with icing sugar and plenty of dust. The *panayiri* is a commercial expression of religion and therefore, like most money-making religious affairs, it attracts the reverence of the faithful. And this year (1997) for the first time, the Cypriot roulette, the *kazanti*, will make its first appearance legally. The lucky stainless steel ball may bring to the punters interesting winnings like Chinese panda bears, Scotch whisky, live canaries and pickled, illegally caught birds. The chief of the village,' he adds, 'is usually the *kafedji* who has a license to charge twice for his sweet or *metrio* coffee, or sticky, hot almond juice with water.' For all that the festivities are religious in context and character it seems that a rollicking good time is had by all.

But back to the church. The devout visitor, having fulfilled the rubric of icon kissing, goes to a box with a store of pure wax candles of different widths. The thinner ones cost five Cypriot cents, the thicker ones ten. The candle, or candles, for they often buy several, are then lighted from ones already burning and placed upright in an oblong receptacle containing some kind of sand mixture, whereupon the intercessor prays to the saint represented by the icon for a favour he wishes granted. Should the favour requested be, say, the recovery of a child from illness, or the healing of an ailing limb, or the safe birth of a baby and it be granted – or, at any rate, so transpires – the grateful intercessor often has a wax sculpture made of the previously ailing limb, or of the previously sick child, and, in gratitude, hangs it from a nail to one side of the icon, much, I suppose, as cripples cured at Lourdes surrendered their crutches to be displayed for the edification of others. In this small church I saw one waxen face looking like a death mask, several waxen infants, almost life-size and a stout leg, foot and all, that must have belonged to a weighty person. It looked sexless. Perhaps all waxen images do. I have to confess I got an eerie feeling looking at them. They seemed ghostly and grotesque, not at all like cuddly dolls.

Under Georgia's supervision we took a closer look at the iconostasi. To the right of the 'royal door' there is always in Greek Orthodox churches an icon of Christ, usually flanked by one of St John the Baptist, while on the left an icon of the Virgin is flanked by one of St John the Evangelist. Other icons of the local church's choice spread right and left from those of the Baptist and the Evangelist respectively. Above the royal door a series of smaller icons depict scenes from the life of Christ and above those another series tell of happenings in the lives of the apostles and martyrs. A large crucifix centrally placed over the *iconostasi* is an obligatory feature of all Greek Orthodox churches and completes the standard design of the *iconostasi*, in front of which hang a number of silver tabernacle lights that look like ancient thuribles.

The church itself was unspectacular in design – oblong, one-roomed and barrel-vaulted. Many larger churches, however, have a beehive dome usually placed in the centre of a cruciform transept and surrounded by several smaller satellite domes either clustered around it or hop-scotching down one side of the nave. Especially in the old monastery churches, frescoes, some dating from as far back as the 13th century, adorn the insides of the domes and vaults as well as the walls of the church itself. Many orthodox churches are dark inside, having only clerestory windows, but during the liturgies they are lighted by rows of sparkling chandeliers which provide, at one and the same time, a warm, intimate and solemn atmosphere.

The seating, strange to those whose religious upbringing was conducted in the pews of Western churches, is comprised of separate, wooden stalls with high arm-rests on which worshippers can lean during the long three-hour liturgy, nearly all of which is spent standing. When the seat is turned up they can also snuggle their bottoms on to the edge of the seat-ledge to take the weight off their feet, a practice not unknown to the monks of the West whose chapter seats had a misericordia (mercy) projection on which they too could rest while feigning to be still standing. The assumption is that the Lord, with a divine wink, condones these practices. I'm sure He does. The churches are generally full to the doors with worshippers on Sundays and saints' namedays. Men, young as well as old, are present in equal numbers to women, though relatively few of either sex nowadays attend a full liturgy. Some time ago the faithful requested a shortened service but the authorities were not prepared to change one iota of a liturgy that goes back more than a thousand years. They did, however, concede that attendance for the whole three hours was not required. One hour would be enough.

In some churches there is a partial demarcation in the seating arrangements for men and women. In the church we were in a section of the seats near the altar on the deacon's side was reserved for men, while in other churches the gallery is open only to women and small children. At the back of the church of St Michael the Archangel there was an open space called the narthex which was for the accommodation of those who were still catechumens and could not, therefore, be full participants in the liturgy. As nearly the entire Greek Cypriot population is Greek Orthodox, I can't imagine who the catechumens might be. In fact, in St Michael's, the space was used as a kind of children's play-pen.

There is no organ, no accompanying instruments whatsoever, in a Greek Orthodox church and no women sing. The only music is that of the male, human voice projecting in strong, rhythmic monotones, punctuated with occasional swells and deep-throated diminuendos, the age-old chants of the Church. If one closes one's eyes for a minute one hears a choir of broad-chested, bearded monks, black-clad, standing in a semi-circle, giving rich, masculine renderings of prayerful homage to a presumably attentive God. There is a control and uniformity and strength in this Byzantine chanting that bespeaks not only a common purpose but also a measured grace and an immanence of worship. Of the angels these chanters are the Thrones and Dominations, not the Cherubim and Seraphim that Gregorian chanters are. Powerful, not exquisite; splendid, not ethereal. Pure and stirring, melodic, without harmony, this one thousand year old chant, heard first in the Greek monasteries of the Mount Athos peninsula, depends on an interplay of voices. There are eight basic sounds and four symbols, or levels of energy, for the raising of the voice, all depicted in complex notation. Byzantine chanting is deeply reverential and, in a peculiar way, audience-embracing and compelling. Would I feel the same after three hours? Possibly not but then I get restless at any solemn service of more than an hour's duration.

The Church is a powerful institution in Cyprus, historically, politically, financially and socially. Although small percentages of the population belong to the Maronite, Armenian and Latin (Roman Catholic) rites, overwhelmingly Greek Cypriots are Orthodox Christians. If not the oldest, and there are substantial claims that it is, the Cypriot Orthodox Church is one of the oldest in Christendom, having been founded by Saints Paul, Barnabus and Lazarus in the decades following the Crucifixion. And yes, in case you're wondering, it's the same Lazarus whom Jesus, in a loud voice, called forth from his tomb after he had already been three days buried. The Orthodox Church of Cyprus is a self-governing (autocephalous) Church and has been since the 5th century (by order of the Byzantine Emperor Zenon). The archbishop, who is its head, resides in Nicosia and wields much power and influence.

Early in 1996, however, a serious crisis between the Church and its faithful, rocked the entire country. Briefly, it happened like this. The people of the diocese of Morphou, then vacant, voted in diocesan elections for the appointment of the archimandrite (assistant bishop) Meraklis as their new bishop. Archbishop Chrysostomos, the ruling authority, refused to appoint him, accusing the cleric of 'immoral conduct', more specifically, of his having been involved in homosexual practices. There was uproar. Charges of bribery and corruption were levelled against the archbishop and the holy synod. Meraklis was suspended and fled to a monastery in Greece. The archbishop threatened to defrock him if he returned but return he did, claiming the right to trial before an ecclesiastical court. While the investigative process was being carried on inside the yellow sandstone archbishopric, angry crowds began gathering outside. Despite the barbed wire barricades which the police had hastily erected, bloody clashes occurred. Rocks, molotov cocktails, metal pipes, bottles, in fact, anything the crowd could lay hands on, were thrown across the barricade at the riot police, who by now, protected by riot shields, had taken up positions in front of the palace gates. The crowd, at least 2,000 strong, tried to storm the archbishopric; the police used tear gas and smoke canisters and, in the words of one observer, the normally quiet square became 'a war zone'. This went on for several days with more or less intensity. The whole country became involved from the president down. Charges and counter-charges were made on radio and TV. Threats were made against the archbishop's life. There was a bomb scare. It was the worst scandal ever to hit the Church in Cyprus.

Eventually, the holy synod, after days of negotiation between the archbishop and his supporters on the one hand and the archimandrite and his defenders, on the other, came up with a compromise 'solution'. Meraklis was permitted to return to Morphou in his former capacity. He was, however, reprimanded for occasionally doffing his cassock, a practice which, he said, made it easier for him to do pastoral work in bars. Meantime the vacant see would not be filled and the diocese would be 'overseen' and administered by another bishop. Meraklis, 'at the benevolent discretion of the holy synod', would be allowed to 'run' for bishop, when new elections were held at some future time. So a kind of peace was restored and the Church retired to lick its wounds.

The whole affair was brutish, murky and nasty. No one came well out of it and the consensus afterwards was that 'relations between the Church and its people will never be quite the same again.' There are some who would say, of course, that a Church whose faithful take such robust interest in its proceedings is alive and well but that's like saying that an occasional, fierce rebellion against the legitimate government of a country is good for the nation, hardly a recipe for peace and prosperity that historians would agree with.

Yet still in the villages, the priest, always in his cassock, is the most revered and important person. Apart from his church duties, he is also the mender of marriages, the counsellor of both young and old, the solver of disputes, the readily available consultant of all, in fact, the spiritual factotum of the entire village. He is often married and his routine, daily life differs little from that of the other villagers. Even in Nicosia you can see priests walking in the streets, carrying home their plastic bags of groceries. The great wealth of the Church, much of it from bequests of property made in earlier times, is spent on schools, hospitals, a TV station and other public amenities, as well as in paying the salaries of the priests and in the upkeep of monasteries.

Another crisis, this time financial, came to light in 1998 and resulted in the resignation of the bishop concerned. An overwhelming majority of Cypriots (78% according to a recent survey) now believe that the church has a 'morality problem'.

It was warm outside as we walked back to the bus. On our way Georgia showed us the little railway station that once upon a time was the starting point for the narrow-gauge railway that ran between Kaimakli and Famagusta. Three hours or more. Reminiscent for me of the West Clare line in Ireland that is immortalised in Percy French's song 'Are ye right there, Michael, are ye right?' Do ye think that we'll get home before the night?' They must have been built about the same time and both closed in the mid 50s. I had not known that Cyprus ever had a railway.

6

A WALK AROUND LAIKI GITONIA

A week or so later I walked around Laiki Gitonia with a different guide and seven other people. The name refers to a small, reconstructed area of the Old City, the city within the walls, and can loosely be translated as folk area, or neighbourhood of people. The problem is that not many people any longer actually live there. Despite successful efforts to renovate and restore some of the old housing, large segments of the Old City are still semi-derelict with many narrow streets and alleyways full of dilapidated buildings, their facings gone and their roofs leaking. None of this whole area is very far from the Green Line and there is understandably a reluctance to live in a potentially dangerous place (there have been incidents) and an even greater reluctance to put money into doing up buildings so close to the Line, assuming that some of the poorer inhabitants who live in Laiki Gitonia had the money anyway. Daytime, especially back a few streets from the Green Line, the situation is quite different. In the pedestrian area of Laiki Gitonia, for example, there are oodles of shady, street-side cafés and good restaurants. Of the several pubs the one called Plato's is the most popular. It's only open at night and in streets as dark as Montmartre you could miss it. Apart from an unobtrusive shingle it is hardly distinguishable from the other shuttered buildings in the street. Inside, however, it's got character and atmosphere, beer on tap, a huge range of spirits and cocktails and hundreds of bottles of wine wrapped in brown paper and stacked to the ceiling in racks. Broken glasses are displayed, with some pride one feels, on a ledge over the bar which is tended by a friendly, burly Armenian who could tell tales if he weren't so busy. There's also an *ad hoc* restaurant of limited menu but plentiful fare. You can have a large wooden platter of chips, pork or chicken kebab as well as other goodies for less than US$10. Enough for two. Excellent value.

All kinds of art and craft shops stretch cheek by jowl with the more mercenary kinds of souvenir and trinket shops, many proliferating on to footpaths and into the streets of mall-like, recessed areas. During the eight months of the tourist season, especially in the pedestrian area, there is a kind of open market with almost a carnival atmosphere. Many street vendors demonstrably but politely push their wares, and touts offer bargains at the nearby restaurants. Jewellery, ceramics, lace and leather goods, as well as some excellent Cypriot pottery, are all in plentiful supply both in Laiki Gitonia and on busy, bustling Ledra and Onasagorou streets. Strangely, however, I found it difficult to get Cypriot-made T-shirts with Cypriot insignia on them, or good, large calendars (there are a few quite good small ones) that depict Cypriot scenes. Though there are name cards in plenty in Greek and stacks of cards of all descriptions in English, often incongruously depicting English rural scenes and in many cases using corny, English humour, there are few greeting cards of any description in Greek, or even in Greek and English, if it were felt necessary to use both languages. In shop notices and advertising signs, too, whether these be wall posters or sign-written information, English still seems to be the language of prestige. Is this a mark of pragmatic, commercial reality, based on a proud bilingualism, or is it the long tail of a cultural imperialism that still survives in Cyprus? A former minister of education, Claire Angelidou, would like, despite her name, to see such 'anglicisations' disappear. In France and, more recently, in Russia, official bodies have been set up to preserve the purity of the French and Russian languages and to outlaw an intrusive English. Is there a Cypriot language cleansing body in the offing?

On our tour we visited two other churches quite similar in design and interior decoration to the ones I had already seen. The Greek Orthodox religion, which is the religion followed by approximately 80 percent of the people of Cyprus, including the Islamic North, has historically played an important role in the lives of Cypriots. It has always been a banner held high against Islam but also one that Cypriots did not hesitate to wave against Rome as well. During the Lusignan period the Latin Church exercised ascendancy and took over a great number of Greek Orthodox churches, keeping for themselves the prestige ones in populated centres and relegating the Orthodox clergy to the countryside. The Ottomans, for their own political reasons, sided with Orthodoxy and re-instated its clergy in the Latin churches with the result that Roman Catholicism disappeared almost completely from the island. Today, besides the flourishing Maronite and Armenian churches, there is only one Roman Catholic church in Nicosia, Holy Cross, which juts out into the Green Line near the Pafos Gate. This church is served by the Franciscans under the Patriarchate of Jerusalem and follows the Orthodox ecclesiastical calendar. Of its two priests, one is Italian, the other Polish and by far the majority of its communicants are Filipino and Sri Lankan women who come to Cyprus as domestic help. Of the 26,000 foreign workers in Cyprus, 6,500 work as home help, a job which, outside their own families, Cypriot women consider menial. They would prefer to be unemployed.

There is, too, as inalienable a link between Orthodoxy and patriotism in Cyprus as there is between Roman Catholicism and patriotism in Ireland, or Poland. In 1754 the archbishop of Cyprus was appointed 'ethnarch' by the Sublime Porte, that is, he was recognised, not only as head of the Greek Orthodox Church but also as leader of the Greek Cypriot people. All matters concerning the Greek Cypriot people were henceforth to be referred by the Ottoman governor of Cyprus to the archbishop. Not that the two always saw eye to eye and in the bloody events of 1821, the archbishop of the day, Kyprianos, was one of the first to be executed. The British, too, had no end of trouble with Archbishop Makarios III and at one stage had him exiled to the Seychelles. He, of course, won in the end and became the first president of an independent Republic of Cyprus.

Under the Ottoman rule of Cyprus (1571-1878) the second most important man, after the governor, as far as the Greek community was concerned, was the dragoman. Originally a clerk with the duties of interpreter – the word comes from the Arabic through the Turkish *tarjaman*, meaning interpreter – the dragoman was a functionary of the Ottoman governor of Cyprus. The office gradually grew in prestige and importance as, according to Murphy's law, offices do if they last long enough. The dragoman became an appointee of Istanbul and was the recognised liaison between the Ottoman administration and its Christian subjects, principally in the imposition of levies and the collection of taxes. He worked in tandem with the archbishop. Taking a lead, no doubt, from a line of corrupt administrations, including feather-nesting governors, the office of the dragoman succumbed to bribery and corruption. Inevitably elements of the Church, too, in the exercise of its material interests, were drawn into the same morass of corruption and venality. Such times have long passed but the Orthodox Church of Cyprus remains today one of the wealthiest institutions in the land. It employs a whole coterie of accountants and bookkeepers to manage the revenues collected from its land and property resources. As well as distributing its wealth in supporting a wide variety of charitable institutions and donating to worthwhile causes, the Church looks after the upkeep of its churches and pays an appropriate stipend to its priests many of whom are married men with children. The absence of a dependence on parochial funds, collected Sunday after Sunday by pledge or plate, for the housing and sustenance of its clergy, as happens especially in Roman Catholic churches in the West, removes, in my view, a barrier (and too frequently a bone of contention) between priest and people. Donations may be offered, of course, but here the essential relationship between pastor and parish is spiritual and not in danger of being perverted by a preoccupation with money.

The new and imposingly large palace of the archbishop, modern Byzantine in architecture and seeming more ostentatious because of the modest buildings surrounding it, is, appropriately enough, not far from the house of the dragoman Hadjigeorgakis Kornessios. You may be wondering about the 'Hadji' honorific but Christians who had visited Jerusalem, their Holy Place, appropriated the same title for themselves as Muslims who had visited Mecca. There are still hundreds of 'Hadjis' in the telephone directory! The dragoman's house, typical of the architecture and house design of the residences of well-off people in Ottoman time, is worth a visit. I went there. Hadjigeorgakis, I found out, became dragoman at a time – 1779/80 – when the whole country, Muslim as well as Christian, was seething under the heavy and illegal taxes imposed by the ruthless governor, Hadji Bakki. The lives of the people were pretty miserable and there had been several anti-tax revolts over the previous fifty years. Hadjigeorgakis, however, working in close co-operation with the archbishop, succeeded in stabilising the situation somewhat and continued in office for nearly thirty years. During that time he became a man of considerable wealth, a fact not warranted by his modest government salary. In 1794 he began to compile an inventory of his property, which, he said, 'I have acquired with the help of mighty God.' It included houses and farms, ships and flour mills, jewellery and 'other valuable personal objects'. It can be rightfully assumed, I think, that God was not his only benefactor. He was unable, however, to put down another revolt in 1804 when an attempt was made to set his house on fire – a rather lackadaisical attempt it must have been as they only managed to scorch the main door. Though the city was sealed off he and his family succeeded in escaping to Constantinople, where he reported on the situation to the grand vizier and begged for more troops to put down the uprising. Things went well for him at first but political changes in Constantinople saw the fall from grace of his friend, the grand vizier, who was dispatched into exile. His replacement, unhappily for Hadjigeorgakis, was more responsive to the accusations and demands of his enemies back in Nicosia. The upshot was that this controversial man, manipulative, devious and self-serving to some, religious, compassionate and generous to others, was convicted on corrupt administration charges and beheaded in Constantinople in Easter week 1809.

The dragoman's house is probably the most important 18th century building in Nicosia. It is built of local, hewn sandstone and its floorplan is in the shape of the Greek letter *pi*, with its cap toward the north, fronting the street. This was the typical layout of nearly all buildings of the era. From outside, the dragoman's house has a monumental appearance and with its high, iron-barred, ground floor windows looks more like a fortress, or maybe a 19th century prison than a residence. The first storey windows are half-barred, the top ones merely latticed. Above the main entrance is an enclosed, wooden balcony, a box-like projection, called a kiosk. It has slatted, wooden shutters which make it possible to view goings-on in the street below without being seen oneself. A similarly enclosed and covered veranda was a popular feature of all Muslim houses as it allowed the women of the house to sit outside in the cool of the evening, unobserved but still keeping an interested and watchful eye on life in the street below. A pleasant compromise, not without elements of romance and intrigue. A young woman could open the lattice a fraction and secretly attract the attention of a chosen gallant.

The arched main door has a slab of marble immured over the lintel. If you look closely you'll see the winged lion of Venice carved on it with his right paw resting on an open Bible bearing the inscription in Latin 'Peace unto you, Mark, my Evangelist'. In the centre is a shield with a double-headed eagle, symbol of both the empire and the Orthodox Church. Three hills are carved on either side of the eagle above branches bearing five pomegranates, part of the crest of one of the Venetian families of Cyprus. Where the slab came from is not known but it is certainly older than the house. Either it was an embellishment of an older house on the same site, or Hadjigeorgakis picked it up somewhere and 'adopted' it. You have to be a bit careful if you're looking closely at the marble plaque. The street is narrow, more so with cars parked on one side. Even if wealthy Greek Cypriots no longer live in this area they certainly drive through it and twice in ten minutes I had to scamper back under the lintel as large, luxury cars claimed the road. Hadjigeorgakis would have been proud!

Inside, above the main entrance, is another marble plaque which bears the monogram of Hadjigeorgakis and the year 1793 written in letters and numbers. This suggests that he began using the house as his residence at that time; he had been appointed dragoman for life in 1790 and must have felt secure enough to have had the house built.

Opposite you as you walk in is a marble fountain, no longer working and almost completely covered in ivy, though you can still see a carving of the ubiquitous double-headed eagle on the main slab. The cooling sound of the water falling into the trough beneath would have been particularly pleasant in high summer. I'm assuming, of course, that severe droughts didn't hit the island in those days as they do now. From mid-1997 the whole country was put on alternate-day water supply with the possibility of further restrictions in six months time if the rainy season failed again. It did to the extent that reservoirs are now, in May 1998, only 15 percent full. In January 1999, despite an above average rainfall in December-January, the reservoirs are still only 10.5% full. As Barbara Lyssarides, wife of one of the candidates in the 1998 presidential elections, wrote recently ' you can't always wait for the rain king to do something.' The water problem is itself another 'Cyprus problem' and one 'that any new government has to deal with right away.' And it was, of course, a woman who had to point this out!

The two wings of the Hadjigeorgakis house, the legs of *pi*, stand in marked contrast to each other; the west one continues the fortress-like appearance of the outside, while the opposite, eastern wing is of a much lighter construction, with wide wooden eaves, wooden window frames and lattices and white washed walls. Arches and their supporting columns of hewn sandstone are the main features of the spacious *cortile*, elements that are still common today in Italian architecture both public and domestic. The Venetians would have been at home in this building. Shrubs and pot plants would have provided relief from the grey, hot cobbles of the colonnade.

A steep, covered staircase, wooden on stone, takes you up to the first floor and immediately to the large waiting room, or ante-chamber, with its several pillars and arches supporting a log ceiling. The walls, now a dull green, were once brightly painted with multi-coloured decorations. The dimensions of the room are impressive and suggest that the dragoman must have envisaged that from time to time there would be a line-up of visitors and delegations with their entourages waiting to be received. A number of doors lead off from the waiting room to the other main rooms of the house of which the most important, at least from an official point of view, was the *oda*, or reception room, situated on the south side. This is typical of Ottoman reception rooms everywhere: raised floor, wood panelling, built-in cupboards, an ornately carved and decorated ceiling, fluted curtains and a continuous, low, uninterrupted seating arrangement on three sides. This armless, sofa-like seating would have been clothed in rich red, with large, tasselled cushions strategically placed for the comfort of visitors. A spread of Turkish carpets and bright floor-rugs, with scattered cushions, would have completed the furnishings and decor. Apart from one small item

– there would have been a secret passage-way leading to the roof, in case of emergencies! It all still looks sensuous and grand, a place where important people might with some comfort and dignity discuss important matters, a room for compromise and unhurried discussion – a far cry from our more solemn and portentous committee rooms with their straight-backed chairs and tables with blotting pads.

In a room to the right of the *oda* various letters and documents are displayed. Most of these refer to official business with the archbishop and others and deal principally with levies and taxes. One, however, I mentioned it previously, gave the dragoman's property holdings and a listing of his precious possessions, much as we might do today for insurance purposes. Apparently on a few vacant pages at the back of this inventory he also listed his children, giving their dates of birth, their star signs and a brief commentary on each. Two of his children were born in September, one, Michail, in 1791 and the other, Miriam, in 1793. Their star signs were Virgo and he adds after each: 'it follows that because of the nature of the Virgin he/she – Michail or Miriam – will be of sound disposition, will love chats, sophistries, scandals and praise and may God guide him/her in his commandments.' I, too, was born in September under the same star sign. I think my children might agree that Hadjigeorgakis had my measure.

The most interesting building outside is the *hammam*, or Turkish bath, which, as you walk towards the garden, extends into it on your left. It comprises three inter-connecting rooms, the first of which, small and square, is the cooling-off room, the second, a longish, narrow room is the *tepidarium*, or tepid room, which leads by a narrow, pointed doorway into the *caledarium*, or hot bath-house room. There was an underfloor hot air heating system and in the hot room a cauldron in which water could be boiled. The women and children, boys included, had first go each evening. Later on, when the boy was turning into a man and his mother observed a certain, alert and discerning glint in her son's eyes, he was given his marching orders and told to join the men for the second session. In the meantime, however, he had not only become familiar with the female body as naturally and unobtrusively as he had with his own but had also on many occasions become privy to the special 'secrets' that women tell only to other women. According to an Egyptian friend it was assumed that, as a result of these experiences, the boy would grow up more informed and more sensitive. Certainly beats sex education in school. By the way there's a functioning *hammam* in a nearby street should you feel like a thorough cleansing.

After she had taken us to a small, upstairs studio where fine jewellery was being made (and sold) we said goodbye to another helpful and charming guide. I enjoyed both these tours and thoroughly recommend them.

The Cyprus Museum, housed in what looks like a colonial villa, right next door to the British Council in Mouseiou Street is well worth spending a morning in. Whether your interest be jewellery or coins, ceramics or ivory, sculpture or sarcophagi the Cyprus Museum contains the best and most complete exhibition of Cypriot antiquity from the Stone Age onwards. Most complete, that is, until we get to the 19th century and the early years of this one when European archaeologists filched from the island many of the discoveries they made; these are now prime exhibits in museums all over the world. But you will be consoled by a fine, muscular bronze of the Emperor Septimus Severus and, possibly even more so, by the equally evocative, more distinctively Cypriot statue of Aphrodite brought here from her shrine at Kouklia.

7

LOST ON THE
ROAD TO AGIA ANNA

We've had only one experience of driving on country roads at night. It wasn't dangerous and, if anything, we ourselves were the traffic hazard. Let me tell you about it. Many ex-pats here prefer, if they can manage it, to live in villages and small towns rather than in the larger towns and cities. Each village has its own cherished identity, its own special character and, in some cases its own peculiar patois. In recognition of the importance of the village in Cypriot life there is a whole special section of the telephone directory entitled 'Villages and Small Towns'. Before we left New Zealand a friend gave us the address of a New Zealand woman who lived in the village of Agia Anna about 30 kms from Nicosia. Jean was well into her 80s and lived alone with a rectory of pigeons and two cats, one called Peter, the other, Boy. In matters of gender identification Jean was rather conventional, so I've no doubt that Peter was also a boy. Jean was probably reverting to a usage she would have been familiar with in her youth when, in her native land among the Maori people, grown men were sometimes called Boy and grown women, Girlie. The usage still exists but is less common nowadays. We were not long in Nicosia before she invited us to dinner and gave directions over the phone which seemed complex to me but we had no worries as my wife considers herself an experienced navigator. For the expedition we had borrowed an ancient Austin 1100 from an Australian friend and, as it took us some little time to coax the thing into jerking, spluttering, heaving life, it was coming on dark when we left Nicosia. The car wouldn't do above 40 kph and we were reluctant to push it to its limit, so progress on the old back road to Larnaka was slow. First we had to find Mosfiloti, the nearest large village, where, according to instructions, we had to turn off for Agia Anna.

Darkness fell quickly as it does in Cyprus at the end of September and we were soon stopping under street lights in very small towns and even smaller villages to consult the scribblings on the back of an envelope and match them up with a map which, when spread out, covered the entire two front seats of Tony's car. Several times we thought we had pinpointed where we were *and* where we were going with radar-like precision. Not so. The names of places hitherto unnoticed on the map, or not on the map at all, appeared on road signs before our disbelieving eyes. Where a name was written only in Greek we had to stop and decipher. Distances became either telescoped or elongated and where a road forked we invariably took the wrong fork which usually petered out on us after only a few kilometres. Where two or three were gathered together in small tavernas or cafes we pulled over and asked for directions. At that time our combined Greek was not up to holding a conversation lasting more than 15 seconds and the little English the rustics once possessed hadn't been exercised for years. *Kalispera*, we said, *Agia Anna, parakalo?* They were most helpful, not just telling us the fork of the road to take at every crossroads but demonstrating it for us, repeatedly pointing, *aristera*, to the left, to the right, *dexia* (two new words we quickly learned) and raising their voices in the way that some people do when speaking to the deaf. After further reference to the map and more finger-pointing we felt that, at last, we knew and, using up our entire remaining vocabulary, we thanked them. *Efkaristo poli.*

But ten minutes later after a signpost we'd been expecting went missing, and the junction Jean had been so specific about 'with a restaurant on the left and a plant shop on the right' hadn't materialised, we stopped again, this time in the middle of nowhere, and approached a house with a light showing. Or rather one of us did as the other had to stay behind, one foot on the accelerator, to make sure the car didn't die. *Kalispera* – then map in hand, fingers pointing, we'd try to discover where we'd gone wrong. Brushing the map aside as if *it* were the cause of all our problems we received new directions from a friendly husband and wife team. *Kali Tichi!* they shouted to us as they waved goodbye. To my unaccustomed ear at that time I thought they were offering us one last piece of well meant advice – 'call a taxi!' Later I found out it was the Greek for 'Good luck!'

Of course, we eventually found both Mosfiloti *and* Agia Anna

– after all Cyprus is rather a small island and we seemed to have been driving for hours. Following enquiries in the village (Jean had lived there for more than 20 years and was well known) we drove up a narrow, winding hill-street and there, at last, around a corner, to our immense relief and satisfaction, was the carport and the Morris Minor which Jean had given us as our final landmark. Not that she drove it anymore but the car was precious as an old photograph. We breathed a loud sigh of relief as a gentleman appeared in the open doorway of her lovely, old, stone house.

'The MacHughs, are you?'

'Yes, does Jean live here?'

'She does but I'm afraid she's not here at the moment. Come in and I'll explain.'

Peter, an Englishman, perhaps in his 60s, who had been principal of a number of British schools in different countries of the Middle East, was staying as a house guest of Jean's for a couple of weeks. We silently took our seats round a table on the covered veranda overlooking a *cortile*.

'Bad news, I'm afraid.'

He stopped to have a pull on his drink. Peter, an old hand, who had taught English for many years, had a sense of theatre. He cleared his throat.

'About an hour ago Jean fell over her cat, lost her balance completely and hit her head heavily on the floor' – he took his time lighting a cigarette – 'luckily I was here, in my room actually, about to change for dinner. When I found her she was unconscious' – he flicked his cigarette once or twice before continuing – 'and bless me I couldn't find any pulse. So I got on the old blower immediately and called a former nurse, an English woman, who lives not far from the village. She got here in double quick time, found a faint pulse and decided that Jean should be taken straightaway to hospital. So that's where she is now.'

'How awful,' we chorused.

'I managed to contact all the other guests,' Peter continued, 'but I couldn't catch you – you were obviously already en route [were we ever!]. So here we are, just the three of us,' – he paused and I wondered if he were going to add 'left' in the idiom of surviving mourners – 'anyway, now you're here, you'd better have something to drink. Jean's got everything.'

The nurse from the hospital soon rang to say that Jean had recovered consciousness and beyond having two black eyes and lots of bruises didn't seem to have any more serious injury. The hospital was treating her for shock and would check in the morning for hairline fractures. All three of us were relieved. Peter turned out to be a gracious and excellent host – we even got our dinner – and best of all he showed us how to return to Nicosia via the motorway. Some weeks later we finally got to meet Jean, a bright, birdlike, delightful person who'd lived in Nicosia for many years before retiring 20 years ago to Agia Anna. This time she'd invited us for lunch and we, more prudently, took an inter-city taxi.

These communal taxis are a feature of the travel industry here. They are usually stretch limos, carry up to 8 passengers and charge a flat rate per person equivalent to the total cost per person to the taxi's destination. For example, the 20-25 minutes ride to Mosfiloti cost us US$5.00 each. It would have cost exactly the same had we gone on to Limassol a further 40 minutes away. The justification is a fine piece of the best Greek sophistry. Here's how it goes. We ring up the taxi hire at noon the day before our planned trip and book two seats to Mosfiloti. They agree to take us. At 1 o'clock somebody else rings up and tries to book two seats to Limassol. He can't – our two seats to Mosfiloti were the last two available on that taxi run. Now, the explanation continues, if there were a price differential between the fares to Mosfiloti and the fares to Limassol the taxi company would lose out and, human nature being the same for taxi drivers as for stock brokers, the company might be tempted to 'cancel' our booking in favour of the more remunerative one. To avoid the possibility of such a temptation and remove the taximan's dilemma, all fares are set at the fare of the longest stretch of the ride. The driver explained this to me on our way to Mosfiloti with, I thought, a certain amount of superior intellectual pleasure at the neat logic of the argument. 'Isn't it a good person,' he asked, 'who can foresee temptation and take the steps to avoid it?' Of course! Logic aside however, this communal taxi service is a great boon to travellers. Where else in the world could you travel 85 kms in a taxi for only $5.00 *and* be picked up at your home *and* dropped off at your particular destination?

City taxis, 90 percent of which are Mercedes, are also very reasonably priced. We can go anywhere in Nicosia, day or night, for under US$5.00. This is one reason we prefer not to have a car. Another, even more valid one, would be the difficulty of parking it. We can walk into the centre of the city in 15 minutes, about the same time, we reckon, that we would spend looking for a parking space. Taxi drivers are invariably male, invariably friendly and all have, at least, a smattering of English. Almost always there is an icon, or some other religious symbol, either on the dashboard, or hanging from the roof. The same applies to private cars and, judging by the few I see with dings, despite the hazardous driving and narrow streets, there must be something to it!

We had the pleasure of visiting Jean several times over the following two years. She was renowned for her parties and continued to give them even when, invalided home after a heart attack in France, she was in poor health. A widely read, indomitable lady, with old world manners, I learned a lot about Cyprus from her. Sadly she died when we were 'off-island' in the summer of 97.

8

MAKHERAS – MONASTERY AND CAVE FIKARDOU – A VILLAGE RESTORED

The road to Makheras, 40 kms south of Nicosia, offers a pleasant drive into the mountains to a level of 700 m. Apart from its other attractions, Nicosians find a run out there an agreeable way to spend a Sunday afternoon, especially in the hot months when, in contrast to the city, it is cool and invigorating. There are also plenty of shade-providing trees both outside and inside the walls of the monastery. And the monastery has walls, an enclosing rectangle of them, which, slope-roofed for snow, fall inwards to cap corridors of Spanish arches. The church, of hewn stone, roofed, as all the buildings are, in Mediterranean red, with its single dome and attached belfry, stands central in the *cortile*. Situated on the edge of the Pitsillia, as the eastern chain of the Troodos is called, it probably derives its name from the 'cutting wind' that channels down from the heights in winter. Makheras is close in sound and spelling to the Greek word for 'knife'. When we visited on 25 March, late in the morning, the overnight snow had melted and, though there was still plenty on the hills, thankfully there was no cutting wind.

As with most 12th century monasteries in Cyprus this one, too, is associated with a miracle-working icon of the Virgin Mary, found, the legend tells us, in a cave nearby. One version of the legend speaks of a sword, or knife also being found there, goodness knows for what purpose but presumably to guard the icon. Perhaps in some vague way it pre-figured the presence in the area in the 50s of Gregoris Afxentiou, second in command of the underground EOKA movement, who was most certainly associated with a cave and may have had a bayonet attached to his gun. Afxentiou, who has become something of a national hero, fought his last action here from his cave hideout just below the monastery. Forty years ago exactly and in this same month, – it was 3 March 1957 – he held at bay for ten hours the British soldiers sent to capture him. The end of his heroic resistance came only when the British set fire to his cave and burnt him alive inside it. The cave has now become a national shrine and those who visit the monastery rarely omit making a pilgrimage to it. Inside the monastery itself there is a small museum dedicated to him. The items of his kept on show there, both military and personal, could, I thought, have been more impressively displayed.

Under the gallery on the upper floor of the monastery, its history is recorded in illustrated texts. There is another text on the main entrance door to the monastery, which, in both Greek and English, reminds us that we are about to enter a holy place and, among other things, stipulates that women in trousers would not be allowed entry. Sandra and our German friend, Kathy, had brought an acceptable change of attire with them, wrap-around skirts or some such. These they religiously put on, successfully hiding their jeans, only to discover when they got inside that Cypriot women, great numbers of them, were parading about in trousers. And not just in slacks, they pointed out to me, but in those slinky, skin-tight tights that might catch the eye of a man who wasn't even a monk. We concluded that either the holy men were turning a blind eye, or the notice needed changing. Or, both.

On our way back to Nicosia we noticed a prayer tree in an orchard. At least we concluded that it was a prayer tree and not a device, like an improvised skeleton, for frightening off birds. There were, in any case, few birds about. In fact, a search turned up none. Whilst all the other trees were planted in rows and were tall and in full and glorious blossom, our prayer tree was leafless, out of kilter in the rows and stunted in growth. It had to be special. Strings of white cloth, cut like jagged ribbons, were attached haphazardly to the bare branches. Two long, broad, red pieces of cloth like scarves, were thrown lazily over opposite sides of the tree. Viewed against the background of orchard blossom, those scattered and strung out pieces of cloth seemed enigmatic and prayerful like the yellow ribbons some people in America hang on trees to crave protection for warriors, or to welcome them safely home. This tree may have been the ostentatious prayer of a pious orchardist seeking heavenly protection for his fruit.

Some 9 kms northwest of the monastery is the tiny village of Fikardou (the signpost may say Phikardhou) which is being restored as a typical, indigenous village, one too that was favoured by the Venetians during the hot summers of the 16th century – at least until the Turks came in 1570! You can walk around it on your own but the custodian who lives in the taverna overlooking the square will willingly be your guide. Several houses have already been restored and two of them serve as *in situ* folk museums, exhibiting winepress and handlooms, old village-made furniture, earthenware storage jars *(pithoi)*, wooden bowls, gourd containers and other paraphernalia of a former peasant culture. Like the mountain *baitie* used as summer 'cottages' by shepherds in northern Italy, these houses are double storied with the ground floor reserved for animals, or sometimes for bulkier equipment such as a winepress. The upper storey uses a light mudbrick and the roof is of terracotta tiles. There is usually a stone courtyard and a barn whose roof provides a wide veranda at first floor level. The whole structure is compact and practical though a few of the more prosperous ones run to lintels and arches. Each house is almost indistinguishably joined to the house next door in a cosy pattern of familiarity and support. The short, winding streets are cobbled. Our guide told us that a number of the houses were now being prepared for agritourists, whether local or international. The thought struck me that one could live delightfully in any one of these houses, granted the essential mod cons and work in Nicosia. Once when we visited the village with friends I wrote Kathy's name in snow on a giant *pithos*. The hill behind was white and Fikardou had become a fairy village, our guide its troll.

I visited the small graveyard, paid my respects to the war dead and noted the ages on four simple, white, Greek-cross grave stones lying side by side, 80, 97, 94, 85 – 356 years between the four of them. No wonder the government is restoring the village – some of them might have an eye to retiring there.

Nearby on a marble slab set amid the pebble of a grave well cared for I read the following apologetic, comfort-giving epitaph:

So you are dead

They told me so today
Then I recalled too late
All that I'd meant to say.
But all that I'd never told you
And all I never said
You will be aware of, Now that you are dead.

We returned to the taverna, warmed up with some generous wine tastings and took a small selection home. This taverna also does a brisk trade in honey and compotes. It would be a pity to miss Fikardou if you're anywhere near.

In and Around Larnaka

9

LARNAKA AND LAZARUS

L arnaka, one of the oldest cities in the world and certainly
the oldest continuously inhabited city in Cyprus, has had
over the passage of time many different names. Recent archaeological
excavations suggest the presence of a Mycenaean settlement there
in the 2nd millennium BC, but if we are to believe the long memory
of human kind that pre-dates all historical and archaeological
evidence, Larnaka was founded by Kittim, the great-grandson
of Noah of the Ark. No proof, of course, except why else would
it have been called Kittim in the Bible, Citium by the Romans and
Kition by the Greeks! We know with greater certainty why it
was called Salines, or Salina, during part of the Frankish period
– very prosaically, because there was a salt lake nearby. There still
is. For a year or two Larnaka gloried in the wonderfully evocative
name of (La) Scala, or 'The Landing Stage', designating it functionally
as the nearest port to trade from during the siege of Famagusta by
the Genovese in 1374-75. About 1600 its current name of 'Larnaka'
came into vogue, a Greek word, meaning either a tomb or a hollow
place. In one way, I suppose, a tomb is a hollow place and the
accuracy of the derivation can be saved under both headings but
I rather think that the reference here is to the contour of the land.
But, whatever way you look at it, Rome, Dublin and Berlin are
new kids on the block as far as the antiquity of their names and
their settlements is concerned.

From the 9th century BC Larnaka was occupied by the Phoenicians.
It had a good harbour (at that time it may even have been enclosed)
which was used by the Phoenicians to export the copper, mined
about 25 kms away at Tamassos and for which Cyprus, 'the Copper
Isle', was widely famed and eponymously named.

In the mid 5th century BC a Greek fleet under Kimon, a very
famous Greek general of the time (they didn't have admirals of
the fleet in those days) besieged the town trying to flush out the
Persians. They failed and Kimon himself was killed in the attempt.
As he lay dying, however, being also a bit of a psychologist, he

forbade the Greeks to announce his death, fearing such news might become a morale booster for the Persians. So the fleet set sail under orders from their now dead general. At the command of the gods, however, the Cypriots (were they under some duress, or were they mostly Persian-Cypriots at that time?) honoured him with a monument. What became of it nobody knows but memories of heroic deeds die hard in this part of the world and so 50 years ago, in 1927, nearly 25 hundred years after the event, the citizens of Larnaka, this time entirely of their own volition, erected another one, a marble bust, which you can see on the waterfront. Translated, its inscription reads appropriately,

'Though Dead he was still Victorious'

A reminder, perhaps, that more than once in her long history, Cyprus has snatched victory from the jaws of death.

An interesting expression said to be used even still in Larnaka is 'Go tell it to Kimon', to indicate the same incredulity and disbelief that we express in English by saying 'You can tell that to the marines!' Why? I can only surmise that it's because both Kimon and the marines have a reputation for toughing it out and are not easily deceived. Of course, it could mean the exact opposite – 'you can tell it to the marines (or, to Kimon) – they'd believe you, I wouldn't.' Somehow, however, I don't believe Kimon was that credulous.

Over the arc of almost a millennium Larnaka's citizens went about the business of their daily lives with few dramatic interruptions. There was a huge fire in 280 BC and sporadic Arab raids in the 7th century AD. Nothing much in between. During the Crusader period the importance of Larnaka gradually increased but it really wasn't until the middle of the 19th century, under the Turks, that it became to all intents and purposes the commercial capital of the country. Though Nicosia remained the administrative and political capital, most of the embassies and consulates were located in Larnaka, as were the traders and their entourages of bankers, insurance agents and purveyors. For a time Larnaka, with 13,000 people, was larger than Nicosia and more cosmopolitan. In 1847, for example, there were approximately 400 Europeans living in Larnaka as against no more than a dozen each in either Nicosia, or Limassol. A hundred years later, however, as the ports of Famagusta and Limassol became more favoured and the political representatives moved to Nicosia, the political capital, Larnaka, a trifle down-at-heel, became a semi-tropical coastal city, quiescent in the sun.

The Turkish invasion in 1974 changed all that. Almost overnight its population trebled to 60,000, swollen by the influx of refugees fleeing from the north. Shortly thereafter, a new international airport was built there, the one in Nicosia having been made inoperative by the war (it still is inoperative, lying now in the Buffer Zone, patiently waiting the settlement of 'The Cyprus Problem'). More recently, many trade missions, in the form of off-shore companies, have set up offices there and its tourist potential has also been developed. Larnaka has undoubtedly benefited from the tragic turmoil of the post-war years. Pulled up by the scruff of its neck, as it were, it received a vigorous shaking and is now back in business. It could be said, that Larnaka has had three apogees, one in the Mycenaean period, one during the Turkish period in the mid 19th century and the current one instigated by the 1974 invasion. This one shows all the signs of becoming more permanent than either of the other two.

Because of its international airport (more recently an additional one was built at Pafos) Larnaka is often the first place that a visitor to Cyprus sees. Again, as more than six centuries ago, it fulfils its function as a 'Landing Place' (La Scala) a place many tourists only too briefly see before hiving off elsewhere, frequently to over-crowded Agia Napa, for their week or two in the Mediterranean sun. But Larnaka has its own sandy beaches, its own beautiful, palm-lined, seafront boulevard, ideal for the Cyprus *passeggiata*, and, running alongside, its string of good hotels and restaurants, not to mention the many nearby places of historical and cultural interest.

At the southern end of the promenade there's a small Turkish fort, built early in the 17th century and now a museum exhibiting artifacts found at Kition and elsewhere in the vicinity. There are two cannon ports and a huge conch, replete with sea anchors, embedded in the sea wall. Up the stairs there's a parapet walk where, for a sweet moment of delusion, you can feel 'monarch of all you survey'. During the first years of the British administration, however, most of the fort's inhabitants weren't able to survey very much at all, for they, the British, that is, turned it into a prison, something they were wont to do with old castles and towers. The fort is now also used as the Larnaka Municipal Cultural Centre. Quite a multi-purpose building it has turned out to be.

There are four other things for which Larnaka can justifiably claim greater fame. It's the place of which Lazarus, newly risen from the dead, was bishop for 30 years; it's the birth place of Zeno, founder of the Stoics; on its outskirts there's a salt lake and on the edge of that lake is the fourth most holy shrine of Islam. What better way to spend a pleasant afternoon than to visit these four in turn.

The church of St Lazarus (Agios Lazaros) is a short walk from the fort toward the city centre. It was built by the Emperor Leo VI in 900 AD or thereabouts, firstly, to acknowledge that the tomb or sarcophagus of Lazarus was found there. It bore the brief and simple inscription 'Lazarus, friend of Christ' and secondly to compensate the Larnakans for filching the remains and relics of the saint, barring a few small items, to Constantinople. There they remained for just over 300 years until stolen by the greedy Crusaders for their own church in Marseilles, also dedicated to Lazarus (St Lazare), who, exercising the dubious property of episcopal bi-location, is said also to have been bishop there.

Two things seem agreed: Lazarus left Palestine and there is an empty tomb. The story of Lazarus hardly needs re-telling. He was the brother of the sisters, Mary and Martha, also friends of Jesus, who were distraught at his early and unexpected death. When Jesus, knowing of the death, went to Bethany to offer his condolences, there was such sorrow expressed by the sisters, their relatives and friends, all gathered together to support each other, that He was Himself deeply touched. He wept. And when He visited the grave (a cave blocked by a boulder – you can see scores of similar ones at Petra, in Jordan) he instructed some of the bystanders to remove the stone. Martha, ever the practical one, reminded Him that Lazarus was already four days dead and, in that hot climate, would already smell. Not surprisingly the 17th century painter of the icon – the Raising of Lazarus – in the Larnaka church, has one person holding his nose. That trivial possibility did not, however, concern Jesus. The stone removed, he simply told the corpse of Lazarus, in a loud, clear voice, to re-vivify itself and leave the grave. Imagine the fright of the people, however expectant, however grateful, when Lazarus appeared at the cave opening, blinking, and still wearing all his death wrappings. They were astounded, totally awed – in a word, flabbergasted. So much so, that Jesus had to say to them, perhaps chidingly, perhaps with a smile, 'Why don't you loosen him up and let him go?' They did and it's not hard to believe that many of those Jewish friends of Mary and Martha were immediately converted. Comforting to know, however, that they still kept up with the 'old crowd' and hadn't limited friendship by belief.

As you can imagine, news of this extraordinary happening spread quickly, even to Jerusalem, which, after all, was not much more than eight furlongs – a mile or so – from Bethany and Lazarus, trying to go about his normal business, trying to pick up, as it were, where he'd left off, became a bit of a *cause célèbre* among the people. He was the kind of 'walking miracle' that the priests and the Pharisees could do without and they certainly didn't want any truck with him. So they immediately began planning the judicial murder of Jesus and began also to make life uncomfortable for Lazarus. In both respects they succeeded. Jesus was executed and Lazarus was forced into 'voluntary' exile.

It wasn't far to Cyprus – I've even read one account that claims he was born there, in Kition, as Larnaka was then called – and once he'd arrived and settled down it wasn't long before Barnabas, a native Cypriot and himself also a Jewish convert to Christianity, caught up with him. Barnabas had a penchant for consecrating bishops on rather short acquaintance, so Lazarus soon found himself bishop of Larnaka, a role he fulfilled with holy distinction but never, or so 'tis said, with a smile, for 30 years or so. Local Christians so revered him that on his death they buried him in a sarcophagus and built a little church over his tomb. This time he stayed dead.

The larger church built on the same site by Emperor Leo VI is a very good example of mid-Byzantine architecture. Three aisled and three domed over a central nave, with a crypt under the sanctuary, the church was extensively restored in the 17th century, still faithfully adhering, however, to the lines of the original one. The wood-carved, baroque *iconostasi* is among the island's most interesting wood carvings of the 18th century. The belfry was added in the second half of the 19th century.

The actual use of the church provides an example of early ecumenism. The Roman Catholic (Latin) community shared its use in the late 16th century, entering by the north door and holding their ceremonies at an altar in the northern apse. On one of the buttresses outside all the stones are carved in Armenian letters – so a visitor noted in 1625 – suggesting that the church was also used by the Armenians. One hopes they weren't restricted to the outside! Lazarus, a victim of segregation himself, would, I think, have approved of inclusiveness.

The tomb in the crypt, with its empty, broken sarcophagus, speaks for itself. It's interesting to note that the feast of the Raising of Lazarus, who is the patron saint of Larnaka, is held on the Sunday before Easter, when his icon is carried through the city in solemn procession. It is as if the events which his feastday commemorates, specifically his being raised from the dead, are meant to remind us of other events about to be commemorated on the following Sunday when another tomb was left empty.

Many churches are closed for the siesta period (often from one to four pm) so it pays to visit them either in the morning, or in the late afternoon, otherwise you may have to cool your heels for an hour or more, as we had.

Zeno, the Stoic philosopher, would have discredited the idea of episcopal bi-location. And rightly so. But he would have understood the decision of Lazarus 'to go with the flow', even if that meant self-exile. Zeno believed in 'following nature'. Rather than seek to shape circumstances to our own desires, he considered it better to allow ourselves gracefully to be shaped by them. Quite non-stressful, if you can manage it.

More certainly than Lazarus, he was born in Larnaka, or Citium, as it was then called, in 336 BC. Not surprisingly he grew up to be a merchant but unhappily for him lost all his possessions in a shipwreck in 314 BC on his way to Athens. That kind of misfortune concentrates the mind, so, rather than continue in business, he decided to take up the study of philosophy. After some years of reflection and discussion he came to the conclusion that nothing ever happens quite by chance (not even the fall of a sparrow?); rather, he opined, there was a divine intelligence at the back of things, directing and guiding them towards what is good. Why then get upset, he asked. Better to live in harmony with nature. As was the practice of the time he spoke to those students who came to him whenever and wherever it was convenient, in his case in the Colonnade, or Stoa, of the market-place in Athens. Hence the name by which his philosophy became known – Stoicism.

The joys and sorrows of individuals were as nothing when weighed against the laws of nature and the unfolding of history. One should, therefore, practice positive indifference to suffering and pain, love and even death itself. A pretty joyless philosophy, you may think, and certainly one which, in the end, didn't prevent Zeno from committing suicide. While wondering what circumstance could have so upset the equilibrium of his much vaunted indifference, one is inclined to say *'Magister, cura teipsum!'* (Master, cure thyself). Still, all in all, an appropriate enough philosophy for Cyprus which has had to endure so many vicissitudes over the centuries, pulled this way and that by opposing ways of thought, at one time, Roman, at another, Greek, with the Crusaders, the Turks and the British all having their own wheelbarrows to push. It also helps when the mail takes two weeks to cross Nicosia.

Now to the Salt Lake, which, according to one delightful legend takes us back to the day that Lazarus put ashore outside Larnaka. The story goes that, as he plodded along through the heat of the day, he was both hungry and thirsty. He was even hungrier and thirstier as the day wore on and he neared the little town towards evening. But his luck, it seemed, turned at last and he saw a thriving vineyard on the site of the present Salt Lake.

'Could I have a bunch of grapes, please?' he asked a very old woman, sitting in the sun, the *padrona* of the vineyard. Would she have been dressed in a long black garment and been wearing a black headscarf, as so many old women still do in Cyprus today? 'I'm sorry, stranger,' the crone replied 'but this has been a hard, dry year and my vines didn't produce anything.'

Lazarus, hot, tired and thirsty and seeing with his own eyes the healthy state of the vineyard, got mad at the old woman and, in the traditional way that the saints seem to use when dealing with a combination of deceit and meanness, he berated the woman and cursed the vineyard.

'Wretch,' he said, 'because you have lied to me, may the tendrils on your vines shrivel up and may your vineyard become forever more a salt lake.'

Which, say the locals, is exactly what happened. And who's to disbelieve them? Even to this day people working on or near the lake occasionally pull up the rotting roots and runners of vines that once flourished in the mean old lady's vineyard.

Whether or not the above account is true, out toward the sea, on the airport side of town, you'll find the main Salt Lake which has a perimeter of just over seven miles and is seven or eight feet below sea level. After the dry, hot winds of a Cypriot summer, the shallow water evaporates, leaving a crust of salt two to four inches thick over the surface of the lake. Scraping and raking the salt, done in the blazing temperatures of August, must be hot and back-breaking work for the hundred or so workers recruited for the job but there is little or no slacking as each worker is paid for what he or she collects. Nowadays a series of trolleys pulled by a farm bike have all but replaced the donkeys with their panniers. Despite the 'progress' one feels a little as Hardy felt about the 'Big Red Tyrant' of a threshing machine that, in the middle of the last century, usurped the traditional winnowing methods of harvesting grain in Wessex and all over England. Though Larnaka was once named Salines and salt was exported to places as far away as Venice, now only four or five thousand tons are harvested each year, all for local consumption. Salt farming and processing is a government monopoly.

The lake in winter, newly flush with the overflow from mountain streams, becomes for several months the home of pastel-coloured flamingos and long-necked, white swans which come down in flights from the Caspian Sea to hibernate. The long-legged stepping of hundreds of elegantly pink flamingos and the graceful circles of their flights over the lake provide a more scenic picture than dried salt.

Almost at the edge of the lake, surrounded by palm trees,

fountains and gardens, is a small octagonal mosque, called either Hala Sultan Tekke, or the Tekke of Umm Haram. A word of explanation. Tekke is the Turkish for 'monastery', Hala Sultan means 'Great Mother' and Umm Haram is the lady's name whose tomb lies inside. This is the most sacred Muslim shrine in Cyprus and, as previously mentioned, the fourth most prestigious one in the Muslim world. The Arab raids of the 7th century AD have been frequently mentioned in this story.

Where did they come from, these Arabs? Also called Saracens, these warriors and adherents of the Prophet had come up from the deserts in the Arabian peninsula and, with the militant enthusiasm of the newly converted, had by the middle of the 7th century spread into Syria, Egypt and Palestine. Many of the raids on Cyprus were certainly piratical in nature with their full concomitants of raping, looting and destruction which, not surprisingly, caused fear and consternation among the Cypriots. One was organised. Mu'awiya, governor of Syria, constantly sought permission from the Caliph 'Uthman to take a fleet into Byzantine territory, more specifically to Cyprus. The caliph, however, a quintessential landlubber, didn't trust the sea and it was only when Mu'awiya offered to take his wives and children with him as an earnest of his confidence in the survival of the fleet, that 'Uthman consented to an expedition. Others of Mu'awiya's officers, following suit, brought their wives and children, which was how Umm Haram, the pious lady and wife of his second-in-command, came to be in Cyprus. She, reputed to have been an aunt of the Prophet on his father's side (this is disputed) accompanied her husband on the first of the these expeditions in 647 AD. She was riding a mule at this very location when, for some unknown reason, most likely a stumble on the part of the mule, she fell from the animal and broke her neck. She was buried where she died, fortunately a picturesque location and later the site of a mosque, which the Turkish governor of Cyprus built in her honour in 1816.

There were only a handful of people visiting when I was there with friends on a tranquil Sunday afternoon in April. We observed the customary protocol by removing our shoes and were received inside the door by the portly custodian who seemed a trifle bored. He pointed out the *mihrab* facing towards Mecca and the raised and fretted womens' gallery to our right. Opposite the main door was the *minbar*, or pulpit, with below it some votive offerings. The columns were painted green, a colour that with blue, seems favoured by Muslims in the decoration of their mosques but is also associated with death, burial and the afterlife. Why green? I don't know but, for a desert people, it would not be surprising if the green of vegetation, growth and fruitfulness signified the serenity and joy of paradise. The green in the Tekke is not, however, a lively green.

From the mosque proper we went through a 'medieval' doorway to an inner, domed sanctuary built in 1760 where Umm Haram's tomb is. Around the tomb but hidden by heavy, green (again) curtains is a dolmen structure, consisting of two huge, upright stones, each about 15 ft high, supporting a third. The local Muslims have a story as good as that of Lazarus and the lake. Tradition has it, they say, that the top stone, the horizontal one, came originally, self-propelled through the night-sky from Mecca and took up a position of unsupported suspension 15 ft above the tomb and remained like that for many centuries. Public men of lesser faith, however, keen to demonstrate their solicitude for the safety of the faithful (was some kind of election in the offing?) declared the miraculous self-suspension dangerous and had the two supporting megaliths inserted as props. Now, of course, it's a test of faith to believe that the miracle ever occurred at all!

Another important tomb lies in an adjacent chamber. It is that of Khadija, grandmother of King Hussein, the present ruler of Jordan. In 1930 Khadija also died while visiting Cyprus. The tomb is of alabaster with a gold inscription.

There's an interesting story about Christian and Muslim naval salutations in Larnaka harbour. Whenever a warship of a Christian power entered the harbour it was appropriately saluted by all the Christian merchantmen in port at the time. The warship replied with a series of gunned salutes to all and sundry, making a lot of noise. There was more to come because a runner was sent forthwith to Nicosia and, with the governor's permission, the fort got into the act, banging out a barrage of its own. A lot of sound and fury – one wouldn't want to have a migraine while an entire fleet anchored one by one. All Turkish vessels, on the other hand, were instructed simply to dip their flags on entering or leaving Larnaka harbour, in homage to Umm Haram and her holy shrine. I'm sure I'd prefer this silent and more dignified greeting. But then what would be the point of trying to intimidate the dead, as surely the Christian mariners were out to do to the living?

About a quarter of a mile to the west of the mosque the ruins of a recently discovered Bronze Age village are being excavated. Many interesting finds have been reported, some on exhibit at the Fort Museum.

10

OF FINE LACE AND OLD STONES

About 40 kms out of Nicosia on the main Nicosia-Limassol highway and within similar easy access from both Larnaka and Limassol, there's a turn-off on the right for Lefkara, a twin village – Pano Lefkara and Kato Lefkara, Upper and Lower – located about 10 kms up a twisting road and 600 m up in the foothills of the Troodos Mountains. The less prosperous lower village has tiny, narrow streets, a shop, a church and two coffee houses (males only). The church is dedicated to the Archangel Michael and has some fine 12th century frescoes. Looking up, the stone-built houses with their red-tiled roofs have a southern European aspect. No dowry apartments go atop these but then the village is so rich that parents can probably afford to build separate houses for their daughters. My wife was struck with the similarity between the older parts of Lefkara village and the neolithic settlement of Khirokitia, which we visited that same afternoon, in that the houses, there, too, were built from a plentiful supply of local stone, were huddled close together as if for comfort and the alleyways were narrow and winding.

In the upper village, Pano Lefkara, there were plenty of shops and restaurants galore as tourists come here by the busloads in summer. It was, too, a favourite spot of the Venetians, especially of the womenfolk who came here to get away from the oppressive heat of the coast and of Nicosia in July and August. They brought their embroidery with them to while away the time. The local girls picked it up and, in a manner of speaking, have been at it ever since, so much so that the lace made here has a centuries-old, world wide reputation for its delicacy and refinement. Tradition has it that Leonardo da Vinci, no slouch where fine art work was concerned, visited Lefkara in 1481 and picked up an altar cloth here for the cathedral in Milan.

The embroidery is done by the local women often, in the warm weather, sitting in the narrow streets outside the shops that sell their work, chatting and gossiping. Several of the streets in the village look like never ending clothes lines as shop after shop proudly displays its lace and other work of fine needle point. Table cloths and serviettes, cushion covers and antimacassars, children's dresses and women's slips are all here at a fraction of the price you'd pay in fashionable shopping centres the world over. The linen they use – I have to tell you this – is imported from Ireland. I asked one woman who owned three shops in the village and one in Nicosia why this was so. 'We use only the best,' she said, 'and there is a long tradition of partnership between Lefkara and Ireland'. We talked for a while and I told her that I'd grown up in Limerick where there is also a famous tradition of lace making. She knew of it and seemed delighted to meet somebody from there. If I'd had my cheque-book with me I believe I could have got a good bargain that day!

The men are involved, too. They travel extensively lugging their heavy suitcases to all parts of the world, selling not only Lefkara lace but the fine silver and gold jewellery also made here. Not unsurprisingly, it is said that, within a relatively narrow vocabulary range, the men of Lefkara speak many languages among them; indeed their village has the reputation of being the most polyglot village in all Cyprus. I've also been told that there is a community penchant for playing contract bridge here. Add that accomplishment to its linguistic ability and you surely have a village of rare sophistication. Could it be that the *signore* and *signorine* of medieval Venice left more than a tradition of lace making behind them? Indeed, walking along the narrow, hilly side streets, with their stone arches and wooden balconies, a quick leap of the imagination could easily transport me and set me down in any one of a hundred hill-top Italian villages.

Lefkara gets into the history books for another less refined reason. In Crusader time the Orthodox bishop of Amathous and Limassol was sent into exile there by the Frankish (Roman Catholic) administration in Limassol. The period of exile spanned 250 years, from 1222 to 1470. A hundred years later the pain and humiliation still rankled and when the Turks landed in 1570 an Orthodox priest led a contingent of the army to occupy Lefkara. The Venetians, alarmed that such insidious actions might spread, despatched a cavalry regiment from Nicosia to raze the village and slaughter the inhabitants. Later, under the Turks, the village was re-established and granted special concessions by them. Despite the traumatic upheaval in their lives the surviving villagers returned to lace making, thus preserving for the world an art and a skill that is still universally admired.

About 55 kms south of Nicosia, 15kms farther on from the turn-off to Lefkara and just 500 metres or so off the main Nicosia-Limassol highway, lie the neolithic ruins of Khirokitia, the remains of what were considered until recently the oldest settlement in Cyprus. It has however just been announced (January 1999) that French archaeologists have discovered at Parekklisia, about 10kms northeast of Limassol, the remains of a human male, 1000 years *older* than the human remains found in Khirokitia. The settlement at Parekklisia was occupied between 8200 and 7000 BC. The remains bear similar characteristics such as artificial skull deformation, to those found at Khirokitia.

The flat-roofed, circular, stone houses, when 'plastered' on the outside, as in the reconstructed models in the area to the right of the site, look for all the world like old-fashioned, flat-roofed, cement water tanks. These rounded dwellings, which some call beehive, were tightly packed together on the steep slopes of a hill. Their ruins were discovered in the mid-30s and excavations still continue. But where, you may ask, did all the stones come from, thousands upon thousands of them? This is not too difficult to answer. Many would have been lying about, on top of, or just below the surface of the hill, as, indeed, is the case over so much of Cyprus today. The smoother rocks and larger slabs would almost certainly have been hauled up from the river-bed of the Maroni, a river, which, when in flow, borders the settlement in a loose loop from the north to the southeast. It is worth noting that a form of mortar was used to bind together the outside stones and occasionally, too, the sun-dried mud bricks which were used on the inside of the houses. It is amazing that, despite the buffetings of wind, rain and time, the mortar is still in place in such foundation walls as still remain. The floors, too, were plastered and you can see, inset, little ledges that must have provided seating around a central hearth. Pillars on which a loft could rest are visible in one hut. Here and there, outside the houses, you can see stone querns in which wheat and barley were mortared into flour, enough to supply a ring of houses which presumably were occupied by the extended family. Deer, sheep, pig and goat bones have been found.

Why did those first settlers, one estimate puts their number at 2,000, choose that particular place to make their home? The short answer is we don't know but we do know that 7,000 or more years ago the settlement was surrounded by dense vegetation, making it more likely that the inhabitants wanted to isolate themselves rather than overtly defend themselves from marauding pirates up from the coast. The river, of course, besides providing water, also acted as a kind of natural moat and the hillside slope offered some protection from attack should their hillside 'hide-out' have been discovered. They were farmers who cultivated wheat and barley and hunted pig, deer, sheep and goat. Some of these animals they had also domesticated to the extent of becoming stock-breeders. Grain was harvested by flint sickles and, as we mentioned above, stone saddle querns were used for grinding it. Exhibits of all these findings can be seen in the Cyprus Museum in Nicosia but there are several clearly identifiable querns still to be seen at the site today.

The stone structures, sometimes grouped in complexes of two or three, around a central court with only one exit, varied in size, from the smallest of 3 or 4 square metres, to the largest, of something like 25 sq. m. The smaller ones might have been bachelors' quarters; the largest could have accommodated a husband, wife and perhaps two children, a nuclear family in a non-nuclear age! Other structures were used as granaries and communal kitchens. In addition, a long dividing wall runs vertically through the settlement, for what reason we don't know. One surmise has it serving a functional purpose, separating, perhaps, the generations, or doing duty as a retaining wall to prevent soil erosion. A simpler and more likely explanation is that it was the original perimeter wall, which was allowed to remain after the group's numbers increased and the settlement expanded on the other side of the wall. It reminded me of those stone walls in Connemara that are used as hedges to mark off fields or property.

These earliest settlers were a short people, the men, on average, about 1.6 m tall, the women shorter. In a strange reversal of present day trends the men outlived the women but neither possessed longevity as most were dead by 40. They were buried in crouched or congested positions in shallow pits under the living room floor and sometimes there were earth-holes which permitted the living to communicate with the spirits of the deceased. And vice versa, one supposes. These holes also allowed libations to be poured from time to time, keeping the spirits below happy on a kind of intermittent drip feed of attention, thus securing their continuing involvement in family affairs and ensuring better protection and counselling for the living. Do we express wonder at such far off, primitive customs? When I was in Tanzania in the 60s it was widely believed that the Makonde tribe from Mozambique, who were 'imported' to work on the sisal plantations near Tanga, used to bury their dead under the 'lintel' of the 'door', or entrance way to their huts. Though Christian, they rarely, if ever, used Christian, or any other communal burial grounds. Their dead still lived and they wanted to keep them close by. Not awfully different, is it, when one comes to think about it from the desire of bereft loved ones to keep an urn containing the ashes of a deceased spouse, child or dear friend on a shelf in their bedrooms?

We know little about the features of these early settlers except that their skulls were almost as wide as they were long and that nature was assisted in achieving this symmetry by artificial cranial deformation. From an analysis of skeletal remains it seems that the back of the head was flattened by having a wooden board bound tightly to it. Beauty in the eye of the beholder? Hard to be sure but this kind of primitive mortar board is probably less offensive to Westerners than the practice of some of these same Makonde women mentioned above, who, even today, pierce their upper lips and insert through them a variety of gadget-ornaments that look like the flywheels of large watches. Should nose studs fall into the same category of facial embellishment?

I left Khirokitia with a strange feeling of unease, of eeriness, almost. What I had looked at on that sunny Sunday afternoon was not an aseptically presented exhibition in a museum, neither had stone been placed on stone in frivolous vanity to create, as in Egypt and elsewhere, monuments of megalithic grandeur. Here I had touched stone placed upon stone exactly as 'my ancestors' of 7,000 years ago had placed them. These were their houses, their homes, the streets where their children played, the ledges they sat on, the querns they used to grind their corn. A whole world of history had passed since then – the Ptolemies and Caesar, Troy and Rome, Alexander and Napoleon – but on this rock-strewn hillside I was able to touch events which had preceded them all. It was a bewildering thought and a humbling prospect. Where will the houses be that we inhabit now in 7,000 years' time or even in 700? Were the thoughts and aspirations of the men and women who fashioned these buildings any different from ours? A safe place for the family in an environment that would sustain it? We have added leisure, competitive consumerism and huge military complexes that have the power to destroy everything, even these ancient houses and the world that for a while sustained them.

As with other aceramic settlements the end of this one was sudden and inexplicable. We do know, however, that the site was occupied by a ceramic culture 1,500 years later. If you're at all interested in the remnants of a Neolithic civilisation then Khirokitia is worth a visit. This ancient site was placed on UNESCO's World Heritage List in December 1998.

Both Lefkara and Khirotikia can be comfortably visited in a morning or afternoon from Larnaka, Limassol, Agia Napa or Nicosia.

11

STAVROVOUNI –
THE OLDEST MONASTERY

In 45 AD when Saints Paul and Barnabas founded the Church of Cyprus they proclaimed themselves to a people, Greek both in language and culture. Over the ensuing millennia, the Church preserved that Greekness, thus insuring, despite the roll-on effects of successive occupations, the survival of Cypriot Hellenism.

Throughout its long history, monasticism has been an abiding feature of the Church's practice of Christianity. Out of the 19 active monasteries in Cyprus today, 11 are Greek Orthodox; the others belong to the Maronite rite (4), the Latin (3) and the Armenian (1). Despite the recent allegation of His Grace, the Bishop of Pafos, Chrysostomos, that 7 percent of monks are homosexual and that a number of the heterosexual ones spend nights away from the monasteries with their mistresses, the sanctity of monks and nuns has always been revered by the Cypriot people. They are seen as conduits between the faithful and God and both their intercession and their spiritual guidance are routinely sought.

The oldest monastery in Cyprus is Stavrovouni, the Mountain of the Cross, situated on a hilltop, more a crag, really, about 660 m above sea level, and about 7 kms off the main Nicosia-Larnaka road. It's 37 kms west of Larnaka. The road up is quite a climb, even for a car and should be avoided by a human on foot during the summer months. The monks follow the rule and revered canon of the Monastery of Mt Athos in northern Greece, a rule of strict observance, which forbids the entry of women, including nuns and female infants, within the monastery precincts. It is the only monastery in Cyprus to do so. Should they make the journey, however, there is some compensation for them in the cool, clean air and the superb view. On a clear day you can see the great Troodos mountain range, the extensive Mesaoria Plain and beyond it, the Mediterranean. A Canadian friend told me that she saw so much of the island from up there that ever after she suffered from 'insular claustrophobia'. I suppose that's understandable if you're from Canada.

The annual military training exercises of the Reserve Army were taking place in the area at about the time we went there. Sunday, however, as in more chivalrous times, was a non-fighting day and the monastery was full of soldiers in camouflage, sightseeing, visiting the chapel, buying books, icons and honey from the small, well stocked monastery shop. I didn't see any sultanas, though, according to legend, here is where they were first cultivated on the island. It was momentarily strange to see soldiers and monks mix briefly together in their different uniforms. I would have liked to have taken a picture but photos are not permitted (neither by the monastery, nor by the military) and, if you bring a camera up to the entrance, you must surrender it there.

The monastery was first built on the site of an ancient temple dedicated to either Aphrodite or Jupiter (opinions differ) in 327 AD by order of St Helena, mother of the Emperor Constantine. Apparently she visited the island on her way back from Jerusalem and gifted to the inhabitants a small part of the True Cross (some say only a nail) as well as the entire cross of the Penitent Thief, with instructions that a monastery be built to house them. Hence the name, Stavrovouni, 'Cross Mountain'. One tradition has it that the cross of cypress wood in which the fragment, or nail, of the True Cross was inserted, remained suspended for several centuries in mid air, without any visible form of support. The English traveller, John Locke, was one of the last to see the relic in 1553.

During the Lusignan period Benedictine monks replaced the Orthodox ones but, despite imposing fortifications, the monastery was overrun by the Mamluks in 1426, after the rout, near Khirotikia, of Good King Janus, one of the last Crusader kings and the relics destroyed. The silver reliquary we see in the church today is said to contain a splinter of the True Cross, found and salvaged in some uncertain way. It is venerated accordingly by both monks and people. The fate of the cross of the Penitent Thief is unknown but a wandering Dominican friar claims to have seen it, still intact, in 1486. Perhaps it was stolen.

The monastery suffered rampage and another burning during the Turkish conquest and was only re-built in the last century when it was repopulated by monks and, to ward off the snakes, a cattery of cats! Both are still there. About 20 monks (most of the ones I saw looked relatively young) form the community today and, as well as chanting the divine office, they spend their time in study and hard work in the surrounding fields. Some of their devotions are nocturnal and their two meals a day are vegetarian. They all dress in traditional black robes, cylindrical black hats and wear beards.

Inside the monastery, sitting on a ledge in a small, inner courtyard, I met a man from Nicosia. He was grey-haired, perhaps 55, and stout. He suffered, he told me, from a chronic blood disorder and had been coming to the monastery most weekends for the past 20 years. While I sat beside him on a vacant part of the ledge, he told me about his wife and family, his work, his illness and his hopes. A monk brought me a glass of fruit juice and some of those hard, figure eight biscuits that Cypriots like. He sometimes spent a week there, he said, and knew all the monks by name. He stood whenever the abbot passed. By the Friday of each week he was, he said, so exhausted and his blood count so low that he could scarcely drive to the monastery but after a weekend of quiet discourse with one of the monks, of sharing their fare with them in their tiny refectory and drinking their home-made juice, he became re-invigorated and 'miraculously' able to cope with the following week's strenuous work. I wondered what his wife thought of this timetable. I thought it a pity that she couldn't accompany him.

This gentle man showed me around, pointing out some outcrops of rock that had been 'chiselled' smooth and were, he said, part of the foundations of the temple to Aphrodite (or Jupiter), that pre-existed the 4th century monastery. We visited the small, dark, over-furbished church where the relic is and walked through the narrow, low-ceilinged dormitory where each monk has a bare and simple cell. I imagined how cold it must be up here when winter winds blow down from the Troodos.

The monks, he told me, followed sun time and showed me a sundial high on a white-washed wall. It was approaching lunch time and would I like to eat there, share a meal with the monks? I told him I would but had better rejoin my patiently waiting wife outside, otherwise my lunch would do me no good at all. On the way out he showed me a sign that says in Greek 'If you die before you die, then when you die, you won't die.' Cryptic but message-laden and a consoling reminder to the monks that, in renouncing the pleasures of this life, they will be assuring themselves of whatever joys await them in the hereafter. I have a suspicion, however, that it was meant more for the pilgrims than the monks and that, indeed, is what you are when you visit Stavrovouni. Not a tourist. My ailing friend took gracious leave of me and hoped we would meet again.

On the way down we called in at a little studio by an S bend, where one of the monks spends his time painting icons. Inside there was a large range on rather haphazard display. Those done in gold leaf were quite pricey, up to and above US$200. These are the ones on which ultra thin sheets of 24-carat gold are laid over the wood and brushed with a thin coat of glue. We bought a lesser priced one, a copy of one done in 1898. It is of St Barbara whose haloed image dominates the icon. Then, as is typical of this form of didactic art, there are, from half way down on either side, five, one-inch, square panels, ten in all, depicting with a fair amount of realism, scenes from the life of the saint, her accusation, suffering and ultimate martyrdom. It still hangs on our wall. Icon painting has sometimes been called the 'supreme art of the miniature'. 'What makes the miniature unique,' says Nikos Paleo, a highly respected 90-year-old Greek painter of miniatures 'is that it forces an artist to focus.' Certainly the intricate drawing and delicate, polychrome brushwork of an icon, some of which are no larger than a matchbox, concentrates the faculties in a unique way. 'A large work of art tends to reflect many of the artist's moods,' Paleo continues, 'because of the many days it takes to complete. But with a miniature an artist sits down as if at prayer, drawing and reflecting with the energy that is inside him at that particular time.' A non-believer, he says, could not be an icon painter.

There is a static, presentational quality about many icons, it seems to me – they first of all make a statement about, say, the majesty of God reflected in the majesty of Christ, the Son of God, or about the relationship between Virgin and Child in a reflection on some aspect of the Incarnation and only secondarily and, as it were, vicariously, is there an intent to modify, or appeal to, the emotions. Nevertheless, to witness a row of people before the *iconostasi* in a Greek Orthodox church, kissing each icon in turn and lifting up their children, one after the other, to do the same, is to witness an emotional response; whether this be due to religious culture, or personal devotion is another matter. Perhaps both. Few would be the Greek Cypriot homes without an icon or two on display.

12

AGIA NAPA – OUR LADY
OF THE FOREST

The ancient Greek word 'napa', used by Homer in the Iliad, means 'wooded valley' and it would seem that in ancient times this southeast coast of Cyprus was covered in thick forest, mainly of junipers, with a goodly supply of natural springs. But what of the 'agia' which in Greek means 'holy' or, 'saint'? As so often in Cyprus the explanation lies in the discovery of an icon. Or, so Michael, a grey-cardiganed, middle-aged, articulate Greek Cypriot told me. He was seated behind a donations table in the cave – he insisted I call it a cave, not a grotto – that, like a catacomb, was used, he said, by Greek Orthodox Christians over several centuries as a place of refuge from iconclastic Byzantines, piratical Arabs and Catholic Crusaders. It seems that sometime in the 11th century a hunter, following his dog who was following a hare, came upon an opening up there, small but large enough to allow him to enter – Michael pointed to the rock ceiling to his left – and enter he did, whether out of curiosity or persistent search for his dinner I do not know – but inside he immediately found himself face to face with an icon of the Virgin on which shone some miraculous light. It is thought that the icon was hidden there to save it from the 8th century iconoclasts. The narrow opening gave way to the cave we were now in except that as the numbers of Orthodox increased they had to tunnel deeper into the rock. Once when pirates stayed around for longer than usual, the cave dwellers were suffering severely from the pangs of thirst and prayed to the Virgin to save them from certain death. According to tradition, said Michael, the Virgin appeared to them and pointed to a corner of the cave where water was already beginning to burble. This was the icon's first miracle and the reason for the 'agia' in Agia Napa. The water is still burbling and the cave-shrine has expanded into a semi-subterranean church.

Outside and above the cave is the monastery which, in its spacious, terraced gardens shaded by a 600 year old sycamore fig tree with below, an attractive black and white pebble-pavement courtyard, is the Still Point in a rather brash, new town, 'a point of intersection of the timeless with time', as Eliot might describe it. The Monastery, in a strange, coincidental way, perpetuates the idea of refuge, this time of a wealthy Venetian lady who, in the early 16th century when she was being forced into a marriage not of her choice, fled from Famagusta to Agia Napa to become a bride of Christ, whom even the Venetians dared not take on. There she built a convent which continued to flourish for more than a hundred years until in about 1668 it was converted into a monastery which lasted another 90 years or so. After 1758, for reasons unknown, it ceased to be inhabited by a permanent community of monks. The church, however, was used by the local Orthodox community until the building of the fine, barrel-vaulted new church with its wide colonnaded portico in the late 1980s. Of the remaining buildings some have been turned into a conference and social centre for Christian Churches of Cyprus and the Middle East. On the eastern side the Roman Catholics have an oratory, a favour being returned by the Orthodox Church for a similar accommodation offered to them by the Catholics when the country was ruled by diehard, Latin rite Lusingans. In fact, as I wandered through the cloistered courtyard I heard the sounds of what I took to be a Pentecostal service. Instead I found a small group, no more than half a dozen Philippinas, with guitar and tambourines, belting out in loud voices totally disproportionate to their number, upbeat hymns of praise sung in English - the El-Shaddai Chapter of Agia Napa at worship.

Before the Turks arrived in 1570 the Venetians had an elaborate plan for doubling the size of the monastery but the only part that was built was the double storey gatehouse. Below the gatehouse an old irrigation channel still spills water through an antique (some say Roman) boar's head. The octagonal, domed fountain in the centre of the partially colonnaded courtyard was, it appears, built by the family of the Venetian lady who first founded the monastery. Sculptural representations of her and of her family are carved into the marble sides. Memorials writ in water that prevail? The honey-coloured masonry, the flowing fountain and nearby cistern, the leafy, unspoilt garden, the cobbled stones and gigantic old sycamore tree, 30 metres high and of ample girth, all contribute to an aura of prevailing serenity that contrasts discordantly with the busy square and crass consumerism of the town's main street. There gaudy invitations to eat, drink and be merry stretch out like one-armed bandits from almost every building. Crude, glittering, competing shingles, all written in English, beckon you inside. There is a proliferation of restaurants, takeaways, bars, inns, coffee shops and yes, yet another Orange Grove Hotel. On this Sunday afternoon in late November with ominous clouds gathering, the streets look lonely and abandoned but I've no doubt that during the long summer season the tens of thousands of tourists who come here from Britain and elsewhere get exactly what they want, a home away from home, plus sun, sea, comraderie, disco music and palm trees. Children are well catered for. Besides the usual fun fairs there are spine-tingling waterslides at WaterWorld.

Once, not much more than 20 years ago, you could see the sea from the monastery. No more. In an understandable effort to provide food, entertainment and accommodation as close as possible to the shore all the intervening space has been gobbled up by buildings. I walked along the harbour pier. The fishing boats are still there, side by side, sardine-packed, scores of them, snail-like winches lifting from their prows, well cared for, indicating that Agia Napa still maintains a fishing village's tradition. Many fishermen will have known it as nothing else since it was only when Varosha died, in the afterwake of the 1974 invasion, that modern Agia Napa was born. Though it was first mentioned in historical records in 1366 it remained for 610 years a picturesque fishing village, site of a famous monastery, visited by discerning tourists from Famagusta/Varosha, 15 kms up the road. After 1974 the refugees poured down, quintupling the population and out of their distress built a new resort by six sandy beaches almost as if in retaliatory compensation for what they had lost. Now the quiet harbour shelters day-cruise boats and glass-bottomed boats. On the day I visited a government fishery patrol vessel was also moored there. On the adjacent 900 metre wide stretch of Agia Napa Harbour every imaginable variety of water craft, from windsurfer to ski boat, awaits the water enthusiast providing a sea-paradise unrivalled on the island. Agia Napa may not be everybody's cup of tea but, if building sand castles is your thing, Agia Napa is your heaven. On a summer's day the small beaches are crowded with mostly European sun-worshippers baked every shade, from pink to deep mahogany, lolling on chaise longues under umbrellas, reading and relaxing and enjoying the warm clear sea. Should they feel the need of more strenuous activity, there is the standard range of Mediterranean amusements, from paragliding to banana boats. In the balmy evenings they can enjoy the delights of their hotel or tourist apartment amenities or dine in a range of restaurants offering international cuisines and afterwards move on to a bar or disco for further revels. Agia Napa is one of Cyprus' livelier playgrounds.

As we left for Pyla a tropical downpour darkened the rich, red soil of the fertile plains around Agia Napa called by Cypriots the Kokkinochoria, the Red Land. Here it is that farmers can grow three crops a year of some of the best potatoes in the world and that's high praise coming from an Irishman.

13

PYLA – VILLAGE ON SHOW

A nybody home? I shouted up the staircase.

Come on up! – the big voice boomed in an unmistakable Irish accent.

In the day-room, a tall, balding man looked relaxed, his dark blue tunic thrown over the back of a chair.

I'm on my own here – the rest of the lads have gone down the road to play a game of football. It was a Sunday afternoon.

'The rest of the lads' were all members of the Irish police force, the Garda Siochana, as they're officially known in Ireland, or, more commonly the guards and 'down the road' was the British sovereign base of Dekelia.

Sandra and I, with some friends, were in Pyla, an inland village northeast of Larnaka, unique in Cyprus as the only mixed village, where Greek and Turkish Cypriots live side by side (almost) under the discreet, friendly supervision of the 'Guardians of the Peace', as the Gaelic name of the Irish police translates. Pyla has the further distinction of sitting right on the demarcation line, the so-called Green Line that runs across the Island from Kato Pyrgos to Famagusta. On the hill overlooking the village you can see clearly a Turkish pillbox and, close by, on an out-spur of rock, even more clearly, the colossal, menacing likeness of a Turkish soldier with fixed bayonet, silhouetted against the skyline. The purpose of the 'sculpture' could only be to intimidate.

He's a bit close, I ventured, looking out the barrack's window, after we had discussed football for a while.

Neither he nor they should be there at all, he replied, they've been told by the UN times without number to pull back but they take no notice and nobody does anything about it. I suppose they can't, he added, short of a skirmish and anyway it's a good drawcard.

Pyla, which is one-third Turkish Cypriot and two-thirds Greek Cypriot in a total population of 1,200, has, indeed, become a 'show' village. Visiting UN officials have it on their list, tourists make a point of going there and foreign dignitaries are taken there, all of them to witness the strange phenomenon of two different, ethnic groups of people, both Cypriot, living together in relative harmony. I had taken a stroll around the quiet streets earlier. There seemed to be two of everything. Certainly there were two schools, each proudly flying its own flag, one Greek, the other, Turkish.

There was a mosque, complete with minaret, and a small Greek church, complete with bell tower (a new and much larger church was being built).

There was a Turkish *cafeneion* on one side of the street, old, with a graceful colonnade of arches and an old man sitting outside letting his beads slip between his fingers and, on the opposite side, an 'upstart', modern rival, garish by comparison, a Greek taverna. A few Turkish Cypriot boys were exercising themselves by pushing and occasionally, with great sound and fury, riding a couple of mopeds round the streets, racing. Otherwise, there was nobody about.

I asked if they had any problems in Pyla, any trouble?

Nothing to write home about, he said, then, chuckling to himself, he added, oh yes, there was one incident.

He walked over to the window, had a quick look around and returned to his chair by the table.

Late one night I was at home, on call, you might say. We don't staff the station at night unless when things get a bit tense-like. After the murders on the line near here in August-September last year (1996) we stayed overnight for a while.

(I remembered that it was one of the female officers of the Irish Police contingent who, putting her own life in danger, went to the aid of a stricken Greek Cypriot.)

Anyway, to get back to my story, the phone rang and it was a Turkish Cypriot I knew from the village warning me that a Greek Cypriot who'd had more than too much to drink was on his way up the hill to take the Turks and their pillbox single handed. So I ups and leaps on my motor bike and was here in two shakes of a ram's tail. Then I phoned K15 – that's what we call the outpost up there – and told them I was coming up. And up I went, looking about me, it was a lovely night, with the moon shining like a harvest moon at home but no trace nor sign of the hardy boy. The Turks on duty swore they hadn't seen a hair of him either. So, what to do? Anyways, I returned to the barracks, believing yer man to be stretched out somewhere on the hill, dead to the world and that he'd be clambering down at first light in the morning. Though it was all a bit of a laugh, something told me to put in a report and – lucky for him – I did.

How was that?

Well, when he didn't appear the next day, nor the next after that, the UN decided to launch an inquiry and the upshot was that the Turks had captured him alright and taken him into custody and poor man would be appearing before a court. He was lucky to get away with a week, loitering behind the lines, they said he was.

And if you hadn't sent in a report?

If I hadn't sent in a report – he hesitated a moment – anybody's guess, the Turks don't have a polite way of askin' what you're doin' on their side of the line. But it's his Turkish Cypriot 'mate' he should be thankful to and I don't suppose he's said a word of acknowledgement to him.

It's like that, is it?

It's like that – below the surface, of course. How else could it be with the ring of Turkish army posts up above and yer man looking down with his threatenin' bayonet and down here, the Greek Cypriot army telling visitors not to cross the street to buy a cup of coffee. It's not a great augur for the future, I suppose, but it's lasted nearly a quarter of a century now and it's a good beginning. You have to begin somewhere.

We chatted on for a while longer. It was all a bit nostalgic for me as my father had for many years worn just such a uniform. With apologies I rejoined Sandra and our New Zealand friends, Sue and Margie, who had spent my absence surveying the village and looking at the mostly shuttered shops.

A large, new Greek Orthodox church was under construction on the right hand side of the village. Will its twin towers, I wonder, and central dome outbalance the mosque on the left hand side of the village with its single, tall minaret? The cost of the new church, more than £800,000 sterling, is being heavily subsidised by the government and the president of the Republic, in the first ever visit of any president to the village, himself laid the foundation stone. The Greek Cypriot *mukhtar* of the village (there is also a Turkish *mukhtar*) stated at the ceremony that the purpose behind such an elaborate and expensive project was to show the many tourists and visitors to the village that there are Greek Orthodox people living there. One could hardly have been in any doubt about it though it was still the trio of Turkish boys who were making all the running in the streets.

Northern Cyprus

14

CROSSING THE LINE
IN A BORROWED CAR

The border crossing. Cypriot side, Sunday morning, 8 am. Passports in hand we parked outside the immigration building and walked inside. A man in civilian clothes got up from behind a desk. Unsmiling.

'Wait your turn outside and park your car over there' – he pointed to a space to the right of the building. We did as we were told. Though it was a bright, sun-blessed morning, with little or no traffic at the border (the couple inside were walking across, they told us later) the tone of this official was gruff and peremptory. Soon it was our turn and we were called inside. The man flicked several times through our passports.

'You tourists?'

'No.'

'Do you work here?'

'Yes, one of us does.'

'Which one?'

'Me.' (Sandra also believed in brevity.)

'Where's your pink slip?' He wasn't asking about her underwear.

'The immigration people have it. They haven't given it to me yet.'

'Hm ... Where do you work?' She told him.

'I see. Is that your own car?'

'No,' she answered truthfully, 'it's a borrowed one.'

'You're not allowed to cross here in a borrowed car.'

'It's not really borrowed' – I cut in – 'it belongs to the institution and those who need it share it.' After that he spoke only to me.

'Where's the insurance?'

'It must be in the car somewhere, or maybe it's in the office at the ... do you want me to go and search for it?'

Silence, while he toyed with the passports.

'I shouldn't but ... Ok, you may go in but you must get your immigration and work permits fixed up immediately.'

'We'll see about them straightaway,' I fibbed placatingly.

'You are not allowed to buy anything, anything at all, in the 'occupied territory' and you must be sure to be back here before five. Absolutely.'

We thanked him and left.

On our way through No Man's Land, passing on our left the Ledra Palace, headquarters of the United Nations, Sandra said, 'This is Marlboro Country, you do all the talking for the rest of the day.'

'That'll be a neat change', I quipped. But I did. The teasing expressed our relief.

In other parts of the divided city the Green Line consists of barbed wire, sandbags piled one on top of the other, wrecks of cars, rusty barrels of cement and the derelict, dilapidated houses and shops that prior to 1974 were part of a street now split in two. It is a sight more poignant than even the Berlin Wall was, because the dividing line here was sloppily improvised and has the decayed appearance of emptiness and neglect that one associates with an unreconstructed bomb site. One also gets more immediately the feeling of panic fleeing and the human tragedy of lives suddenly cut apart. Perhaps, on reflection, it is better that we are left with such a cheap and shabby reminder of how the Green Line was shaped.

The ramparts and bastions of the Venetian walls of the old city, built to integrate and protect the citizenry of Nicosia, now also act as dividing walls. At times of tension I have seen small groups of Turkish Cypriot youths approach the rampart edges, not more than 100 m from a UN outpost, to jeer and shout abuse at the Greek Cypriots below.

At the Turkish crossing the officials couldn't have been more pleasant or accommodating. They must have been individually selected by the Northern regime for their low key amiability. The girl who took our money gave us a 'Good morning' smile and continued munching her breakfast. The soldier-policeman who came ambling over to our car, leaned familiarly on it and told us we were welcome, that we could stay as long as we liked and wished us a pleasant time in the Northern Republic. Neither side stamped our passports, the Greek Cypriots because they don't recognise the North as an independent state, the Turkish Cypriots because they're poor and need tourist dollars. Had they stamped our passports we would not have been allowed to re-enter the South. So we paid them two Cypriot pounds for each of us and two for the car, a total of about US$12. And on both sides the fiction that we'd passed the day in limbo prevailed! Please note that the crossing fees have recently (1998) increased and seem to vary by nationality.

Since the tragic deaths of two Greek Cypriots that were so graphically displayed on TV screens world-wide in August/September 1996, there is an atmosphere of greater tension at the crossing. On the Greek Cypriot side huge posters depict the brutal killings, one of a young man who was shot as he climbed up a Turkish flagpole, clamping the pole with his feet like an electricity board repair man, cigarette in mouth, the other savagely cudgelled to death at the barbed wire perimeter, both now, understandably, national heroes in the south. Militants, organised by an outspoken member of parliament, and mostly relatives of the missing 1,619 prisoners of war who never returned to their homes after the 1974 invasion and are now sadly presumed murdered, stop all traffic, especially at weekends, hand out leaflets and, in a forthright, occasionally aggressive manner, seek to persuade tourists from going over to 'the other side'. Their contention is that people crossing over, spend millions annually in meals and purchases of much cheaper goods in the North, which they then have mailed home. This, they contend, is giving support and succour to an illegal regime. The government in Nicosia, while disapproving, has not stopped the interference with people's perfectly legal rights to travel to the North under the restrictions laid down. While one has sympathy with those who have lost loved ones and some understanding of their motives, private harassments of this nature seldom win friends and do nothing to enhance tourism in the South. Statistics do show a reduction in the number of crossings but what effect that is having on the income of the northern treasury we are unlikely to find out. Even as I write, Mr Denktash, in retaliation for Britain's making it compulsory for all his 'citizens' to have entry visas to Britain, issued by the High Commission in Nicosia, has raised the daily entrance charge to the north to CP15 (about US$30) for those holding British passports. That should have an even more serious effect on his tourist revenue.

At the Turkish crossing, not more than a stone's throw away, there are more huge posters recalling atrocities committed by the Greek Cypriots on the Turkish minority (one a particularly gruesome murder of a mother and her three children in 1963) and others thanking the Army of the Turkish Motherland for saving the lives of the Turkish Cypriot population and giving them the opportunity to live in peace and security. A pessimist would say 'never the twain shall meet', an optimist, that, from this mistrust, openly expressed, and from these acknowledged horrors, there is a way forward through admission of guilt on both sides and the asking of forgiveness. From the ashes of a discordant past, Cyprus, phoenix-like, as so often throughout its long history, can rise again to become a unitary state where the rights of both its peoples are equally respected. But it will take goodwill and compromise on both sides.

While one appreciates the depth of feelings of those in the South, even with the immigration officer, who was most affable when we met on another occasion, I cannot help wondering whether a policy of non-fraternisation is a good one. This policy is being implemented by both sides for short-term political ends, though in fairness, it should be pointed out that there is no legal prohibition on Greek Cypriots from crossing to the North. It simply is not done. By anyone. The prohibition comes from the other side whose own residents require permission, seldom sought or granted, to come South. In fact, for visitors, there is no land crossing at all from the North into the South. As far as Greek Cypriots are concerned they have entered the country through an illegal airport and will be, therefore, turned back at the Ledra Palace checkpoint. To me this policy of segregation between the inhabitants of both sides of the island, seems to bolster, almost encourage, the distinctive separateness, not so much of the political boundaries but of the sociological differences between the two ethnically different communities. In this context it's not so much religion, language, even culture that I'm thinking of (they will always be different) but a way of looking at life, a mode of thinking, a habit of daily intercourse with their shared environment, that, left alone, without the frequent need to respect, compromise and make allowance for their cultural diversities, can only deepen the divisions between them. With every passing year the present way of life of the Turkish Cypriot in the North, isolated as it is from that of his fellow Greek Cypriot in the South, becomes more precious to him, more a necessary expression of what he considers as his natural and moral right to live in guaranteed security as part of a separate entity. Granted that the North is overall poorer and less technologically sophisticated than the South, the people there will, nevertheless, become increasingly accepting of the *status quo*, wanting henceforth to continue to be bosses of their own destiny, like an adolescent child running away from home and being satisfied to live in a garret as long as he can do his own thing. As long as the increasingly more prosperous South (where not a few make pots of money and pay lip service only to integration) continues to disparage and look down on the lower standard of living of people in the North, they are cementing in the separate and different socio-cultural identity of the people of the North. This, of course, is precisely what Denktash wants to foste and this is why he insists on Greek Cypriots having their passports stamped by his illegal regime, knowing full well that they will not submit to that condition.. Nevertheless,I think, with all respect, that if I were a Greek Cypriot politician I would do all in my power (perhaps in conjunction with the United Nations) not to permit the two parts of the island to develop in isolation one from the other. I would want to swamp the North with their erstwhile co-citizens from the South at weekends, on public holidays and whenever else possible and as a necessary corollary, of course, invite their Turkish Cypriot fellow citizens to come South where they would be welcomed with all courtesy there is an impasse at the moment but if neither side is prepared to budge on this issue I see little chance of amicable integration.

And who would want the other kind? Too many years have already gone by for old conflicts, old grudges, old misunderstandings to be allowed to continue to keep a country's two ethnic groups apart, especially when the quarrels which started the division were not entirely unilateral, not even entirely voluntary, engineered as they too frequently were by a manipulative colonial power for its own political ends. Real re-integration, in my view, can only be achieved by real re-socialisation, never, I believe, by the stroke of a pen, enforced schedules and imposed 'solutions'.

The United Nations has had some significant success in organising reciprocal religious pilgrimages, one from South to North, to the monastery of Apostolos Andreas in the Karpas Peninsula, the other from North to South, to the Tekke Hala Sultan near the Salt Lake, outside Larnaka. There have also been Across-the-Green-Line social gatherings, some of several thousand people, at the Ledra Palace Hotel in the Buffer Zone. And there has been a carefully monitored and overall successful rock concert featuring lead singers from both cultures. Only through such inter-communal meetings of ordinary people can trust and respect be given an opportunity to grow.

But on to Salamis, through the arid, rugged, tufted, sun-drenched plain which stretched for mile after mile, a Mediterranean steppe. One supposed that nothing lived there, but men with guns and gun dogs, some in camouflage that in that barren environment served more to draw attention to them than the reverse, were out hunting. At first I thought they were sentries on patrol duty, as I could see no other reason for their being on these bare, craggy, moorland moonscapes. But then I saw one with a large bird, still dripping, a pheasant, maybe, or a partridge, hanging ostentatiously from his belt – a public statement of success when he returned home to his village later that day. Last week in the South 80,000 pheasants were released into the wild by a government department to enhance the environment and provide easy targets for the hunter-gatherers.

'Christmas is coming and the geese are getting fat
Please put a pheasant in the old man's hat'

– an only slightly changed piece of doggerel from the one we used to recite when I was a child. I'm not sure what's on the Christmas menu in Cyprus. It seems, however, that quail and a variety of other small birds are their usual bags. Quail, in fact, features regularly on restaurant menus here and is not expensive.

Back on the road to Salamis we were held up for a while by a military convoy crossing it. Rumble-rumble. Crunch-crunch. Rumble-rumble. A small dust storm. Four cars in a row behind us, three of them Mercedes. Fully armed and helmeted troops guarding the crossing. Mostly they were guarding army lorries, full of soldiers, and evil-pointing gun carriers, full of guns. Were they out on some kind of Sunday morning manoeuvre near the border – perhaps celebrating in their own quaint way the UN's 50th jubilee which occurred precisely on that day?

We allowed the convoy of three Mercedes to pass, wondering only if the middle one were bullet proof.

15

SALAMIS – OZYMANDIAS OF CITIES

After about 40 minutes we arrived at Salamis and stopped at a restaurant on a knoll with splendid views over the Mediterranean. We parked the car there and enjoyed a soft drink while savouring the magnificent panorama. Salamis, according to tradition, was founded by Tefkros, one of the heroes of the *Iliad*, who was driven out by his father from the tiny Greek island of Salamis because he didn't, or, couldn't, prevent the suicide of his brother Ajax at the siege of Troy. Here on the eastern seaboard of Cyprus he founded his own kingdom, which eventually became the most prominent and prosperous of all the ten kingdoms of Cyprus. Whether in the process he destroyed the nearby flourishing, Bronze Age city of Enkomi, just 2 kms inland, is a moot point. Ironically, though it had withstood previous attacks from various potentates, it was when Greek met Greek, in the person of Ptolemy, one of the generals of Alexander the Great, and Nicocreon its last king, who committed suicide at the turn of events, that Salamis was defeated and the city laid waste.

It rose again and, having an excellent, natural harbour became once more the great commercial centre of the Levant long before the Romans arrived in 58 BC. They, however, removed the centre of local government from Salamis to Pafos and it was only in the 4th century AD, under the Byzantines, that it again came to be the capital of Cyprus. It was, however, subject to severe earthquakes and was flattened, inundated and destroyed on several occasions. Flavian Constantine, son of Constantine the Great, re-built it on one occasion and it was called Constantia after him. During the Arab invasion of 695 AD it was sacked and burned and, in subsequent years, plundered more than once. Understandably the local population got fed up with all these destructive invasions and fled to nearby Famagusta. The city fell into decay, the debris of its buildings being used to build medieval Famagusta. It was never again re-built and today, apart from the area of the ruins, old Salamis, that once thriving metropolis, is covered with a forest of acacias, eucalyptus, pine and other trees. *Sic transit gloria mundi!* Gone the glory that was once Salamis. The ruins are about 8 kms north of Famagusta but we came to them from the west.

From the restaurant it's an easy, dusty walk to the famous ruins. First, as we enter we see, indeed we are already in, the Gymnasium-Palaestra, equivalent to our school playing-fields-cum-showers complex. The Gymnasium proper, which, is only partially excavated, was the place where Roman children went to school. There they were taught to read and write, to use the abacus and to learn the history of Rome. They also listened to great orators and themselves were taught the elements of discourse and debate, eulogy and panegyric. Outside but adjacent to it is the rectangular *palaestra*, so favoured of photographers, with its wonderful marble floor, paved in geometric patterns and inner courtyards surrounded by columns. There the boys were taught wrestling, and the use of arms for defence, offence and public display. Maybe they also practised running and played ball. For those who came to watch the supple and glistening bodies of the boys at play there was a covered, colonnaded walkway, off which were the latrines. These were public and open (males only) and provided sit-down, semi-circular facilities for a large number of people, 44 in the case of the Salamis ones, to use at the one time. Water, in a sewer-like arrangement, ran under the open 'bowls' and there was a trough of water running just beyond the feet of the sitters. Sponges were provided. Though the latrine courtyard was open to the sky for obvious reasons, the actual closet area was covered. A fountain in the courtyard tinkled. The users tended to make the occasion a social one, taking their time and chattering away. What provision was made for the girls and women, if any, is never mentioned.

Whatever physical activity they were engaged in, it was all hot work especially during the long scorching, Cypriot summer. What more convenient then than to have the baths nearby. There were three, a cold, a tepid and a hot, much as in Roman baths anywhere, or in a present-day Polynesian pool in New Zealand, or Hawaii. If you felt really macho you could, no doubt, dawdle in the cold one and in summer I expect it was the most popular. Then there were the public baths after which the boys gave themselves a thorough anointing with olive oil, rubbing it in vigorously over their entire bodies. Olive oil is good for you! – said the ancients – a slogan, modernised and given a different twist by a well-known beverage company. Expensive it was, too, but the wealthy head of the gym (the appointment, as now for presidents of golf clubs, was for one year–he probably couldn't have afforded a second one) picked up the tab for the scholarship boys.

In Classical times there are thought to have been three gymnasia, two for boys and one for girls but only one has so far been found and excavated. After all this activity the students would have been ready for a stroll, *passeggiata*-like, around the agora – the market place – a few paces to their right. The Salamis agora, the second largest in the Roman empire and the largest in the Mediterranean area, is 700 x 200 ft and ringed to this day by tall pillars, many still with their Corinthian capitals. I walked all round it imagining the shrill cries of the sellers of fruit, vegetables, oils, nuts, fish and wine. 'Take a little wine for your stomach's sake', Paul said and he was a Roman citizen and must have heard a similar slogan in the agora many times, not that the old Romans needed much persuading. The agora was a supermarket – it was only in a flash the other day that I recognised the strange word printed in capitals over 'Johnny's', our name for the local supermarket we patronise – HYPERAGORA IOANNIDES ... JOHNNY'S SUPERMARKET. Some things never change. Continuing on my rounds I saw the young boys, just out of the pool, hair still wet, boisterously swaggering while girls, twittering in groups, seriously gossiped. I saw an orator addressing a crowd from a rostrum in one corner and advocates in another consulting with their clients. My inquisitive eye spotted deals being struck and assignments being arranged hugger-mugger behind the stalls. Life in all its interesting dimensions was on parade and in such a beautiful setting who could not thrill to it! But my young boys had had enough of the buying and selling, the small envies and petty jealousies, the parading and counter parading. They came over with me to the semi-circular theatre, 100 yards or so south and to our left. It's the largest theatre in Cyprus, has a diameter of 90 ft and 18 hundred years ago, in its heyday, could accommodate close to 20,000 spectators. The building is free standing according to the canons of Roman architecture and is supported by massive stone arches, not cut into the side of the hill as would have been the Hellenic practice. Despite twice being destroyed by earthquakes, 18 of its original 50 tiers of seats are still in place. Fortunately much of the rest of it has been restored so my young boys, accompanied, if you like, by a class of their modern day Cypriot descendants, could see today, as they could have seen when Augustus was alive, Sophocles' *Oedipus Rex* or, Euripides' *Helen*, and understand them both if they understood Classical Greek. Classical Greek is not, in fact, too difficult for a Cypriot child whose language is more Homeric than the Greek spoken today in Greece. In our time, on yet another night, Shakespeare's *A Midsummer Night's Dream*, might play and, though the language didn't exist at the time of Augustus, many high school Cypriot children today could follow at least the gist of it, English being part of the compulsory school curriculum. In fact, many schools in Cyprus prepare students for English GCSE and A level examinations. In September-October 1995 Nicosia was celebrating the 5,000 years of its history with a European Culture Month and one of the many attractions was, indeed, a performance of *The Dream* by the London Shakespeare Company. The Municipal Hall which holds 2,000 was packed on two successive nights and judging by their response, the audience followed every word of it. Cypriots are avid theatre goers and on any one night there could easily be four different plays playing in Nicosia theatres.

The acoustics at Salamis are still perfect, we tried them, one of us reciting 'To be or not to be' in a voice barely above normal, while the other paraded along the topmost seats, listening. It was an advantage, of course, that we both knew it! It must indeed, I thought, be aesthetically fulfilling to watch great theatre in the round of an ancient auditorium with, in the background, the dark blue Mediterranean shimmering silver in the decline of the sun, or dancing ghostly in the early moonlight. One would not even have to understand the language I thought and more than a year later proved when we saw Euripides' *Bacchae* performed by an American company mostly in Greek in a similar theatre in Kourio. But now in Salamis I said goodbye to my charges and headed back to the restaurant where Sandra and I had what no Greek or Roman ever had, a huge cone of multi-layered ice-cream.

On another occasion we visited the ruins of a Byzantine church, quite a little distance away from the theatre but still within the boundaries of the old city, a fact that brought home to us once again the very large areas of Salamis that have still to be excavated. Built in the 4th century the church is noteworthy for one mosaic floor, in good condition, of intricate design and varied in colour. How it survived so well the ravages of wind and sun and rain, as well as the looters' greed, is in itself a small miracle. The church has a spacious courtyard in the centre of which was a well used for ritual washing, a Middle Eastern custom, abandoned by the Christians but still retained by Islam. The church conforms to the general pattern of Byzantine ecclesiastical architecture with a nave, two aisles and an econarthex, for the unbaptised, running parallel to each of the two aisles. To the east of the church are the ruins of the bishop's palace, also spacious. One gets the impression that the complex, built so soon after the emancipation of Christianity under Constantine, was as much a statement of hieratic pride as the provision of a holy place.

A golden beach is but a stone's throw away. Walking along it, close to the bank's edge, we discovered what, in all likelihood, was a Roman dump. Certainly there were numberless shards about, small and large, of pots, jars and other kitchen utensils. The occasional lid, or piece of neck or rim, suggested a likely spot for a future dig. Yes, I admit it, I did take a small piece or two of the profligate offering to take home as a keepsake. I do not know whether they come from the 7th, or the 17th century but they certainly come from Salamis and would most probably have been washed out to sea had I not 'rescued' them. My conscience is clear.

So, over the hills to Kyrenia. But first a quick visit to the monastery of St Barnabas about a mile down the road from Salamis. Barnabas, who travelled on his missionary journeys with St Paul, was a native of Salamis and became its first bishop. Salamis, the largest town on the island at that time, had a substantial Jewish population and it would have been to these Jews that Barnabas and Paul preached, without, it seems, much success. The outcome of their mission is not recorded, the only time in the Acts of the Apostles that we do not get to know the outcome of a Pauline campaign. 'If you can't say anything good, don't say anything at all' might well have been a guideline of Luke's journalism!

Unlike Paul, Barnabas was a warm-hearted, genial fellow, who actually had a serious tiff with the more 'difficult' Paul over whether or not they should take Mark with them. The outcome was that Mark stayed with Barnabas and they let Paul go off on his own. Barnabas didn't always get a very good press from Paul in his writings but I suspect Paul might have been a hard man to get on with. Maybe, in this case, Barnabas had an ulterior motive for he did eventually succeed in persuading the reluctant Mark to write his gospel. In the end, however, this mild man, a Jew himself, was stoned to death by Syrian Jews and his body, secretly 'rescued' by Mark after it failed to burn on the pyre prepared for it, was buried in a sepulchre near where the church stands today. You can conveniently walk to the little chapel and visit the catacomb crypt which contains the sarcophagus. It was covered with spring flowers on the day of our visit.

In 478, as a result of a vision to the then archbishop of Cyprus, the remains of Barnabas were discovered and, beside them, in his own handwriting, a gospel of St Matthew. This was presented to the Byzantine Emperor Zeno at Constantinople who was so immensely gratified that he funded the building of a commemorative church, allowing at the same time the Church of Cyprus to be independent and self-governing, which it still is, and permitting the archbishop to wear a purple cloak, carry an imperial sceptre and sign his name in red. I believe these are still privileges of the archbishops of Cyprus but I don't know how often they make use of them. I remember red ink as a schoolboy. Like the archbishop I used to sign my own name in it but it never got me anywhere. I haven't seen it around for years. Zeno's gift of a church was destroyed in the Arab invasions about 700 AD and the present one with its very visible white domes is a later construction. Now it is an icon gallery but most of the icons are recent, within the last century or so. I met an Irishman from Cashel, Co. Tipperary, in the church, though you wouldn't have recognised it from his accent, 'purified' by many years in colonial service. While his wife seemed genuinely interested in the icons, he wandered about with an insouciant air, stopping once to confide in me with some amusement that five English pounds were worth a million Turkish lira.

'Bet you didn't know, old chap,' he added next time round, 'bet you didn't know that 500 makes us all billionaires'. I hadn't, indeed, known that and, following such a revelation what was there left to do but bid hasty goodbyes and head for Kyrenia.

16

OVER THE HILLS TO KYRENIA

The road from Salamis to Kyrenia takes you over the Pentadactylos (Five Finger) Mountains, a range that parallels the northern coastline for about 80 miles. It's a narrow range and, as the name implies, has five fingers, or up-jutting peaks. We knew we had to cross it so, at an appropriate place, we stopped the car and engaged in our map reading routine. We spread it out, more comfortably in our borrowed Mazda than in the Austin 1100, pinpointed where we were and began our study. When you look for roads on a map you look for continuous unbroken lines – no point in going to some distant mountain village and literally running out of road. So we looked carefully at unbroken, thin, black lines and unbroken, fat, black lines and at the more impressive-looking unbroken blue ones – as there are no railways in Cyprus there weren't any red, broken, or unbroken! Like a child confronted with an array of lollies and told he could only have one, we couldn't make up our minds – or rather, Sandra the pilot-driver couldn't, as for technical reasons connected with the borrowing of the car she alone was allowed to drive, much to my chagrin, so in some exasperation we sacked the cartographer (a plague on all his lines!) and decided to ask a native, a local, who must surely know more about traversing the mountain in his own backyard than any map-maker. English is not at all as widely spoken in the North as in the South and the name of our destination had suffered a sea-change to Girne since 1974, making things that little bit more difficult. But we persevered, with repeated gestures of our index fingers towards the mountains – we were quite close to them – and repeated soundings of the two names, Kyrenia-Girne, Girne-Kyrenia, until a man, unaware of our attitude to maps, took a pointed stick and himself drew a map in the roadside dust. All would now be solved, all revealed. The second turn on the right was the one. OK? OK? – the only English words he knew. Of course, OK! The jabbing stick stopped. We thanked him in English as we'd forgotten to find out the Turkish for 'Thank you' and thought it might be indelicate to use the Greek.

So, we took the second on the right and for the first few miles everything looked bright and cheery. Then we ran out of tar and met a narrow, winding, stony substitute that in places was not much wider than two goat tracks. That was to be expected, of course, no point in having a surface that would make life more difficult for the goats on their homeward trek each evening. We were climbing. The scenery was superb, if one had enough peace of mind to enjoy it and it was cool. Some time previously heavy rain had scored the road and the potholes had never been filled. It was acrobatic driving at its best, a quick twist to the right to avoid a deep pot-hole on the left, then suddenly realising we were uncomfortably close to the craggy escarpment verge on the right, a wild swing back to the left, taking care to skirt around that jagged tooth of rock that suddenly had appeared in the middle. And we didn't even have power steering! Should we turn back? Several times we thought of it, recalling the warning of the Greek official on the border not to travel on back roads. But 'we were now stepped in so far that, should we wade no more, returning were as tedious as go o'er'. So on we went.

The Kyrenia mountains have an average height of only 2,000 feet but to us it seemed like 6,000. Corners came out of nowhere, S-bends that would have challenged a rally driver came at us unannounced and always that yawning escarpment on our right. What if one got a puncture on these deserted roads, or holed the petrol tank, or dislodged some tiny, important part out of its usual place of residence in the engine? Neither of us is mechanically inclined and, on questioning each other, neither of us knew where the spare was. And – an additional worry – if we didn't make the border crossing in time, what then? We didn't discuss it. It didn't bear thinking about. Privately I besought St Christopher to take us safely through the mountain passes – helping travellers out of jams has always been his special area of expertise. Then, while firmly gripping the handrest as the car rocketed to and fro, I had a sudden flash of memory – they say your whole life passes before you when you're in imminent danger – Simon the Cyrene, Simon of Kyrenia, the same one who, on another journey, helped Christ to carry the cross, surely he would help us. Without disrespect, a local lad who'd made good would be bound to help a foreigner lost in his own mountains, wouldn't he? I'd hardly ever thought of Simon before, except maybe once a year on Good Friday, but saints are forgiving people. At any rate, I sent up a message. Not all would agree, of course, that Simon hailed from these parts. More orthodox historians prefer to locate his place of birth in Cyrenia, then a province of Libya but in the pickle we were in at that time, any argument contrary to local tradition seemed wholly academic.

One gets a small, lonely feeling as one approaches the crest of a mountain. On our way up we'd passed through numerous, tiny hamlets and small villages where, apart from old men smoking, there was little sign of animation. The goat-herds, at two in the afternoon, were still curled up under some craggy outcrop, dozing, while their charges despoiled the hill side. Here and there a solitary Coca Cola sign, discoloured, crudely nailed to a gable, suggested a shop of sorts. No more. I'd seen such signs in back-of-beyond places in Africa and again wondered at the ubiquity of them. Were there peripatetic Coca Cola salesmen (no women surely) who spent their lives roaming the backwaters of the world raising these insignia of 20th century progress? Some time later when neither of us had spoken for a while and after she had negotiated a particularly steep gradient, Sandra said 'That's it – we're over the top, we've made it. It's all down hill from here on and I think I see the main road in the far distance, over on the left – the one we should have taken'– she added as if it were all *my* fault. I relaxed, in my own mind quite pleased with the prompt response of Simon, the Kyrenian (alias Cyrenian, or not), while not at all wanting to belittle the efforts of Christopher, our more experienced talisman. Not for the first time I thought – 'it pays to know people in high places!' But I didn't tell Sandra that. It was her skillful driving, of course. We stopped for five minutes or so to savour the view and to let the engine cool down. Our hunger began to gnaw at us.

On the way down we passed the signpost to Buffavento Castle on our left, indicating a two-mile hike. We gave it a miss. There are, in fact, three mountain-peak castles in the range, all dating from the Byzantine period which lasted from 395 AD until Richard the Lionheart annexed the island for a week in 1191 and then sold it on. Each castle has a commanding view eastwards towards the sea and westwards over the Messaoria, the central plain that lies between this mountain range and that of the Troodos, 80 miles to the south. These castles in the Kyrenian range, like the castles and towers in the Val d'Aosta, in northern Italy, passed warnings to each other and to the strung-out military installations within sight, of any suspicious circumstances they observed. They were particularly on the lookout for signs of an attack from Turkey, visible across the Mediterranean to the east on a clear day. Later the Lusignans, mainly French, to whom, as we saw, Richard sold the island for the second time when, after a year, the Knights Templar defaulted on their payments, increased the fortifications of the battlements and added an upper storey as a kind of royal penthouse. On another, later occasion we would spend a morning climbing up a hilltop to investigate the Castle of St Hilarion but, for the moment, getting safely down to Kyrenia was our only objective.

Kyrenia with its small horseshoe harbour, flanked by the massive walls of its very own medieval castle and sheltered at its back by the Pentadactylos, is one of the prettiest towns in Cyprus and one of the most picturesque I've ever seen anywhere. Known in antiquity as the 'Jewel of the Levant', Kyrenia has a history going back to the 10th century BC when it was founded by Arcadian Greeks. Later it became one of the original city kingdoms of ancient Cyprus and, later still, the Romans turned it into a commercial town they called Corineum. Weakened by sporadic piratical raids from the 5th century AD onwards it was destroyed by the Saracens in the 7th and subsequently lay dormant for 300 years. The Byzantines in the 10th century noting its strategic, military importance, guarding, as it does, a pass through the mountains to Nicosia and commanding one of the closest crossings to Anatolia, decided to build a castle there and the town revived around it. Using the foundations of the Byzantine castle, the Franks and especially the Venetians restructured it into the form we see today while the Ottomans in their turn reinforced and updated the defences. Later on, the Ottomans used it as a prison and the British followed suit. The Turks now call the town Girne and have turned the castle into a museum of sorts. Early in the organisation of the Orthodox Church it became an episcopal see, which it still remains.

To balance these, on the whole, progressive achievements I must add that twice during the past 450 years it has proved to be the place that provided suitable landing beaches for Turkish invasions – an accident of geography, as Turkey is only 50 kms away across the Mediterranean. Occasional noises from Turkey would have it that Cyprus is geographically and orogenically part of the Turkish tectonic shelf. This is incorrect. A deep sea crevasse of more than 2000 meters separates the Taurus and Anti-Taurus ranges from the Pentadactylos. There is no evidence of any geographical origination at all. Turkey is part of the European tectonic plate. Conversely, the deepest part of the sea-bed between Cyprus and Egypt is only 400 meters. Cyprus is part of the African tectonic plate. Interesting, even ironic, when you consider Cyprus has been accepted for membership in the European Community and Turkey not.

Nothing, however, detracts from the enchanting beauty of this place. Sheltered in the lee of mountains and steep, dog-toothed cliffs, it nestles snugly in the heel of its horseshoe bay. So narrow is the entrance to the Old Harbour, man-made and watched over by the medieval castle, that it has the tranquillity of a lake. Fishing boats and pleasure craft lap lightly in the water. Restaurants ring the bay and, for most of the year, have their tables outdoors under phalanxes of sun-shading umbrellas as welcoming and romantic as you'd see in any Mediterranean town in Italy or France. In the high distance the fortress of St Hilarion looks out at Turkey.

Such beauty did not go unnoticed. Closer to our own times and particularly after the Second World War a new invasion of mainly British 'arcadians' came, settled and enjoyed the good life here. Many of these were ex-colonial administrators, retirees from the disappearing colonies whose working lives had petered out when the countries they worked in gained independence. They were given whopping severance cheques (golden handshakes) and as they couldn't bear the horrors of an English winter – and not infrequently those of an English summer, either – they came to live here in Kyrenia, which took on the ambivalent atmosphere of a town for the prematurely retired. There were in all about 2,500 ex-pats here in the 50s. Their 'oldies at play' lifestyle was intensified by the more serious 'playing' of the jet set crowd from Italy and elsewhere who in the 50s and 60s came here for the season. Writers and artists also made temporary or permanent homes in Kyrenia, the most notable of whom was probably the previously mentioned Lawrence Durrell, whose sometimes patronising but prescient book, *Bitter Lemons*, is required reading for anyone who wants to understand something of what was happening in Cyprus in the 50s.

Today, some of the beauty of this cloistered bay has been eclipsed, not only by the devastating fire of the summer of 95 which so denuded the surrounding hillsides of trees and bush and scrub, but also by the building on these same hillsides of a number of vulgar-looking villas, the ostentatious pride of the *post bellum* (1974) *nouveaux riches* from Turkey and elsewhere. Despite all this the town still looks cosy, albeit in the faint down-at-heel manner of a declining madam remembering still the excesses of her former glory. Since the invasions of 1974 many foreigners have left and much of the glamour of life in Kyrenia has worn away. The insistent presence of the Turkish military both in the town and in the surrounding countryside has had a decidedly dampening effect on whatever *joie de vivre* was left. Many of the houses of the departed British ex-pats are now occupied by Turks who've prospered abroad, others allegedly, by less salubrious characters who have made Northern Cyprus their convenient hideaway. The houses remain, the lifestyle has changed. On the day of our visit, however, the atmosphere was relaxed, friendly and low-key. A modest meal *al fresco* with a beer or a bottle of wine was markedly cheaper than you could get in Nicosia. Those lingering at tables near us mostly spoke German.

We still had some time to spare after our late lunch so we visited Kyrenia castle. Thought to have been built by the Byzantines in the 9th century to stave off repeated raids by Arab marauders it was strengthened and embellished by the Lusignans and variously used by them as a fortress, prison, barracks, detention home for the king's mistress, Joanna, jealously provided by his wife while the king was overseas, royal residence (with the mistress removed) and omni-purpose stronghold. The British used it as a location for gun emplacements during the Second World War and now, of course, it's a museum. The Venetians, as was their wont, added massive towers and bastions in the 16th century but despite these additional bulwarks it surrendered to the Turks without a fight in 1570 after the garrison learnt of the fall of Nicosia. One could hardly blame the governor, however, for seeking terms as the news was conveyed to him in a most terrifying and graphic way. A squadron of Turkish cavalry rode over at speed from Nicosia and, emptying a bag before him, displayed the severed heads of the Venetian commanders of the city. A sensible man, the governor was convinced by that gruesome evidence that any defence of the castle was bound to fail and immediately arranged amicable terms. Two hundred years later its commandant, Khalil Agha, staged a revolt against the then governor, Hafiz Effendi, in a dispute about levies. Many of the Turkish inhabitants joined in his insurrection which was considered so serious that a special expeditionary force was sent from Turkey against him. For two months the castle resisted storming and only surrendered after prolonged blockading when provisions were running out. Khalil negotiated safe conduct for himself but was executed anyway as were 200 of his followers whose decapitated heads were sent to the sultan as proof that the revolt had been suppressed. History does not record how the heads were presented. It is worth remembering that in all its long history the castle was never taken by assault. Restored and garrisoned by the British, it was used in the 1950s as an internment camp for members of the EOKA underground movement.

Inside on the left there is an unremarkable 12th century Byzantine church with a restored dome. A gate house leads into the main courtyard. On your way you can see the tomb of the Turkish naval commander who 'received' the castle in 1570. His name was Sadil Pasha and he died the following year. His tomb is shrouded in a green tarpaulin as is the custom in Islam. On your right, from the courtyard, steps lead up to the royal apartments and, below the tower on your left, other steps lead down to the dungeons, an immediate and salutary reminder to all who had evil thoughts. But by far the most interesting exhibits you'll find in the castle are in two of the large halls abutting on to the east wall, for there, in the Shipwreck Museum, lies one of the oldest vessels ever to have been raised from the sea bed. Some say the oldest.

The remains of this 4th century BC trading ship were salvaged in the late 1960s from their resting place 30 m below the surface of the sea and 1 1/2 miles northeast of the castle. A professional diver named Kariolou first spotted the wreck but the work of raising it, or more precisely, of raising its cargo and hull, was undertaken systematically and successfully by the University of Pennsylvania Museum over a number of years. Sadly Kariolou was later drowned attempting to rescue two divers who were in trouble.

The wreck, 48 ft long and 11 ft wide, is of a single-masted trading ship with a sizeable sail, 33 ft by 20. The trader was half-moon shaped with a high prow and an equally high stern; between its ribbing were cradles to hold the amphora it carried. And apparently it carried a lot – 404 amphorae filled with oil, wine and 10,000 almonds. The almonds, those I saw behind a glass window case in the front hall, looked quite edible and are, or so I'm told; the wine, of course, not having been properly stoppered, has long since gone off, or leaked away to become fish food. The amphorae came from a variety of different ceramic workshops, indicating that they were loaded at a number of different trading posts along nearby coasts. Large, heavy, chiselled grain-mortars did duty as ballast during the voyage but what, I wondered, did they do when these were off-loaded? I don't know, but in Cyprus, at least, no place is without a plentiful supply of rocks. Our boat, however, still had all its mortars. It also had eating utensils for a crew of four – four platters, four cups or goblets, four forks plus sundry other plates. Nothing special for the captain, as far as I could see. Not surprising, I suppose, for didn't the Greeks write the blueprint for democracy?

We do not know where they were going, or coming from. One suggestion, however, is that at the time of the disaster, they were heading for safe harbour in a sudden squall but didn't quite make it. It wouldn't make much sense to imagine them sailing out from Kyrenia into the teeth of a storm. Whatever the precise cause of the tragedy we are reminded once again of man's perennial frailty before the elements of wind and water. The museum is worth a visit, there are detailed descriptions in Turkish, English and French. No Greek–but then there wouldn't be any Greek speaking visitors there.

We found the main road without any difficulty and then, hearing the 'winged chariot' at our back, made haste to Nicosia. When we reached the city, northern side, we discovered there were no signposts to the border and, as we didn't know the word for it, we kept asking to no avail for the United Nations as a far-out synonym. Then, with only ten minutes to go, I stumbled on a combination of two words that saved us: Lefkosa, the Turkish for Nicosia and Ellenika, the Greek for Greek. Greek Nicosia! Four young men simultaneously pointed to a corner about 100 metres from us and made ostentatious leftward swipes. I smiled my thanks and sure enough a pole across a street-end was the border, the Green Line, so called because a British army officer drew a line through Nicosia, dividing North from South, with a green pen! I might add that this line is also known as the 'Attila Line', or the Nekri Zoni, the Zone of Death. I prefer Green. It offers hope.

The Ledra Palace Hotel is centred in the middle of No Man's Land and is the headquarters of the UN. That particular Sunday the UN was throwing a party at its HQ for families from both north and south sectors to get together as a mark of celebration of their 50th jubilee. Five thousand were expected, the largest number ever to cross the border in a single day. When we ourselves reached the border just before 5 pm the road was thronged with people, many tearfully embracing, as they bade each other farewell before returning to their own homes in the different sectors of this divided city. 'Greek and Turkish Cypriots cannot and will not ever live together side by side peaceably again.' Could it be, I wondered that that statement, so readily and frequently repeated by many, especially in the north, might be wrong? What, if the hate machines were turned off?

This time at the Greek Cypriot crossing we were simply waved on.

17

BELLAPAIS MONASTERY – MOST EVOCATIVE RUIN

The Third Crusade (Richard's) achieved limited success and the Christians of Palestine were able to hold on to their lands, properties and possessions for another 100 years – quite a long time really, if we look at the continually changing disruptions and alignments of the peoples of the Baltic over the past 100 years, right down to the tragic 'ethnic cleansings' that we see today. Twenty years before the Third Crusade Saladin had declared a *jihad* to recover Jerusalem and thoroughly defeated the then king of Jerusalem at Hittin in 1187. This now throne-less king, Guy de Lusignan, was the very one Richard, in 1191, sold Cyprus to exactly a year after he'd sold it to the Templars. Many Europeans, mainly French, conveniently called Latins, joined ex-King Guy and so began what has come to be known as the Lusignan (or, Frankish) period in the history of Cyprus. It lasted for approximately 200 years, though you could, I suppose, call the Venetians Latins and add almost another 100 years. At any rate there were Latins in control of Cyprus when, a century after Richard, the Sultan Khalil completed the *jihad* of Saladin and drove the remaining Christians of Palestine into the Mediterranean. Of those who survived some had had enough of it and returned to Europe to await a miracle in the form of another crusade; others chose to join their Latin comrades in Cyprus with the more immediate hope that one day soon they would again be making that short sea-crossing to reclaim their lost lands. A hauntingly similar situation exists in Cyprus today where 200,000 Greek Cypriots now in the South await a return one day soon to their lands and properties in the North, expropriated by a similar autocratic power.

During their time as rulers of Cyprus the Lusignans brought their language, culture and structure of government to the island. They also brought their architecture and Bellapais is a fine example of that, perhaps the finest illustration in Cyprus of cold, northern Gothic 'humanised' in an eastern Mediterranean setting.

Not that the locals, even the local Christians, accepted all this Latin acculturation meekly. They did not and despite pressure from Rome they remained loyal to their Orthodox traditions. The ruling classes, who, of course, followed the Latin liturgy, were in a distinct minority and so welcomed the Latin refugees from the Holy Land when Sultan Khalil sent them packing, looking on them as religious reinforcements. Among these refugees were monks and canons. The first occupiers of the site at Bellapais were Augustinians, an overflow from the house of the order in Nicosia, who established a kind of retreat house there. Sometime in the 13th century they were joined and eventually 'ousted' amicably by the White Canons or Premonstratensians, refugees from Palestine, named either for the colour of their habits, or from the town, Premontre, in central France where they were founded by St Norbert. The White Canons, reflecting, perhaps, their unquiet experiences in the Holy Land where they preached to Jew and Christian alike, decided to opt for a more contemplative, austere and Cistercian-like interpretation of the rule. So, early in the 13th century a simple church was built there with simple accommodation for the monks nearby.

The Lusignans, however, took a special liking to the place – the setting was both attractive and strategically important – and it soon attracted royal patronage, especially that of Hugo III (1267-1284), who initiated the building of a new monastery. He went one further and granted the abbots the rare privilege, usually reserved to knights and nobles, of bearing a sword when on horseback and wearing golden spurs, privileges that one might consider to be directly contrary to those of the abbot's master who rode a donkey and said 'I have come to bring peace not the sword....' Further munificence followed under Hugh IV and later still, in the middle of the 14th century, under Peter 1 who both patronised the monastery, then called the Abbaye de la Paix and had royal quarters there. In fact, it began to resemble more a palace than a monastery.

If power corrupts so does wealth. The White Canons, cosseted and spoiled by the Lusignans over many years, had too much of both and suffered the inevitable consequences, though it may not have seemed like much 'suffering' to them at the time. The locals became in effect their vassals, the abbot, a feudal lord.

Women became their special benefice and not a few of the canons, dispensing with their vows of chastity and, no doubt, also with their white habits, took to themselves two or three apiece, in a bid, perhaps, to make up for lost time. When rumours of these goings-on eventually reached the mother house at Premontre, the French canons were naturally upset and sent an urgent request to the Venetian senate (the Venetians had taken control of Cyprus from the Lusingnans in 1489) to investigate the situation with a view to reforming it. That was in 1540. The windmills of the Lord turned even more slowly in those days and the intention of the governor of Cyprus, Bernardo Sagredo, to replace the White Canons with the Brown Franciscans, was overtaken by the fall of the island to the Turks in 1571. What was left of the abbey after its sacking by the Turks was handed over to the Greek Orthodox Church, which continued to use it until the 1974 invasion, which, incidentally, saw the Turks again land at Kyrenia, four centuries after their first landing there. History on this island has a peculiar knack of repeating itself.

Through a machicolated gateway, grooved to take a drawbridge and inside the compound, past the flower beds, there is an open-air restaurant, sited, appropriately enough, where the abbey kitchens and cellars used to be. Looking north from the garden edge there is a magnificent panorama of seascape and harbour. Though on the day of our visit we were late arriving, lunch was still being served so, helped by an efficient and cheerful waiter, we made our selection from a fairly elaborate menu and ordered a bottle of the local wine. It was old-worldly pleasant sitting there in the warm shade, glass in hand, sipping a deliciously cool, spicy white wine, listening vaguely to the different languages being spoken at the tables around us, and facing the most splendid, Gothic ruins in all Cyprus, not a stone's throw away from us. Lunch or no lunch, hungry as she was, Sandra could not long resist the inviting prospect and soon disappeared into the cloisters. The next I saw of her she was walking on the veranda-like roofing of the arcade, on a level with the clerestory windows of the church and looking down on the cloister. I filled my glass and, as there was no sign of lunch, decided to do some exploring myself. The cloister, with its four tall, trim, elegant cypress trees complementing the pointed gothic arches of the three remaining arcades, is the focal point of the abbey. It provided a common meeting place for all the monks and served also as a kind of running foyer with entrances off it to all the main buildings of the abbey. For their post-prandium community walks on wet days, or on any day in the middle of the hot summer, the monks would have used the arcades. It was in a way nostalgic to walk over the very same cobblestones that the monks walked on and imagine their subdued voices, with only the occasional concession to Gallic excitability, as they conversed in French or Latin, or, later on, perhaps, in the Greek patois of Kyrenia. King Hugh 1V (1324-1359), during whose reign the cloisters were probably built, often stayed there and, though he is recorded as having had 'marvellous apartments', it is not too far-fetched, I think, to see him, too, in the company of his knights and nobles, joining in the evening *passeggiata*. The cool, high-vaulted cloister was carved by local masons and makes up for whatever it lacks in artistic skill by the robustness, liveliness and humour of its decorative work, especially that of the human figures on the inside. The locals obviously had fun doing it and were probably taking the mickey.

Our diligent waiter found us and we returned to the restaurant for lunch. This is where we met the five, proud, white cats I already mentioned. Like good guests at a party they circulated among the tables, stopping a moment here to eye a couple who had eyes only for each other, meowing quietly at another table with children where they knew they would be welcome, at least until the adults discovered what was going on. They took little notice of the shooing of a waiter whose heart wasn't in it. They were spotlessly white. In between bites of quail – too many bones was Sandra's verdict – I asked her if she thought they were descendants of cats the White Canons had. 'Of course,' she replied with a sparkle 'they have the self-importance of the good ones and the raunchiness of the lewd ones'. It was time to return to our tour.

On the south side, the cloister gave access to the church and, across the *cortile*, on the opposite side, to the refectory. The eastern walk led to the chapter house and common room, the western one, now without its vaulting, to the kitchen and service areas, which included a bakery, a brewery, a wine press and a mill. The abbey was self-sufficient. The refectory is in an excellent state of preservation. Even its roof still remains in place, despite the fact that the medieval architects erected a 30m by 10m hall, of only one leaping vault, on the edge of a precipice. That took courage, enormous skill and confidence. When we saw the hall, it was filled with row after row of tightly-packed, aluminium chairs with hard plastic seats and at the eastern end there was an elevated, wooden projection which obviously served as a stage. All a bit incongruous looking. I was shocked to learn that the British army had considered using the abbey as an internment camp during the war and was shown by a friend the bullet marks on the back wall of this 14th century refectory which the soldiers had used for target practice. The monks had to put up with none of that but they did have a reader, chosen, maybe, for his sonorous voice and his ability to project it, or maybe, ghastly thought, they just took it in turns! A lectern-pulpit, still there, was built into the north wall, with access from the rear and set at a height well above the heads of the silently eating monks. From there the chosen monk read from edifying texts. If the cook had an off-day the brethren could nourish themselves on the words of wisdom floating down like manna from above. I recall reading of a deputation sent to the abbot by the monks of a 6th century Irish monastery. The message ran clear and simple 'words don't feed the brethren!' It would seem that they also had a pulpit reader, whose job included the occasional production of manna.

Outside the main entrance to the refectory, in the northwest corner of the cloister, is the *lavabo* where the monks washed their hands before entering. The washing was partly symbolic ('wash away my sins, O Lord') but in the main, I think, hygienic, especially for those of the brothers who worked in the fields, in the byres and in the hen coops. There was probably also a foot bath to the left of the tank – one can easily imagine circumstances in which it, too, might have been necessary. The water was contained in two marble sarcophagi, one below the other. The top one was ornate mainly (and strangely) with pagan motifs and, not to compromise its decorativeness, had no spigots but it did have six holes drilled in its bottom to let the water flow into the lower one, which is quite plain. I didn't climb up to see if the holes were still there but I'm sure they were. No one has yet discovered the system which supplied the water but it most likely came through ceramic pipes under gravity fall from higher up in the hills. As I was leaving the *lavabo* I wondered if the monks dried their hands in a towel or simply rubbed them on their white habits.

Opposite the refectory on the north side is the church, a squat, dumpy, unexciting building which antedates the abbey by more than a century. Like all Gothic churches in the Middle East it has a flat roof. This means that inside the church the nave arcade goes straight up to the clerestory, doing away with the necessity of providing a sloping roof to cover the aisles as in Europe. It's that, I think, that gives the church its stockiness, as well as the fact that the transept does not project beyond the aisle walls. The square choir and the massive, round Norman pillars complete what I might call the 'Middle Age spread' of the church. The iconostasi was, of course, added by the Greek Orthodox Church when, after 1571, the Turks took their side against Rome and handed over the Latin churches to them. Outside there is a substantial porch of three bays and on its roof a quaint belfry with only one of its four bells remaining. Since all the Greek Cypriots of Kyrenia had to leave in 1974 I wonder if it's ever tolled now. If it is, it must be a doleful tolling.

After our late lunch and another walk around the abbey we stopped in one of the beautiful, neighbouring villages and looked in the shops but mindful of the warning at the border, we overcame the urge to buy anything. It was in one of these villages, that of Bellapais itself, that Lawrence Durrell lived when he was writing *Bitter Lemons* in the 50s. He saw then the build-up of animosity between Greek and Turkish Cypriots that would within a decade turn to open hostility and, within two, to war. Durrell's house is in the upper part of the village, past the post office. It is white with brown shutters and has a commemorative plaque. We also paid our respects to the 'Tree of Idleness', under whose far-flung, leafy branches an outdoors *cafeneion* still flourishes. All is not lost. Durrell used to entertain friends there among them Rose Macaulay, George Seferis and Freya Stark. We had no one to entertain but ourselves.

18

ST HILARION –
MONASTERY TO CASTLE

Some months later we made another foray into the self proclaimed 'Turkish Republic of Northern Cyprus', this time as guests of an American Anglican priest and his wife, Bill and Edith, who were hosting two longtime friends of theirs from Egypt with whom, as it happened, my wife had stayed when she was in Alexandria the previous year. Because Bill was well known to border control – they had by now lived in Cyprus for 20 years and he had done parochial work in Kyrenia – we had no difficulty this time in crossing the border. In fact, only the Turks refer to the demarcation line, the 'Green Line', as a *'border* crossing'; Greek Cypriots, not recognising any *de iure* division between the two parts of the island, refer to it merely as a 'crossing point'. Semantics and politics intersect in Cyprus.

About 15 kms out of Nicosia on the main road to Kyrenia there is a signpost on your left which reads simply 'St Hilarion, 3 km'. The name goes back to early Christian times and, though there is some dispute about the time and provenance of the saint, it seems accepted by all that he was a holy hermit who came originally from Syria, or Gaza in Palestine, and lived out the last years of his life in a cave high up on this 730 m mountain peak. That could have been in the 4th, 6th, or 8th centuries – take your pick – according to which account you read. The confusion arises because there is a second St Hilarion who lived in Cyprus though he seems to have preferred the plains around Episkopi. It doesn't matter an awful lot, it seems to me, as time is irrelevant to sanctity; it's only we, lesser mortals, who have hang-ups about it. The earlier century seems the more likely.

According to this tradition, Hilarion, a convert to Christianity, visited the famous desert anchorite, St Anthony of Egypt, and became so enthused about his ascetic and solitary way of life that he himself determined to do likewise and so, finding his own spot in the desert, for all the middle years of his life he followed a rigorous life of prayer, penance and basket weaving. Wandering nomads, finding out about the holy man, a strangely easy thing to do in the desert, especially as Hilarion is believed to have survived on the fruits of a fig tree, came on their camels seeking cures both for themselves and their animals. He obliged with miracles, a fatal mistake for a hermit, leading eventually to his hermitage being overrun by suppliants. It was because of these intrusions that he set sail for Cyprus and, having traversed a great part of the island, finally decided to seclude himself in a cave high up on this mountain, ironically, you might think, near the ruins of a temple to Venus (which is why the Crusaders gave the fortress a second name, *Dieu d'Amour*). It is quite possible, however, that here also, Hilarion, became revered for his penitential life and holiness and there is a strong probability that during the remaining few years of his life he again became a cult figure, a kind of local guru. One wonders if this second time he succumbed to his role. At any rate, people in trouble – provided they were able-bodied – would have visited his cave for counsel and intercession with the strong probability that even then a small cluster of mountain huts would have been built to afford some protection against the fierce sun in summer and the buffeting winds in winter. It is certain, however, that his memory and the power of his intercession persisted and it comes as no surprise that the Byzantines, long after his death, built a small church there in his honour.

A monastery was subsequently added to accommodate those who desired to follow in Hilarion's footsteps and themselves lead lives of penance and devotion, and also to host the increasing number of pilgrims who went there. His relics were kept in the monastery and were still being 'right worshipfully' venerated in the 14th century according to an English visitor. But no longer in a monastery. Toward the end of the 11th century, the Byzantines, worried to death about an invasion by the Saracens, planned a strategic defence of the island by, among other things, building three castles, one looking north-south over the Kyrenia mountain range, a second facing directly north toward the sea and Turkey, while the third, surveyed the great Mesaoria Plain which stretches as far as the Troodos Mountains, 80 miles away to the south. Two of these castles, Hilarion and Buffavento, are close by in this area;

the third, Kantara, is across the island, near Famagusta. Thus did the prayerful shuffle of monks at St Hilarion give way to the noisy drill of soldiers. They're still there, soldiers, I mean, as the Turkish army has a boot camp nearby whose rookies, throughout all the time we were there, conducted shooting practice just below us on a long, level, green patch where joustings used to take place.

Earliest references to St Hilarion Castle are found in contemporary accounts of Richard the Lion Heart's brief campaign in 1191.

Richard, after his enforced landing in Cyprus was, as we already know, angered by the cavalier antics of Isaac Comnenus. Pursuing the ill-equipped locals who used poisoned arrows against his experienced soldiers, he defeated the Comnenus army at Tremethousa. According to one source Comnenus himself was immediately captured, according to another he escaped and surrendered some days later. What is certain, however, is that there were troops loyal to him, holding out in both St Hilarion and in Kyrenia castle. Richard decided to go after them but fell ill himself and deputed Guy de Lusignan to lead the Crusader army in his stead.

Kyrenia fell quickly but Hilarion resisted vigorously and might have held out had Comnenus not given them orders to surrender. Isaac's daughter was, for a time, incarcerated there – to save her, we're told, from her father's soldiers. I can't help wondering if the solicitude of the father for his daughter was part of the surrender deal? If so, it makes the upstart more human.

The Lusignans enlarged and re-modelled the castle, at the same time strengthening its fortifications. It is quite remarkable that they were able to build in solid stone at such a height using only the primitive transport and haulage methods of the day. True, some of their requirements would have been chiselled out of the mountain rock, as was done in the famous mountain-peak Church of San Michele, outside Turin, in whose eerie, stony, door-creaking crypt the illegitimate offspring of the House of Savoy lie entombed. Much, however, would have had to be hauled up from below. Labour, of course, would have been cheap; the 'grunts' of the army would have provided some of it and local serfs, pressed into the service of their feudal lord, the rest. Two 'road-paths' to the summit were built, one, stepped, for humans, the other, straight up, for horses, almost certainly so that these could haul the heavy stones and slabs up the steep slopes. Today, thankfully, there's an aluminium rail on the precipitous side of the human stairway – I would never have got up without it. The equine path is a wider, equally steep gradient, without rails, fit only for exuberant pre-teens and Olympic cross country runners in serious training! And horses, of course.

The castle provided a kind of seesaw sanctuary for those on opposite sides whose lives were imperilled in the wars of the early 13th century. When the Emperor Frederick Longbeard, grandson of Barbarossa, was on his way to Palestine he, too, made landfall in Cyprus (not storm-driven, as Richard was) and demanded on specious grounds to be made regent of the island during the minority of the young king, Henry I. His demand was refused. The defiant regent, John d'Ibelin, accompanied by the boy-king, betook themselves to the Castle of St Hilarion, which, for the first time, in 1228, was readied for war. A truce was reached and, turning the other cheek, as it were, John even joined Frederick's Crusade. On his return to Cyprus the following year he found Frederick's forces in control of the island. He fought them back from the coast, eventually defeating them in a battle near Nicosia. Those who escaped by fleeing took refuge in St Hilarion and held it under siege for nine months, using, perhaps, the plentiful provisions that John had laid in there the previous year.

Four years later when John and the young king again returned from an expedition, this time to Syria, they found that Frederick's forces had once again cut loose in the island. On this occasion, however, it was the king's relatives who had fled to Hilarion and were being besieged there. The young King Henry quickly engaged the imperial forces in battle at the narrow entrance to the Kyrenia Pass, on the road to Nicosia, near the village of Ahgirda and cut them to pieces. He went on successfully and joyfully to relieve the castle. Chastened, Frederick and his Longobards at last surrendered their claim to the island and withdrew from Cyprus altogether. Thereafter, peace returned to the land and for the following 140 years there was quiet at the castle, the only sounds being the neighing of horses, the clash of armour at the joustings and the dulcet tones of entertainment coming of an evening from the royal quarters. Every year for well over a century five successive queens of the noble Crusader family of d'Ibelin and their entourages, escaped from Nicosia to pass the hot summer months at St Hilarion – or, *Dieu d'Amour*, as they probably called it. Of course, the men folk came, too – where would the 'amour' be otherwise – and after the jousting and the hunting, joined their women in the cool of the evening for dinner on the terraces. Those were the halcyon days.

As we looked up from the car park we noticed that this picture-book castle has three clearly visible lateral sections called wards. The lower one, the *bourg*, as it was called, was the largest, containing the barracks where most of the garrison were housed and stables for the animals. The strong outer wall, which runs for over 500 metres before connecting with the summit defences, provides a ring of security around the castle and is also clearly visible from the car park. This wall had seven semi-circular towers and a parapet walkway around the battlements, part of which, to the left of the entrance, has been restored. Today the custodian lives in one of the towers and one of the cisterns is also still in use. As we climbed up the steps we noticed several vaulted passageways of cut stone, tall enough to take a mounted horseman or a camel. The one leading to the middle ward was originally closed by a drawbridge, giving the knights the privacy of their own quarters and, no doubt, also forming a useful part of the defence strategy.

When we reached the middle ward, going up the steps on our right we came to the church, a square Byzantine structure, which once boasted a dome, supported by arches of irregular span. Remains of paintings, perhaps of the 12th century, are to be found on the south wall. The church would have been too large for the needs of a castle chapel and the fact of its existence is, therefore, taken as further evidence of a monastery having been built on that site to replace the original hermitage of St Hilarion. In addition, a vaulted passage, just north of the church, leads into what was probably a refectory for the monks before it became some kind of hall in Lusignan times. Next we came to the belvedere, a vaulted loggia, or balcony, with fine views through its open arches. This is the place where the knights, whose quarters were nearby, would have gathered for a spectacular view of the tournaments played out on the level sward below – when they weren't themselves participating, that is. On the day we were there, seven centuries later, rifle and mortar fire split the silences as, under our full view (no photos) the Turkish army drilled its recruits. Units of 15 to 20 were doing marine-like training exercises thumping up and down the long field – the same camouflage gear, the same senseless plodding, the same rough, group dynamic and the same deep masculine voices answering each other in the same short, rhythmic, staccato antiphonies. The same sweat, too, steamed up off similar, sun-darkened faces. And all the time at intervals went the heavy boom-boom of the guns. Horse on horse, man on man, the jousters would have provided a thousand times more entertainment.

Not far away to our left, the kitchen block is arched over a crevice in the rock to provide an outlet for a row of dunnies. A long, long drop with a cold wind funnelling up in winter! As we passed on to the zigzag path to the upper ward, where the royal apartments were, we saw on our right an enormous tank, a reservoir to store winter rains which spouted into it from the natural catchment area above. The Lusignans were good conservationists, at least as far as water was concerned. They had to be on an island that was, and is, subject to serious drought. There's a restored 'staircase' at the south end which leads to the upper chambers, now open to the sky but originally covered by a steep-pitched, tiled roof. There we found the traceried 'queen's window' with two opposing side seats from which on a clear day you can see forever. Naturally, on the day we visited, though it was only 25°C, there was a haze on the horizon so the snow-capped Taurus range of Anatolian Turkey remained invisible. There were, however, great plunging views of seascape and a perfect picture-postcard view of Kyrenia. It's a good place to take a photograph.

From the courtyard, to which you must return, it's a short, steep climb to the topmost rampart, 732 m above sea level. The views in all directions are panoramic and one can well appreciate the commanding position this castle would have given its defenders in medieval times. The importance and success of communication by flares, northeast to Kyrenia, south, through the pass, to Nicosia, east to Buffavento and, through Buffavento,to Kantara and then on to Famagusta was a reliable Morse code of its time. Little could have happened by surprise, except, perhaps, the gathering of a

Turkish fleet behind the haze.

The Lusignans were always afraid of invasion from the north. They were right, too.

Only the adventurous, on leaving the upper ward, should visit the isolated tower of Prince John in the centre of the castle. I didn't. My wife did and took a picture of me from up there. In it I seem Lilliputian. 'Nice eyrie,' she commented when she came down. Although, when young, I had climbed several respectable peaks in the Italian-Swiss Alps, taking at times what in retrospect seem frivolous risks, I now occasionally suffer from vertigo and prefer not to take any risks at all. Especially not here, because here it was that, during the Genovese War, Prince John of Antioch took refuge with his young nephew Peter II and his troop of mercenary Bulgarian bodyguards. The tower, a vaulted construction, probably built in the 14th century, has sheer precipices on three sides. On this occasion John allowed himself to be persuaded by Eleanor of Aragon, his sister-in-law, that the Bulgarians were planning to assassinate him, so he called them up one by one and, without more ado, heaved the unfortunates over the top into the dizzy abysses below. It was only when the last one, the commander, saluted before himself walking over the parapet, that the prince realised his terrible mistake. I felt I could do without an on-the-spot re-enactment of that scene, even if only in my imagination. Sandra is made of sterner stuff.

Following picnic refreshments by the big tank we descended quickly to ground level. On our way out we had to drive past the shooting range but, thankfully, the guns were silent. Even 'marines', I suppose, take a smoko. I looked back at the massive walls and crumbling fortifications of this once magnificent, mountain-top fortress and tried to imagine life as it would have been then, with all its chivalry and brutality, all its eager romance and quick death, all the tedious normality of life within those encompassing walls, but all I could think of was 'the stale of horses', the long-drop privies in an easterly gale and the lonely elegance of the royal ladies on their window seats.

The castle was back in the news in 1964 when it was occupied by Turkish Cypriots. They fought off attacks by the Greek Cypriots and remained in control of the Kyrenia-Nicosia pass. Ten years later the Turks came, pushed all the way down to Nicosia through the pass and have remained in control of Kyrenia and St Hilarion ever since. The castle itself is, of course, a national monument but it is one of those monuments that, despite its ruinous state, one feels still lives.

19

NICOSIA – THE OTHER SIDE

The medieval walls of northern Nicosia, a continuation of that perfect circle of ramparts, whose other half is in the South, immediately grab your attention as you walk across the Buffer Zone, entering, within a matter of minutes, a time capsule of fifty years ago and savouring a culture so different that you imagine yourself in an eastern city, that somehow or other became attached to what is known as a western island. The massive stolidity of these walls is reassuring even today and their setting, behind open plots and unreconstructed streets, still redolent of ancient markets, is, perhaps, more 'authentic' than in the tidier South. They, like the walls of walled cities anywhere, have a story to tell, heroic or tragic, at one time chivalrous and brave, at another defeated and dire. As soon as you enter the northern city (should you decide to do so) turn right and take a short walk along Tanzimat Sok, between the two bastions Roccas and Mula, renamed Kaytazaga and Zahra, respectively. Walk along side the long row of earth-filled oil drums overlooking the Ledra Palace crossing, there since 1974 and still protecting the street, as it were, from snipers and you will get a feeling of what the Green Line is all about.

Most ancient cities, having cradled themselves for centuries, lean and alert, behind enclosing walls, later, as they prosper and grow, sprawl into a kind of complacent excess. They build themselves outwards haphazardly, or tie themselves by the umbilical cord of a narrow ribbon of connecting streets (in the famed wall city of Carcassone in the south of France by a bridge over a dividing river) to an adjacent 'new town'. Nicosia, a city typical of this contradictory land, did none of that. In fact, it did the reverse.

Under the Byzantines the city had walls, which the Lusignans fortified and extended. For the 297 years of their rule the citizens of Nicosia sat comfortably behind those walls, which had a perimeter of 9 kms. A growing and wealthy city spawned palaces and villas, monuments, gardens and churches in unplanned, leisurely profusion. By one count there were 250 churches, an ungodly number surely for a population of maybe 40,000 (the whole island at the end of the 16th century was no more than 200,000). Then came the Venetians, the island handed to them on a plate by Catherine Cornaro, the last queen of Cyprus, herself a Venetian. These wily and arrogant people, while skilled in defence, suffered the psychological vulnerability of all sea-faring folk when 'caught' inland. With justified prescience, however, they feared invasion from the east, specifically by the Turks. The sacking of Limassol in 1539 confirmed their worst fears. Famous military engineers were called to the island and the two Sanmicheles, uncle and nephew, advised that the existing walls should be strengthened to withstand cannon fire. Their Martinengo bastion, still in existence to the northwest of the city, is considered to be the finest example anywhere of the military architecture of the 16th century. Despite this the apprehensions of the defenders remained and so again in 1565 they summoned the master military engineer of the day, one Count Giulio Savorgnano. His judgement was immediate and decisive: the circumference of the walls was too long. To provide an adequate defence their perimeter would have to be cut by half.

A frenzy of activity followed. Soon the old walls were razed, the outer-rim churches demolished, the palaces and villas flattened. New walls, on a tighter 4.2 kms circumference, were erected, with every 500 m or so a huge bastion, eleven in all (five of these bastions are now in the northern sector, all out of bounds to the tourist as they are occupied by the Turkish military). In order to provide a free field of fire for the artillery, no one was allowed to build outside the walls. There were to be three gates and a moat was to encircle the lot, surely an act of faith in a drought-stricken land. The stone and rubble from the broken buildings would be used in the new structures. When work commenced, the locals were press-ganged into service and soon the defences began to take shape; these same walls, these same bastions, built over 430 years ago, remain on both sides of the Green Line the largest and most visible ancient monuments in Nicosia today. For all the high hopes of the Venetians, however, the Turks took the city after a 43 day siege and, on the same day, 9 September 1570, slaughtered 20,000 of the inhabitants. It was an inauspicious beginning to a stay that would last 308 years.

All three gates led to seaport towns, Pafos, Famagusta and Kyrenia. The latter, the only one in northern Nicosia, is today in the centre of two busy roads, one of access to, the other of exit from, the city. These the British made in 1931 by breaking down the walls on either side of the gate. Once such a focal point, today Kyrenia Gate is hardly noticed by the thousands of commuters who drive past, caught up in the whirl of traffic, but it was not so long ago, not yet 70 years, when, with the walls still adjoining it, this gate was, on the north side, the only narrow entrance to the Old City. A hundred years ago it was still being closed and locked at night and during the preceding centuries it served as both toll gate and immigration check for all wanting to enter the city, man, beast, or goods. There were no passports then; swords, daggers and battle-axes were presented in lieu! Many were granted daytime entry only and, come evening, had to provide, or hire their own tent accommodation outside. Narrow gates and stout walls served more than one useful purpose.

Kyrenia Gate was originally known as Del Proveditore and was built by the Venetians from the stones of the old medieval walls and, as well, of course, from the stones of the churches and *palazzi* they had demolished. A stone tablet, found by the Turks when they restored the gate in 1821, at the same time adding to it the square pillbox structure with the dome on top, gave its completion date as 1562 (MDLXII). This tablet is now embedded in the centre of the facade above the archway. I don't know if its gate is ever opened now. The purpose, by the way, of the pillbox dome was to give extra light to the 'tunnel' beneath. There was, however, another tunnel, a secret one, that connected Kyrenia Gate with a point across the Green Line near the Ledra Palace. It collapsed during heavy rains in 1965 and, believing that they could readily do without another episode of the Trojan Horse, was immediately sealed up by forces of the UN. Just north of Kyrenia Gate is a statue of Kemal Ataturk, the famed Turkish commander at Gallipoli and founder of the modern, secularist Republic of Turkey.

If you walk straight down from the gate along Girne Caddesi (Kyrenia Avenue), you will come, in a matter of minutes, to Ataturk

Square, the hub of the Turkish sector of the Old Town and, for centuries, the political centre of all Cyprus. On the northern side of the square was once, in Ottoman times, the *saray* or palace of the governor. Indeed the Gothic structure went as far back as Venetian and Lusignan times. The British unimaginatively demolished it in 1904 and built a police barracks in its place. In the centre of the square is the Venetian Column, so called, but thought originally to have been part of a temple at Salamis. It's 20 ft tall with a diameter of 2.4 ft and was put there by the Venetians to express symbolically their dominance of the city. Coats of arms of Venetian families adorn the base and there's a copper orb on the top. Originally the orb was a lion, the lion of St Mark, but soon after the Turks captured Nicosia in 1570 the column was taken down and removed, to lie horizontally in some inconspicuous place. Some time during the intervening 344 years, until the column was re-erected in 1915, the lion disappeared and hasn't been seen since.

On the way from the gate to the square you will have passed two large cannons. There are seven more in the public gardens and a number of others scattered here and there throughout the city. These cannons were all used in the Napoleonic wars and were subsequently acquired by the Turks. On some you may even see the emblem of the British crown and the signature broad arrow indicating that they were made at Woolwich Arsenal Ordinance Works. In the last century it was considered that cannon, suitably mounted, added 'class' to entrances, whether public or private. I can't imagine our century adorning portals with replicas of 'Fat Boy'. Such gross indecencies are not for public display.

Spread over the 24 districts of the Old City there are today 14 churches and 18 mosques. The mosques are those of the more moderate Sunni Muslims, the churches mostly of the Greek Orthodox communion, though Armenians, Maronites, Roman Catholics and Anglicans have one each. A few other Christian denominations have also recently acquired places of worship. The often adjacent positioning of church and mosque suggests more or less integrated communities prior to the 1974 invasion. This doesn't gainsay the fact, of course, that, following the 1570 invasion, the Turks took over practically all the churches of the Latins. Chief among these is the majestic Cathedral of St Sophia.

Built in the 13th century by the Lusignans (Franks), and modelled on Notre Dame, St Sophia became the coronation church of the kings of Cyprus from the 13th to the 16th centuries. Damaged severely by at least four earthquakes, it has nevertheless amazingly survived, this, despite the fact that it doesn't have steel girders and that reinforced concrete was unknown 700 years ago. Architects believe that its high flying buttresses, which carry and spread outwards the weight of roof and walls, saved it. These flying buttresses had the further advantage of permitting a high nave, which, in turn, provided artists with tall, large windows to decorate. This they did in stained glass, bequeathing us the most wonderful, natural-light illumination of biblical themes in parade-like sequence. The same light, however, that gave us kaleidoscopic windows also, in part, gave to Gothic churches their somewhat gloomy interiors. Not that this at all bothered the Latins; quite the opposite, in fact – they thought it created an appropriate ecclesiastical atmosphere of reverence, awe and mystery. It didn't bother the Turks either but the display of biblical 'reading material' did. One could hardly preach Muhammad with Christ, his angels and saints, forever looking on! So they took the artistically drastic step of removing the stained glass from the windows of the cathedral. As I walked around the interior I experienced a feeling very similar to that which I felt at my first antipodean Christmas. No log fires, no holly or mistletoe, no carol singing by candle light at 6 pm. Something was missing that a barbecue on the beach couldn't make up for. The little extra light only gives a little extra 'gloom' to the cathedral but it's still very much worth seeing.

The Ottomans in 1570 took over, as spoils of war, all the buildings previously used by the Lusignans, including their churches. Orthodox churches did not suffer the same fate. St Sophia, therefore, underwent a swift change from being the principal church and cathedral of the Latins to become the principal mosque of all Muslims in Cyprus, which it still is. To affirm its changed function it added two 49 m minarets which reach up into the sky somewhat incongruously like spear-headed rockets. To be brutally honest about it, the Muslims did not take over a flourishing cathedral. Though its precincts once housed schools of theology and grammar and accommodated scores of canons and other clerics, by mid-

16th century the great cathedral was suffering a period of almost terminal malaise. It was even difficult at times to find a priest to say mass. This was due in no small part to the appointment of Venetian noblemen as absentee archbishops. From the singular point of view of worship one could, therefore, say that the appropriating Muslims had renewed the original purposes of the building – to give glory to God. Selimiye Mosque, as it's now called, is the principal landmark of north Nicosia.

A guide will take you round the mosque for a small donation. The one I had spoke in rapid fire sentences the most fractured English I've ever heard. If I could, I would have happily doubled the donation to shut him up.

Inside, the mosque presents to the Christian eye, a deceptively bare appearance. Without side chapels (there used to be five of them) benches, chairs, altars, statuary, racks of candles and so on, spaciousness is what first strikes you. It is 216 ft (66m) long by 125 ft (38 m) wide and is the largest place of worship, church or mosque, on the island. If it were full for Friday prayer, which I'm told it isn't, as Turkish Cypriots, in contrast to Anatolian Turks, are not very religious, the sight of hundreds of men bowing in unison towards Mecca would be impressive. And somewhat disconcerting, as they would be facing towards the east in direct contrast to the north-south orientation of the church, presumably in line with Jerusalem. Footwear is, of course, removed before entering and the entire floor of the mosque is covered in vari-coloured carpets, prayer mats and richly coloured rugs with deep piles, any one of which, despite its signs of wear, would grace the hall of a mansion. Absence of noise must be one of the pleasing features of a mosque at prayer, no noisy movement of chairs, no high heels tapping on marble or stone, no acrobatic swinging of censers. And late comers would not distract the early worshippers. A lot to be said for it! Beneath the rugs are many stone slabs – the helpful though inarticulate guide will show you some – indicating places in the cathedral floor where, for their sins, bishops and noblemen lie buried. In life they walked over others, now, in death, they do posthumous penance by allowing others to walk on them. Brief necrologies are carved into stone or marble. Roman pillars, probably also filched from Salamis (amazing how much re-cycling goes on) have capitals, most likely transplanted from a 4th century Byzantine church, painted in rich, sombre brown. Curiously, because they train the eye upwards, they give a lift to the much beloved 'dim religious light' of the Gothic church builders. The imam leads the prayers from a position in front of the *mihrab*, a slightly askew niche in the eastern wall. Rome given a twist towards Mecca. More centrally situated is the *minbar*, a kind of pulpit but with much shorter sides, from which the imam, delivers his weekly sermon. I think I would feel unsafe up there, with nothing to hold on to, if I forgot where I was in the vehemence of my sermon.

Probably the most artistically interesting feature of the building is its western facade with the four moulded arches in the vestibule of the main portal. Adorned with foliage and figurines of kings and queens, saints and ecclesiastics, some of these mouldings have been cleaned of the gypsum plaster which covered them. Others remain still covered. Presumably the revealing of four is a compromise as Islam forbids the portrayal of plant, animal and human life in decorative work. The mouldings are the best you'll see in Cyprus. The three portals, the centre one twice the width of the flanking ones, are fine examples of decorative Gothic. In of them is a covered ablutions fountain (*sadirvan*) for the ritual washing Muslims perform before prayers.

You'll be pleased to know that the muezzin no longer has to climb the 170 steps to his eyrie on the minaret to call the faithful to prayer. Electronic amplification now spares him that job. Five times a day he had to do it! I wonder if he had to pass a fitness test before he was appointed.

Immediately to your right as you face St Sophia are the ruins of another 14th century Gothic-Byzantine church, that of St Nicholas, now known as the Bedestan, a Turkish word meaning 'covered market'. The ruins are quite close to today's market sector and the church itself became a textile sales market under Turkish rule. It was also known as St Thomas of the English, after the Knights of St Thomas of Canterbury, who hurriedly left Nicosia when it was attacked by the Genovese in 1373. Yet another set of knights passing through. During Venetian times it was the principal church of the Greek Orthodox community and is an exception to the rule that the Turks did not confiscate Orthodox churches. Perhaps this one was too close to the mosque! But they didn't destroy the three north doors, the principal features of attraction of the ruin, despite their statuary and mouldings. Built on the site of a previous 6th century Byzantine church, this one had a barrel-shaped roof and an octagonal central dome. Extensions to the north and south were done in the Gothic style with pointed arches. It was the Greek Orthodox archbishop's cathedral, with his residence nearby. Interesting that both Greek and Latin cathedrals should have been almost contiguous, despite some heinous crimes committed against the Greeks by the Catholics. The worst such crime was the burning to death on 19 May 1231 of thirteen Orthodox monks, who refused to accept Roman Catholic doctrine. A friend of mine, an esteemed Cypriot writer, Christakis Georghiou, wrote a play about it called simply *The Monks*. It was broadcast in Greece and televised recently in Cyprus. It is good that such atrocities, like the atrocities of Auschwitz and Dachau, be recorded. The three beautifully carved Gothic doors are, perhaps, the most interesting architectural feature still extant, though there are the remnants of some 12th century Byzantine wall paintings inside between the Byzantine and Frankish walls on the western side.

The Beuyuk Khan was the first 'hotel' built by the Turks, just a year or two after Nicosia fell to them in 1570. Its name literally means 'Big Inn'. It was built by one of the 'storming' generals, Muzaffer Pasha, who became the first Ottoman governor of Cyprus, and with its grim, rectangular exterior and its high-up, small, barred windows looks like nothing more than a medieval army barracks, or a gaol, which, for 15 years, is exactly what the British used it for when they took over in 1878. It was subsequently rented out to individuals, who sublet its 67 rooms to homeless Turks. At one time it is recorded that 70 families lived in the *khan*, a close-knit little community. Friday was wash day, so much a sight apparently that it was a 'must see' for tourists who went there to photograph the fun of the communal clothes-wash and their hanging out to dry.

Initially Muzaffer Pasha built the *khan* for the convenience of foreigners, mostly rich merchants and traders, visiting the city.

This may, indeed, have been the reason for the security windows, as wealthy merchants often carried their 'banks' about with them and then, as always, there were plenty who sought to take advantage of this situation. The two sturdy gates lead into a graceful courtyard with a double veranda of carved stone. The rounded arches support slender, elegant columns which themselves support the pointed arches of the first floor, surprisingly strong enough to uphold a roofing of stone-built cross vaults. Spacious rooms led on to the upper veranda. It is not difficult to imagine the wealthy pashas, in flowing robes, tired after a hard,hot day's trading, taking their ease on the verandas, enjoying what breeze there was, swapping tales of commercial derring-do, with attentive servants serving sherbet. On the ground floor were store rooms and shops. The stables were downstairs from the ground floor.

In the centre of the courtyard is a miniature mosque, called a *mesdjit*. Octagonal in design, with open sides and a picturesque fountain and water tank for ritual ablutions, it was the gift of a nameless benefactor, who, recoiling from total anonymity after death, lies buried beside it. This may have been an idea that came to him after observing the floor burials of its noble benefactors in the cathedral. It is not a usual Muslim practice.

The streets around the Beuyuk Khan are cluttered up with stalls and shops so, as it's a singularly unexciting building from the outside, it's possible to miss it altogether. Vacated in 1963, restoration work, undertaken by the Department of Antiquities of North Cyprus began in 1982 and is making slow progress.I wonder why some enterprising private company hasn't taken it over with the idea of restoring it to its former function. Turkish meals served on the extensive verandas, with traditional dancing and entertainment being provided in the courtyard below, similar to the way the Irish have so successfully 'transformed' some of their medieval castles to provide 'authentic' medieval feasts, would be a no. 1 tourist attraction. Is such a venture awaiting the return of Greek entrepreneurship and capital? I believe the present idea is to turn it into yet another museum.

A little farther down the same street is another *khan*, the Kumardjilar, or Gambler's Inn, which dates from the end of the 17th century. It has 52 rooms and the arched entrance may well have been part of an earlier medieval building. In its present state it's hard to imagine it as a working casino. There were, however, many *khans* in old Nicosia, as people involved in the different crafts and trades, leather, jewellery, spices and the like, tended to seek accommodation with their kind. Foreign travellers, too, preferred to lodge together. The Kumardjilar was obviously the place to go if you were interested in a punt, or a game of blackjack.

Another building that invites a brief look is the Turkish baths, the Beuyuk Hammam in Irfan Avenue. The entrance way, which has a semicircular arch, with carved figurines, belongs to an earlier building, probably of the 14th century. It's certainly pre-Turkish, for reasons I have already alluded to. It's interesting to observe how much below today's street level the building has sunk, although that may be the wrong way to express it. The *hammam* (bath-house) hasn't sunk, the road and surrounding buildings have risen. It used to be common practice simply to level the rubble of demolished buildings to provide the foundations of new ones. The baths were too important to be razed, so, while all about them was upwardly mobile as far as levels were concerned, the baths maintained its *status quo ante*. Such successive 'elevations', with the wealth of information they convey about different historical periods, are an archaeologist's paradise. When I was there a passer-by offered the information that the *hammam* was closed at the moment for restoration and re-decoration and would re-open in a week. He had been, he said, a frequent user when it was open and added, that it was 'good for the bones'. He looked forward to its re-opening with the same enthusiasm as an avid opera goer to a first night of *Aida* in Madrid's restored opera house.

There are other things to see in northern Nicosia, the Tekke of the Dancing Dervishes, for example, near the Kyrenia Gate. With its several low domes it looks more like a bathhouse than a place of worship but it was, in fact, the place where the dervishes, dressed in their white tunics, representing shrouds and tall, brown camel hair hats, symbolising tombs, pursued their whirling rituals. They take their origins from the great 13th century sufi mystic Rumi, also called Mevlana. His poetic and mystic work, written in Persian, is among the most respected and loved in Islam.

After his death his son organised his followers into a kind of monastic order, or brotherhood, which prospered all over Anatolia and exercised much influence for many centuries on the political and economic life of the Ottoman empire. In religious practice they tried through many methods – whirling was one of them – to become mystically united with the divinity and in political philosophy they were conservative and monarchist. Once in Istanbul (or, Constantinople, as Greek Cypriots prefer to call it) I was fortunate to see them perform the ritual, sacred dance, called *sema*. With closed eyes, heads leaning to the right, one hand pointing upwards to heaven. the other downwards to earth, indicating the perpetual predicament of human kind of aspiring to heaven while yet tied to life on earth, they wheeled in their whirling dance for over an hour with only two brief intervals. They would have had to have been in some kind of trance to keep up that continuous, circular movement for so long on such a stifling afternoon, without stumbling, without touching. They were also the only ones not perspiring and the rest of us were merely sitting or standing. The accompanying music played on flute, drums and traditional instruments was pure and evocative. One could not help but be 'spiritualised' in some arcane way by their extraordinary devotions. Sandra and I were greatly captivated by their serenity and gentleness. When Kemal Ataturk came to power, however, he placed them in the same category as astrologers and fortune tellers and, in 1925, suppressed them. The Turkish Cypriots followed suit. Rather a pity, I think – such unique pieties deserve to be seen. The building has now been converted into a Turkish Museum of Folk Art.

The Dervis Pasa Museum, off the former Victoria Street (now Salahi Sevket) was once the mansion of a leading Turkish official. It is reputedly one of the finest examples of Ottoman domestic architecture but is also worth visiting if you're at all interested in Ottoman artefacts – it contains the best and most varied collection on the island.

There are many other museums, mosques and converted churches to see, if you want to, but I would rather recommend, if your visit is short (as it must be for you have to re-cross the Green Line before 5 pm), that you spend time in at least one of the *soks* (bazaars), two of which are quite close to St Sophia. There you will savour the atmosphere of the East. The outdoor stalls with their colourful displays of bedspreads and quilts, carpets, rugs and cushion covers, the shops with their serried rows of cheap brand-name clothes, the leather wear, the Delft ware, the beckoning glint of sun on brass, the clothes lines of woven cloth, the glittering trinket shops, these and more, all with gifts for self or others, begging to be bought at below average prices, which only the innocent or uninitiated would pay. No one expects you to. The essence of the bazaar, whether it be in Damascus, Amman or Nicosia, is to bargain and you have to leave your inhibitions behind in Manchester, Waterford, or Maryland, to do it. Accept the offer of a cup of delicious Turkish coffee, enjoy the jelly-wobble of a piece of Turkish delight but be adamant about the impecunious state of your finances. Offer half the marked price, reject a 10 percent reduction out of hand and approach the equilibrium slowly. At the point of sale the shopkeeper, generally the owner, or of the owner's family, will register his pleasure, though he has previously announced to the whole street how your purpose was to impoverish him and leave his poor wife and children destitute. With the deal finally cut, have another coffee. A word of warning, you can't rush through the *sok* and enjoy it. Neither, at the moment, can you buy anything at all in the North if you come from the South. This is a cold war tactic that will endure until a political rapprochement is reached. As I crossed the Line again, empty handed, I sent up a wish and a prayer that that day would come soon.

20

FAMAGUSTA – CITY SUNKEN
IN THE SAND

Cuma Mertel, a slight, active man in his late 40s, with short dark hair and the almost obligatory Turkish moustache, told me he had two daughters and two vines. He loved all four and, though a Muslim, always managed to keep aside some of his grapes to celebrate Christmas. Sandra and I were in his golden Mercedes 220 taxi on the road to Famagusta. Cuma (pronounced 'Juma') spoke English well and did his best, without much practice, to keep up his Greek. Born in a small village, west of Larnaka, he had moved north following the Turkish invasion in 1974.

Would he like to go back?

No, why go back, life moves on. Here I have my house in a little village on the hillside, we always have water and I bring some every day to my friends. Here are my vines and my two daughters – and one grandson, he added with evident satisfaction. Why go back, my wife and I are happy here but I would like the Green Line to go. I have friends on the other side I would like to meet again, Greek Cypriot friends, he added.

Does he think the Green Line will go?

Only God knows, not the politicians. He stopped a moment to consider further. Maybe, he added, if the Americans wish it.

For him Greece and Turkey were only bit players in the scheme of things and he saw no difficulty in Greek and Turkish Cypriots living together. We are one island, he said, which, for all the frequent yards of political rhetoric on both sides, seemed the neatest way of putting it. He himself went down south twice a year, in a convoy of buses to pay his respects at the Tekke of Hala Sultan, near Larnaka. But these were circumscribed visits, supervised by the Greek Cypriot police. Though he was closer to his native village at Larnaka, in reality he was no closer than if he had stayed at home in the north.

We were driving through the Mesaoria, the great, flat, almost treeless, central plain that stretches from the Pentadactylos mountain range in the north to the Troodos in the south. At this time of year, in early March, when we travelled across it we saw vast meadows of yellow weeds growing among the still short corn. These would fade and in June the first corn harvest would be reaped. A second sowing would follow but lack of rain over the past five years meant poor harvests and sometimes a second sowing wasn't worth it. Then the landscape would become an endless, brown desert which mischievous gusts of wind would catch and whirl from field to field and back again.

We talked education. Cuma had studied for a year at a Turkish university in 1968 but because of ceaseless infighting among the students, he decided to return 'to my own country'. He was, he said, a Turkish Cypriot, not a Turk and this was *his* country. He was happy, he told me, with the standard of education in the North, free and compulsory until 14, costing the equivalent of US$150 a year, books included, for the following three years and about US$3,600 a year if the student chose to study at one of the three universities. Mostly, he said, the university population of about 30,000 was Turkish, or other foreigners. Only about 2,500 were Turkish Cypriot. By now on the outskirts of Famagusta, we passed the tall, white blocks of the faculty buildings on our right.

Famagusta has more ruins for its size than any city I know. One estimate has it that the city once had 365 churches, an unbelievable figure. I wonder if the authorities put a block on building any more after that, skipping leap years. It is certainly true that in the 14th century many wealthy, luxury-loving merchants took out a kind of celestial insurance on their lifestyles by building 'gateways to heaven'. 'He who builds a House of God on earth will be made welcome hereafter into God's House in Heaven' – a fair bargain and a profitable *quid pro quo*, thought the merchants. Many of these smaller chapels and churches were levelled by the Turks after 1571, a few of the more prestigious ones were turned into mosques and others simply became ruins of their own accord. As we drove about (we'd hired Cuma at US$70 for the day) I noticed that of the ruins still extant many of those of lesser renown were neglected and uncherished, their forecourts serving indiscriminately as car parks, or handy locations for kiosks, cafe stands and clothes lines. Around others weeds and grasses grew luxuriantly and children played in and out of puddles after recent rain. Why this blasé attitude to what in other countries would be considered precious? In a poor, Muslim country the only justifiable reason for allocating money to preserve Christian relics would be the tourist industry. And here, at the moment, there are too many ruins, in one small area for too few tourists. There is little cash to spare in the TRNC and with the tourist industry in the north less than 4 percent that of the south there's no great incentive to spend it on the upkeep of less prestigious monuments. Besides Famagusta, the TRNC already possesses some of the finest tourist attractions on the island both in terms of beaches and ancient monuments, such as Salamis, St Hilarion, Bellapais and Ayia Sophia. If these don't bring in the tourists the increased cost of the upkeep of minor monuments certainly won't. The trouble is political not cultural.

One cannot but admire, however, the splendour of the 'grand' ruins that are cared for. Old Famagusta was a walled city and the great 16th century walls with their spectacular bastions are remarkably well preserved and worth a visit in themselves. We parked just inside the walls at the 'new' gate, built by the Turks after they had demolished the old Land Gate at the conclusion of the 1571 siege. Now the Land Gate is a dark tunnel providing access to the bastion above and splattered with all the human debris that one associates with dark spaces; then, in Venetian times, providing, as it did, the only land entrance to the city, it was guarded by a small fortress and further protected by the massive bulk of the Ravelin Bastion which overlooked it protectingly. During the Ottoman siege the gate was burnt out and the fortress completely destroyed. In compensation, as it were, the Turks built a guardhouse inside the new gate and threw a bridge across the moat. All are still there, the guardhouse now functioning as a post office!

From where we parked the car, the cobbled incline up to the walls is steep which gives you an idea of their height, 21 m. The moat, once filled with sea water and forded by a drawbridge, is 25 m wide and now offers itself as a sheltered walkway round the walls for those sated with long-distance views. But it's the thickness of the walls at 7 m that struck me most. You could build a terrace of medium sized houses on top of them, sure of your foundations as the tight masonry of the walls rests on bedrock. And these massive structures go on for 4.2 kms, flushed out at regular intervals by 11 stronghold bastions. It's not surprising that the construction of these formidable fortifications took 20 years, beginning in 1492, the year that Colombus is accredited with discovering America. He, incidentally, was born in that state, fierce rival to Venice, Genoa, which had garrisoned Famagusta for 90 years until finally thrown out by James II, king of Cyprus, known as the 'Bastard', shortly before the arrival of the Venetians in 1489. It was they, the Genovese, who had built the previous pattern of flimsy walls which the Venetians, employing the best engineers of the day and literally leaving no (Genovese) stone unturned, remodelled and strengthened. A truly tremendous undertaking.

And where did they get their manpower? From Venice, it seems, came the engineers, from both there and the Rhineland, the masons and tradesmen and from Cyprus, by conscription, one man from every 30 families, the unskilled. The Venetians were still busy with the final fortifications when the Turks began besieging the city in 1570. Neither did they have time to raze the buildings outside the walls, as they did in Nicosia, to provide their artillery with unobstructed fire power. And here, right in front of us, was where it all happened as the Land Gate is only a 100 m or so to our right. There wouldn't have been flowers on the ramparts then but now in early spring the top of the walls looks like display gardens, so covered are they in buttercup yellow, crown daisies. There are other wild flowers, too, in mauves and pinks but these are absorbed in the waving sea of yellow.

Famagusta's history didn't begin, of course, when Guy de Lusignan, Guy I, took over fiefdom of the island from the Templars, agreeing to pay Richard the Lionheart the 40,000 ducats the Templars still owed him. Long before that, in the 3rd century BC the Ptolemies had a settlement at Famagusta but a settlement it more or less remained, eclipsed for a 1,000 years by its powerful neighbour Salamis, only 10 kms away and for so long the commercial metropolis of the island. It was only after Salamis, already weakened by a series of natural disasters, mainly earthquakes, suffered almost total destruction in an Arab raid in 649 AD that its citizens lost their will to stay there and fled for their lives the 10 kms to Famagusta. An influx of Armenians in the first half of the 12th century, and an even larger influx of Christian Arabs after the fall of Acre in 1291 gave a further enormous boost to the population. In the following 80 years, until the advent of the greedy mercenary Europeans, Famagusta, exploiting its strategic location, its fine, all-weather harbour and the business acumen of its ethnically diverse citizens, became a wealthy trading port. More than that, one traveller, a German, Ludolf von Suchen, visiting the city during its heyday, expressed awe at its splendours and named it the 'wealthiest city in the world'. Such prosperity causes envy and soon the two great European maritime powers, Genoa and Venice, were vying with each other for a piece of the action. The Genovese had first go, were ousted, returned in 1373 to sack the city three times before again occupying it but, as always in times of unrest and instability, the money had poured out and the merchants had fled back to the Middle East. The Venetians took over a veritable backwater. They, however, a maritime power of acknowledged culture, set about embellishing the city and restored some of its former prestige. That's when the Turks came in. The battle for Famagusta became one of the great adversarial contests between East and West, Muslim and Christian in the 16th century.

The Turks, unable to take the city outright, lay siege to it for all of 13 months. Toward the end of 1570 more than 200,000 men, come up from their southern landings and victorious assault on Nicosia, encamped south of Famagusta. According to Sir David Hunt, historian, archaeologist and former commissioner for Cyprus, the defenders had 4,000 regular Italian infantry, 2-3,000 cavalry and about 4,000 Greek militia. Guns favoured the besiegers 145 to 90. An unsuccessful blockade attempt during the winter months was followed in late spring by a month-long artillery duel in which neither side gained significant advantage. Under cover of continuous bombardment of the walls, the Turks then succeeded in planting mines in the vicinity of the Land Gate and the Ravelin Bastion. They also filled in part of the moat. Then on 9 July they hurled assault after assault at the bastion and might have succeeded in making a breach if the Venetian officer in command of the Ravelin defences hadn't taken the desperate measure of setting off one of his own mines, killing 100 of his own men and 1,000 Turks. The defenders were saved for another day. Having licked their wounds and, presumably, buried their dead, the obdurate Turks tried a new tack. They lit a huge bonfire in front of the Land Gate and, under cover of a ceaseless artillery barrage, kept it going non-stop for three days. So fierce and consistent was the heat that even the iron frame of the Land Gate melted. The defenders, reduced to a mere 500 (out of 10,000) were now in a desperate position. Once again they sent an urgent call for reinforcements to Crete. In vain – the state of Venice was preoccupied with organising a more cohesive response to the Turkish threat to capture Vienna. Another concerted Turkish assault begun on 29 July lasted three days. It was the end. The walls had been breached and, inside, provisions were so low that people were dying of hunger. The Venetian commander, Captain Marcantonio Bragadin, having heroically exhausted all his remaining resources, negotiated honourable terms of surrender with the Turkish Commander Lala Mustafa.

When they first came out the Venetian officers were treated with elaborate courtesy. They received a document with the sultan's seal on it accepting the terms. The hospitality continued. Suddenly, when the Venetians were all lulled into a feeling of security, Mustafa gave a pre-arranged signal and the massacre began, first of the officers, Mustafa himself cutting off the nose and ears of the captain, then of the survivors within the city who were cruelly tortured, raped and killed. Bragadin was permitted to survive for two weeks in what pain and agony we can only guess at, then in a final twist of the sadistic knife, he was flayed alive in the city square in front of the cathedral. His skin was stuffed with straw and sent in triumph to Constantinople from where it was later stolen by an Italian patriot and brought back to Venice where it now rests in the church of SS Giovanni e Paolo. Mustafa's victory was complete. Cyprus was annexed to the Ottoman empire and he himself became its first governor. In an attempt to 'explain' Mustafa's obnoxious deception and cruelty, one account (unmentioned by Sir David Hunt) relays that Mustafa was infuriated by the discovery of a boatload of corpses, purportedly of Muslim pilgrims heading for Mecca. That the Venetians, exhausted and defeated, with apparently honourable surrender terms, should have perpetrated such obscene violence seems hardly credible. The irony of it all was that the Turkish fleet was utterly defeated by the Catholic powers at Lepanto, not three months later, in October 1571. One little island was sacrificed to the Turks so that Europe could be saved from them. Had Lepanto occurred three months earlier, the siege of Famagusta would very likely have been called off and Cyprus would never have become an Ottoman possession. Would Cyprus then be an Italian island today with today's Cypriots speaking Italian and preferring gorgonzola to *halloumi*? I doubt it.

In Famagusta itself, thereafter called Magusa by the Turks, (now Gazimagusa–'unconquered' Magusa) several of the largest of the 365 churches (if that implausible number is correct) were turned into mosques, the most splendid being the Cathedral of St Nicholas, which we shall visit in a moment. It became an almost exclusively Muslim city which Christians could only enter with a pass. Its Pyrrhic victory won but its entrepreneurs gone, Famagusta, thereafter, settled down into becoming a quiet, unobtrusive and rather pretty Turkish town of fewer than 10,000 inhabitants. Cuma told me that the town now has about 16,000 people but I'm not sure whether that includes the sizeable university population. During Ottoman times it also became the Turkish equivalent to Van Diemen's Land, a place of exile for 'difficult' politicians, turbulent imams and 'subversive' poets. The national poet of the Ottomans, Manik Kemal Bey, was imprisoned here for three years (1873-76) and we had the quaint pleasure of having a mid-morning coffee in the palace courtyard outside his prison lock-up. There is a fine bust of him to the left of the cathedral of St Nicholas, now the principal mosque of the city and called after who else, but Lala Mustafa.

There is little left of the palace (Palazzo del Proveditore) beyond what we could see from the tree-shaded, *al fresco* restaurant. Immediately behind us was the facade with its three arches, one of which provided entrance to the coffee shop and restaurant. The arches are supported by granite columns brought down here from Salamis. In Venetian times the arches themselves supported a marble balcony on which I imagine the royals would occasionally display themselves. It could also have been used by members of the council to address gatherings of people, much as Mussolini used a balcony in the Piazza Venezia in Rome to address (harangue) 'his' people. Standing in that square, facing the cathedral and with the palace at your back, you could just imagine how life was lived here 700 years ago. The Franks were hemmed in between the temporal power of the palace, widespread and encompassing as the sprawling structure of the palace itself once was and the brooding beauty of the cathedral insisting on the spiritual power of the Church. The two were complementary and the round of daily life was dictated by the prescriptions of each. Generally speaking, if you kicked against one, you were clobbered by both. Life was simple.

The small, contained piazza in front of us was witness to successive landmarks in the history of Cyprus. It was here, for example, that the kings of Cyprus, crowned in Nicosia, were crowned for a second time as kings of Jerusalem, a title more symbolic than executive; it was in the cathedral opposite that countless royal marriages took place and christenings, too, no doubt, to rapturous applause from the square; it was here that Catarina Cornaro, the widowed, young queen, last queen of Cyprus, signed her abdication in favour of her native Venice; and more poignantly, it was here, that, as previously mentioned, the stalwart Captain Brigadin, commander of the garrison, was flayed alive under orders from Lala Mustafa, whose name the cathedral-made-mosque now bears. The square would have resounded to a different sound that day.

We walked across to the cathedral whose facade is the finest example of Gothic you'll find in all Cyprus. No expense was spared on it, or on the cathedral as a whole. Famagusta at the beginning of the 14th century could afford the best, for that was the time in Famagusta when a local entrepreneur's daughter wore jewellery more dazzling and expensive than did the queen of France and kings dined sumptuously at the tables of merchants. The cathedral, whose foundations were laid in 1300, was modelled on the cathedral in Rheims where the kings of France were crowned – just in case anybody failed to make the connection.

The western facade (the one facing the square) has three ornate portals and two bell towers, one of which has been elongated to become a minaret. Though several of the buttresses were ineptly restored after an earthquake, in their original structure, dressed in the skillful carvings of imported artists, they were state of the art for that time. Some concessions were, however, made to the Cypriot climate. The roof, if you could see it, is flat, not pitched as in northern Europe and there are balconies from which flags could fly, helpful also for ventilation. The golden, filigree magic of the exterior with its rich stalagmite carvings is not replicated in the interior. Even taking into account that what was once a Christian church has now become a mosque, you are surprised, I think, by the lack of ornamentation and clutter, some of it structural. There is neither transept nor apse and no side chapels either. By Muslim canon, there are no banners, flags, paintings or flowers. Just a nave of three aisles. The large, rotund, unadorned columns, painted white, seem inappropriate in relation to the fine lines of the high, vaulted roof, now also painted white between its tracery of arches. The image it gave me was of a tall, slim, very elegant woman, standing on legs that were far too stout for her. Despite these rather negative comments there is about the cathedral-mosque a robust simplicity that is not altogether unappealing.

The single most dulling factor and the sorriest change in transition from cathedral to mosque is, however, the replacement of the original stained glass windows by carved gypsum screens. I found it dispiriting. Colour has gone. A richness of impact has disappeared to be replaced by a low-key, uniform, diffused yellow light. I opt for a brighter, more colourful heaven. The coloured, geometric designs of modern Islamic glass in the west window give you some idea of what is missing. Were such glasswork to be incorporated in all the windows it would do something, I think, to redeem the absence of the original masterpieces. The effect of illuminated glass on the interior of a Gothic church is integral to its lines and artistry. Almost it is its *raison d'étre*. Without it the architecture is bare and inadequate.

The furniture of the mosque itself is purely functional with little or no concession to aesthetics. On a raised, unadorned platform an old man, in *zuchetto* (skullcap), prays from the Koran, his voice low, his body moving to and fro, absorbed, intent. To his left a latticed, green screen shields off female worshippers. The floor is covered in wall-to-wall, light-green carpet, showing wear in places – a much less preferable covering to the more usual, multi-coloured rugs. The *mihrab*, as is the common Muslim practice, swings the orientation of the mosque towards Mecca but, in this case, rather clumsily. No one could be distracted by the decor of the Lala Mustafa mosque. Maybe God prefers it that way.

We drove to Othello's Tower and apart from two or three Turks we were the only visitors there. In Act II, Sc. I of his well-known tragedy, Shakespeare has Cassio say,

> Great Jove, Othello guard
> And swell his sail with thine own powerful breath,
> That he may bless this bay with his tall ship,
> Make love's quick pants in Desdemona's arms,
> Give renew'd fire to our extincted spirits,
> And bring all Cyprus comfort.'

The scene was set in a seaport in Cyprus. No more. So, was it Famagusta? We don't know for certain but how many other seaports in Cyprus could have filled the bill at that time? To the English of Shakespeare's time accounts of the siege of Famagusta were familiar – indeed, the story of the siege was a runaway best seller in a dozen countries. He himself would have been about 6 or 7 when the siege took place about 30 years previously and his audience would certainly have understood the charge given to Othello by the Venetian senate to defend Cyprus against the 'infidel Turk'. In all likelihood they would have extrapolated from Cassius' 'And bring all Cyprus comfort', to a more universal plea for the security of all civilisation, as they understood it, against the inroads of Islam. The play does require a citadel and certainly Othello's Tower occupies only a small area of what was once a fortified palace and became, under the Venetians, a redoubtable fortress, a citadel.

Shakespearean historians have tried to identify one Venetian officer or another with Othello, to my mind unconvincingly. A combination of the two most likely characters gives us a dark, mercenary fellow from Calabria, called il Capitano Moro, appropriately, a man of some passion, who was unaccountably dismissed from the service and from an earlier time, a Venetian nobleman, also called Moro, who was governor of Cyprus for two years and who returned to Venice wifeless but apparently also scatheless of any wrong doing. Fictional characters are nearly always composites of several real life characters. I noticed on the road leading to the citadel a little cafe that specialised in *mezes* and kebabs and was enticingly called 'Desdemona'. Nothing that I saw commemorated Iago.

The citadel, of which Othello's Tower is a part, is the oldest building in Famagusta. Before it became a citadel, it was a watchtower which looked out to sea and spotted pilgrims, refugees, or even men-of-war make landfall. The citadel, built under the Lusignans, has figured in several episodes of Cypriot history. It was where the Genovese, in a sly, Trojan Horse operation, talked themselves into conducting negotiations with the authorities, then overpowered the guards and took possession of the city. It was the citadel's walls, too, that protected the Venetians from a local revolt in the 16th century. In the meantime they had, of course, made it more of a fortress and less of a palace. Finished in 1492 (that date again!) the gateway entrance was adorned with a marble relief of the Lion of St Mark. It's still there.

We tramped on the rampart walls, also buttercupped with daisies and saw in the courtyard below a full size statue of a man with a cannonball replacing his head. Who was it originally? As I approached a small turret on the ramparts, a flutter of half-a-dozen pigeons flew out in fright. They looked as if their ancestors, too, might have come from Venice and, showing the same kind of ingenuity as those in St Mark's Square, they had made a coop out of the turret. Perhaps, seeing nobody about, they had taken an early siesta after gorging themselves on grain spilled from a ship unloading at the closeby docks. Sandra pointed out a ladybird, wings folded, spotted red 'carapace' shining in the sun, sampling tiny spikes of grass on the stones. Walking the walls I thought of the scion of one of the ruling families of Verona, the last one, imprisoned here by the Venetians. Accustomed to taking his *passeggiata* on the walls he, one day, saw down below him a lovely concubine going about her daily chores. He attracted her attention and then, taking the opportunity of this daily period of exercise, he did the one thing that the Venetians couldn't prevent him from doing – he fell in love with her. The Venetian commander, obviously having a feeling for the romance of the situation, allowed them to set up house together in an empty apartment, provided the Veronese produce no legitimate heirs. Presumably that ruled out marriage but they went ahead anyway and produced a number of illegitimate ones, one of whom subsequently married a Dutch doctor thus assuring for her father the best of medical care in his old age.

A closed passageway on the dock side led to a round watchtower, whitewashed, standing out on its own, about 50 m out from the citadel. It looked towards the open sea, with Varosha, the one time Greek sector of Famagusta, clearly silhouetted on the right. A sign in Turkish, English and German read 'MILITARY SECURITY ZONE. ENTRANCE FORBIDDEN'. I thought that for old time's sake they could have put it in Italian as well. From the courtyard there was entry to a long, narrow, medieval hall with a high vaulted roof and ribbed arches. It looked as if its windows had been blocked up, though ledges still protruded inwards. The hall had five bays and a small, round, recessed apse, cut into the stone, at one end. Impressive but gloomy. I don't suppose the gatherings there were hilarious.

At one end of the traverse courtyard there was a raised platform, suitable for orchestral ensembles and choirs and a clear area in front where portable seating could be placed. The 'hall', however atmospheric, is too small to accommodate Verdi's *Otello* but we were given a brochure telling us that, in late summer, the opera would be staged in the Greek theatre at Salamis. The choir and orchestra are coming from Nuremberg. The setting is magnificent and I should say that at only 10 kms distance, Salamis is close enough to catch the atmosphere.

All the medieval buildings in Famagusta have been constructed out of a fine, yellow sandstone, which, Cuma tells me, comes from the Karpas area, known as the Panhandle of Cyprus. The stone, though soft and malleable and pitted as a pock-marked face, still stands firm in the walls of the citadel. Walking about, I saw on one wall, sculpted by rain, wind and time, open fish mouths, scabrously grinning skulls, gargoyles leering, dogs' snouts snouting and here and there the gruesome cranials of horses. A whole macabre necropolis awaited my discovery but instead I climbed up to the ramparts again to look at the wild flowers. I turned to look down at the docks. One ship was stacking containers, another unloading grain, while, before a third, a lorry load of oranges waited patiently. I noticed that one ship had a name in Cyrillic script, another was called simply 'Roma' – good to see that the old connection was being maintained. It must have been at this docks, in this harbour that Desdemona, Iago and Cassio braced themselves against the wind as they waited for Othello's ship to pull aside. A hundred squawking gulls were enjoying an animated lunch in one particular sliver of harbour. Directly beneath me Cuma was having a smoke. I looked back one more time at the marvellous skyline of the old town, tall and golden and gaunt with the ruins of what were once majestic buildings. It was time for our lunch, too.

At Cuma's suggestion we chose an off-street restaurant with an inner courtyard roofed with a large, circular trellis of four different varieties of vines. On that day the tendrils, which urgently needed pruning, snaked overhead like interlapping, brown intestines. The waiter brought us a family photo album to show us what it looked like in summer. Heavy with falling bunches of grapes and bowery. The picture was in colour so one could see the black and white varieties. He was obviously proud of the trellis in its summer wear. A waterless fountain was the centrepiece of the courtyard – here, too, water was short. We had a substantial lunch of stuffed aubergines, fried halloumi, toasted white bread and mixed salad, followed by chicken kebabs, lamb chops and a heaped plate of french fries. A neatly segmented orange, complete with toothpick, brought our meal to a close. All that plus beer and coffee for US$10 each.

After lunch we drove to the ghost city of Varosha little more than a kilometre to the south of the old town. In the early years of this century Famagusta got a new lease of life. A railway ran between it and Nicosia, and the port was dredged allowing coastal and more distant trading to begin once more. This was where the Greek Cypriot community lived. Famagusta, especially south around Varosha, has also some of the best beaches on the island, so it's not surprising that gradually it became the city of first choice for holiday makers. After the Second World War unrestrained development took over and filled the skyline of Varosha with high rise buildings, graceless, white hotel and apartment blocks, catering mainly to the packaged tourist trade. In the 50s and 60s Varosha boomed. Its population soared to 37,000 in 1973, 34,000 of whom were Greek Cypriot. Of the remainder, 3,000 were ex-pat British who formed an overseas colony of more or less retired and refined hedonists. All that changed in 1974, changed utterly, when, after the second Turkish invasion, Famagusta-Varosha found itself in the Turkish area of a divided Cyprus. Greek Cypriots fled south in a stream of terror-stricken refugees, leaving behind their homes, their businesses and their grandiose property investments. It was a form of psychologically imposed ethnic cleansing that, within the shortest time, completely shut down the busiest resort in the country. Declared exempt from occupation by the UN, Varosha remains to this day a stark, silent, mocking city, unoccupied except by the patrolling Turkish military. No one else may enter.

We drove to the five star Palm Beach Hotel, a splendid pink and white structure that somehow escaped incorporation into segregated Varosha. Sitting on its sunny, seaside deck we were able to see at close hand the empty spectre of a city, 'idle as a painted ship upon a painted sea'. This lifeless town is what you might expect after an attack on it by the latest weapons of modern warfare, designed to kill humans but leave buildings standing. Yet, by contrast, the nearest building to us, not more than 30 m away, had its innards hanging out, possibly as a result of heavy artillery fire in 1974. The rest stood forlorn, cheek by jowl along the seafront, like giant sentinels, gaunt and day by day deteriorating. And behind them wasting in the sun were the supermarkets, the shops, the emporia, the whole panorama of restaurants, recreation areas, salons, curiosity shops and boutiques that once catered to tens of thousands of residents and visitors alike. This city of 10,000 tourist beds has not seen a single tourist in 24 years. 'Let them come back,' says Cuma, 'otherwise it is too much of a waste.' Not all share that view. Once, a year ago, the Grey Wolves, an extreme army contingent imported from Turkey, declared that they would lead a march on Varosha. All they asked was that their followers arm themselves with spray cans, each family to choose its own apartment by spraying it with their own identification. The government of the TRNC stepped in to thwart that helter-skelter appropriation but just recently the 'president' of the self-declared Northern Republic, Mr Rauf Denktash, announced that he himself had plans for it. Dead Varosha could yet provide the spark to some very real-life conflict. On our way out I was a little surprised to find the Irish flag among a dozen or so that hung limply outside the entrance to the Palm Beach.

We made another tour of the old town, stopping to look at the church of St Peter and Paul, which was closed. It's another of those 'gateway to heaven' churches built in the 1360s by the merchant Simon Nostrano from just one-third of the profits of one trading venture. No doubt like Signor Nostrano himself, it is a more pragmatic and functional building than aesthetically pleasing. Typical is the row of simple, solid buttresses supporting the roof. This church, too, served as a mosque for centuries and you can see the remains of a minaret, built atop the turret on the south west of the church. It fell into disuse as a mosque and the British, ever inventive, used it to store potatoes. It is now the occasional venue for theatre, concerts and exhibitions.

Sandra insisted on visiting the Nestorian church built by the enormously wealthy father of the girl whose jewellery topped that of the queen of France but if she was looking for some lavish and ostentatious edifice she was disappointed. The church, again dating from the 1360s, was built to serve the community of Syrian Christians who had fled to Cyprus after the defeat at Acre. It began as a single-aisled chapel with a triple apse and a neat belfry, probably modelled on the traditional Nestorian churches of the Middle East. It grew by additions into its present stockiness and is now more of historic than aesthetic interest. The Turks, also inventive, used it as a camel stable. At present it stands neglected in a courtyard of weeds. It was, of course, closed.

We could have spent more time in and out of ruined churches, or simply mooching around the old town, a pleasant place to wander in. We could have window-shopped in the *sok* but, because of the warnings at the Greek Cypriot crossing, we couldn't have bought anything, however attractively priced. That didn't appeal to me.

We did try to sample the offerings in the 'Old Town Pub Disco', formerly the Hammam, but it, too, was unfortunately closed, possibly for a lengthy siesta. This was Sandra's chance – 'let's go see the 4,000 year-old ruins at Enkomi!' These were not far away and we had an hour to spare so, though I'd had my fill of ruins for one day, I succumbed to her enthusiasm.

Enkomi/Alasia

The first question I asked myself when I got out of the taxi at Enkomi (also sometimes called Alasia) was 'who on earth would want to build here?' and the second was 'who on earth would want to come here to see the ruins?' Certainly we were the only people there and, though there was a custodian, he didn't appear until we were leaving. But, in fact, the US$1.00 each we paid was well worth the hour we spent wandering among the ruins. Enkomi is vaguely reminiscent of Khirokitia, except that, unlike Khirokitia, Enkomi was built on the flat and its dwellings, consisting of an open courtyard and rooms on three sides, are rectangular. Yet thousands of years separate them, Khirokitia being by far the older.

Enkomi is the second city on this site as the first was destroyed by fire around 1200 BC and the second, the one we were looking at, probably by marauding tribes, two centuries later, though Dr Vassos Karageorghis, in his erudite contribution to *Footprints in Cyprus*, says that the silting up of the harbour had a lot to do with the city's ultimate demise. It's surmised that the inhabitants, over a period of time, moved down the road to Salamis. At Enkomi, too, the ruins were a feast of wild flowers, yellow daisies being again predominant, though here scattered groups of short poppies added a dash of red. Occasional, giant fennels looked down on them both.

The city, perhaps, of 15,000 people, built after the fire, was constructed on a rectangular grid pattern and surrounded by a high wall, itself constructed of sundried bricks and buttressed at regular intervals by great, hewn blocks of stone called ashlars. In fact, all public buildings were built of ashlars. Even the ruins of the foundations are impressive. The dwellings – and these include workshops and shrines, as well as houses – were also built in rectangular form. So regular were they that the first archaeologists to excavate the site in the mid-30s, initially thought they had discovered a necropolis, more especially as they found a skeleton in every 'tomb'. Later they concluded that, like the Khirokitians, the people of Enkomi also buried their dead under their homes and allowed that the ruins were of a town after all. No excavations have been done since 1974.

Though wandering through these evocative ruins was in itself rewarding one really ought to have an archaeologist in one's pocket. I particularly wanted to know what the large, round 'doughnut' stones were. They were carefully carved and the hole in the middle made them look like a toilet seat. Dr Karageorghis confirms that not only were there toilets at Enkomi but bathrooms also, both served by a well organised sewerage system. Bathtubs of clay and limestone point, he says, to the high standard of living of the inhabitants. Querns were easy to identify and it wasn't difficult to imagine fields of corn growing in the surrounding area, as the site is part of the easternmost section of the fertile Mesaoria plain. Water was not the problem it is today as the whole surrounding area was forested and a freshwater stream, probably perennial in those far off less environmentally destructive days, flowed nearby. Judging by the number of wells on the site, most houses, or small groups of houses, seemed to possess one. They're still there, waterless now, though Sandra is convinced she heard the soft plop of stone landing in mud when we threw one down.

The city would have been quite wealthy as, apart from its agricultural products, some of which could easily have been exported, copper, taken down from Tamasos and, perhaps, from even further afield, was smelted there. The sea was 2.5 kms further inland then than now and would have provided safe anchorage and convenient trans-shipment opportunities. Trade in copper, mainly with the Mycenaeans, was, as most trade then was, on a barter basis, copper, that is, exchanged for gold ornaments, ivory and alabaster vases, and luxury jewellery. Such *objets d'art* were found routinely in the tombs of rich merchants at Enkomi.

Many of these treasures can be seen in the Cyprus Museum in Nicosia; others are in the British Museum in London and in the Ashmolean Museum in Oxford. Some, like the gold ring with a lion in relief, the gold pendant in the shape and form of a pomegranate and the necklace of gold beads in the form of figure-of-eight shields, all in the Cyprus Museum and all found at Enkomi, are exquisite. There are also Mycenaean vases and bowls as well as other treasures all indicative of both wealth and refinement. As far as religion goes, for at least 700 years, the inhabitants of Enkomi worshipped the 'horned god' of fertility.He is depicted as a youth wearing a kilt and a horned helmet (no bagpipes). A statue of him cast in bronze was found in one of the cult shrines at Enkomi and is now in the Cyprus Museum.

Baked clay tablets, found at Enkomi, used a Cypro-Minoan script which has not yet been deciphered and the interesting thing is that these tablets are not all to do with business transactions. Some have continuous texts and are, possibly, poetry. Maybe that, in retrospect, answers for me the second question I posed at the beginning – why come here? Put simply, any society that produced poets and cherished their poetry 3,500 years ago is worth an hour of my time. Pity we can't read the poems.

We said goodbye to Cuma at the Turkish crossing and gave him a little present for his grandson. We then walked hurriedly across No Man's Land, arriving at the Greek Cypriot crossing with two minutes to spare. It had been a full and interesting day.

21

VOUNI – PALACE ON THE HILL

On a beautiful, warm day in late April my wife and I, along with some friends, availed of an opportunity to visit Vouni, an ancient palace whose foundations are spread out over the summit of a conical hill about 65 kms west of Nicosia in the part of the island at present under the control of the Turkish Cypriot regime. When we got to the border crossing we found 450 Turkish Cypriots, men, women and children, gathered there, preparing to cross over to the south and go on a unique pilgrimage to the Hala Sultan Tekke mosque, near Larnaka. It was the Eid el-Adha festival and the crowd was milling around, happy and excited. They blocked the road and, were it not for the good offices of a United Nations friend, we would have had to wait a long, long time before crossing. It was an historic occasion, the first time that such an experiment in good neighbourliness and religious courtesy was taking place and it went off successfully. Sadly, a corresponding pilgrimage, arranged also by the UN for Greek Orthodox Christians to visit the monastery of St Andreas in the Karpas peninsula a week later, did not go ahead. Despite this first Greek Cypriot disappointment, the crossings have continued in both directions with up to a thousand a time from each community paying homage at their respective religious shrines, one in the North, the other in the South. Could these be the first, small steps towards reconciliation?

On the way to Vouni we had a breakfast of chicken kebabs, served by a cheerful and voluble Turkish Cypriot, at the sleepy, little village of Morphou. His native village, he told us, was near Pafos. He had been reluctant to move north in 1974 but now his little café was doing well and he seemed to have neither regrets nor bitterness about his 'enforced' move. Our Cypriot money was welcome and we even received change in Cypriot currency. In fact, I think he was glad we paid in Cypriot pounds as the Turkish lira fell in value literally every day. One building, close by our outdoor table, which claimed to be a bank had great, weather-stained, wooden doors, padlocked. It looked down-at-heel, insecure and uninviting in contrast to the bank across the street which looked as spruced-up as the shop next door. This direct contrast between old and new is a feature of many villages in Cyprus, more especially in the North. Turkish lira notes were, for the most part, tatty-looking and soiled – understandably when even then it took 250,000 of them to make one Cypriot pound. Two years later it takes 420,000. That's a lot of paper.

Morphou, an ancient settlement, was the biggest village in Cyprus during the period of British occupation and prior to 1974 it had become a flourishing town with its own mayor and bishop. The demise of its most recent bishop, as I've mentioned elsewhere in this book, caused a stir that rocked the Orthodox Church in Cyprus and this had nothing to do with the Turks. When the people of the diocese chose as successor to their deceased bishop a man whose life style the archbishop of Cyprus didn't approve of and, therefore, refused to appoint, serious civil unrest occurred outside the archbishop's palace in Nicosia. Most people who have only recently heard of Morphou will probably have heard of it in that context but the countryside around it, having an excellent underground water table, is best known for its citrus orchards. It seemed a pleasant enough place and did not deserve to have its honourable name brought to the prurient attention of the world.

But on to Vouni – the road, which runs for stretches by the sea, is a pleasing, scenic drive. It's worth going to Vouni for the view alone. Built on a rocky hill, which rises steeply from the sea to a height of 250 m, the palace dates from the 5th century BC. Looking out to sea, we saw the wide-armed sweep of Morphou Bay and had, as well, a catch-all view of the entire hinterland. A haze, joining horizon to sky, prevented us from seeing Turkey. It was easy to imagine why the Turks chose that locality as one of the landing points for the invasion in 1974. They have, of course, delineated and embellished the actual spot, which is now a picnic area. The two flags, one red with white crescent, the other white with red crescent, representing respectively Turkey and its satellite 'republic', fly high overhead. Flagpoles in this part of the island for some reason always seem twice as long as those in the South. And far more numerous. When we turned around, the rolling

176

hills to our back were almost equally impressive.

The palace was quite luxurious for its day, containing 137 'rooms', if you count kitchens, bathing rooms and small sanctuary areas. There was also a central court. Only ruins remain, few, as I recall, taller than a tall man's shoulder, unless you climb down into the bathing rooms. The stones are hewn and carefully laid, the foundations solid. A wide and graceful set of steps leads down to the inner courtyard, giving it a sunken terrace appearance. Opposite them, at the far end, its back to the sea, is a time-worn sculpture of Athene. She now adorns the front of a windlass, poised over a deep well but was once the capital on one of the columns of the colonnade that surrounded the courtyard. One of our friends that day was a young Australian physicist who timed my dropping of a stone into the well and calculated that its depth was about 70 ft. Though excavations in 1928-29 discovered a number of statues and statuettes, none but Athena's pockmarked, half-sculpted visage remains on site. Numerous artefacts, ornaments and coins in gold and silver were also discovered, a number of them in a black pot hurriedly hidden, as family treasure might be, at a time when the palace was overrun by the Greeks of Soli.

History tells us very little about Vouni. Even its name is non-committal – it means simply 'mountain peak'. It is presumed, however, that, as there are oriental features to its early style, especially in its grandiose entrance and its bathing complex, it was built, if not by the Persians themselves, then under Persian influence. Some have it that the king of Marion (Polis) was in the pay of the Persians and built it to keep a watchful eye on the Hellenic city of Soli, only a few miles away to the east. When the Marion dynasty fell in 449 BC the palace came into Greek hands and changes were made to the architecture. The grand entrance was blocked up, giving the palace a large, closed, *cortile*-style courtyard with rooms leading off it, more in the Grecian style and, indeed, much as one might see today in some Italian *palazzi*. The blocked-up entrance is still there.

Men, much like me, I thought, sitting on a ledge in the noon-day sun. with similar desires and disappointments in the pursuit of happiness, had designed these buildings, over whose flagged floors I had just walked, had built the clever conduit system that provided water for a more than adequate bathing facility, had dug the wells and worshipped at the altars, had admired the view and taken refuge from the heat. Their spell of time they had spent purposefully, if not always admirably, any more than I do mine, or modern nation-states, theirs. As they looked on Soli and guarded themselves against her, so do the modern occupants of this countryside look on Nicosia and guard themselves against her. We have planes, not chariots and incomparably more destructive weapons of war, yet do not the children of these hills pick anemones and mallow and crown daisies to make their garlands today, as did the children here 2,500 years ago? Does not that shepherd, a stone's throw from me, tend his goats in much the same way as did his ancestors so long ago? What, I asked myself, as the warmth of the day shimmered around me, what, in the long interim, have we learnt? And will we learn no more in the expanse of time ahead?

If you're a lover of old stones, or simply interested in quietly meditating over a splendid, panoramic view, Vouni is worth an hour or two of your time.

In and Around Limassol

22

LIMASSOL – CITY OF DIONYSUS

The second city of the island, Limassol, with a population of about 140,000, is situated in the middle of the south coast of the island. How old is it? Nobody knows, not for certain, anyway. There is some archaeological evidence which suggests that its origins go back to the early Bronze Age, around 2,300 BC. There is further evidence that in its western hinterland, both at Sotira and Erimi, jugs and jars have been discovered pre-dating that time by a further 2,300 years and then there are the skeletal bones and beads found only in 1961 in a cave at Akrotiri that go back as far as 8000 BC. Whichever date you go for does not change the fact that the people in the settlements in and about present day Limassol lived quiet and peaceable lives for thousands and thousands of years, even after the Emperor Theodosius, in the 5th century AD, elevated their town to city status and called it after himself. For much of those long centuries, two ancient, closeby cities, Amathous on the east and Kourio on the west, squeezed it out and it wasn't till those two were destroyed by the Saracens in the 7th century AD that Limassol got its chance though it took a severe sea-storm and the near wrecking of the Crusader fleet of Richard, Coeur de Lion, at the end of the 12th century to give it the historic boost it needed. Indeed, according to tradition, it was in the old Byzantine castle, precursor on the same site to the present Crusader one, that Richard married Berengaria of Navarre in 1191 to the great jubilation of the city. More of this later.

In the years following Richard's take-over of Cyprus and his immediate sale of it, first to the Knights Templar, then a year later when they defaulted on payments, to the Franks in the person of Guy de Lusignan, exiled king of Jerusalem, Limassol grew in importance, becoming a centre of Crusader power. In the 14th century, however, the Genovese, who favoured Famagusta both as a port and a home base, raided Limassol on several occasions, despoiling it. Earthquakes, in the ensuing centuries, did some more levelling, so that, when the Ottomans conquered the country in 1571, Limassol was a poor relation of the other cities. They, in any case, favoured Larnaka and raised the Limassol harbour dues so high that ships couldn't afford to berth there.

It wasn't until the British came in 1878 that Limassol began to thrive. Cyprus was the only wine-producing country of the empire at that time and most of it, then as today, was produced either within the Limassol administrative district or as close to it as made no difference. The British built a harbour pier and pretty soon oceans of wine in barrels began flowing through the port. Thereafter, Limassol became an important trading centre and a busy harbour town. Its population, containing a high proportion of Turkish Cypriots, had grown to 43,600 by independence in 1960. After the war of 1974 and the subsequent division of the island most of the Turkish Cypriots went north to Famagusta to be replaced in Limassol by the far more numerous Greek Cypriots fleeing from the north. This enforced population switch increased the numbers in Limassol to more than 100,000, effectively making it the second most populous city in the island and its chief port.

Limassol, the province, covers a wide range of terrain, from coastal stretch to hilly hinterland with above, the mountainous backdrop of the Troodos. Its population of 173,319 in 1992 represented nearly 29 percent of the population of the free part of the island and almost one quarter of the whole island. It incorporates 114 villages.

Limassol, the city, especially down by the Old Port, reminds me of many 20th century coastal cities in Africa, presenting, as it does, an attractive seafront of luxury promenades under palm trees, charmingly lit by night, flanked on its off-sea side, by a string of restaurants and old, half-pretentious 19th century houses, with, behind this facade, a labyrinth of narrow, winding streets, small workshops and individual family businesses. In Africa this latter would be a shanty town of dusty, potholed, earth-beaten streets, alive with colourful, noisy, trading by day and dead by night with shuttered shops, guarded by *askaris* dozing in doorways. In Limassol the streets are still narrow, but the shops are solid, there is a modern arcade or two and the road is tarmac yet, for all the efforts at rehabilitation and modernisation, you are constantly surprised by dilapidated buildings, vacant lots and flaky down-at-heel premises.

By day these winding streets – some might call them quaint – have a busy, unaffected, folksy air about them that I found especially agreeable. Passing through them in mid-morning you can hear the hammering of coppersmiths, see tailors sewing, smell the glue and polyurethane from furniture workshops and admire the skill of shoemakers at their lasts. Where else these days will you find a bespoke tailor who will run you up a suit to measure in a matter of days, at a fraction the price you'd pay in Saville Row (that is, if you could afford to shop there), or a 'bespoke' shoemaker who will shod you in fine leather even more quickly? This is the kind of service that all towns must have provided a hundred years ago, before buying 'off the peg, or off the shoe rack' became more cheaply fashionable. If you have a nose for it, you can probably find the best bargains in Cyprus in these back streets in Limassol. No one in his senses would want the old buildings demolished but perhaps the decrepit ones, the shoddy ones and the vacant ones could be given a face lift and a daub of paint. Of course, if it's the latest *haute couture* you're after, be it from Milan, Paris, Madrid or London, there's always Agio Andreou and Leoforos Makariou, the former running a block behind and, in part, parallel to the seafront, the latter bisecting it not far from the Archaeological Museum. Limassol, like all Cypriot cities, has an old and a new town. I prefer the old for all its occasional shoddiness.

Earlier that morning I had gone for a walk down the one kilometre long seafront promenade. I counted 12 ships moored in the harbour, a reminder that, beyond its tourist image, Limassol is also a busy port. The seafront itself, from just below the Catholic church of Agia Ekaterina to the Old Port, has the widest prom I've seen anywhere, in fact it has four walkways, five, if you count the sea wall on which people were also walking that morning, all paved, separated from each other by rectangles of grass, flower planters, or children's play areas, with rows of palm trees adding a tropical touch. Looking further east towards Amathous, there is a 15 km ribbon of hotels and apartment blocks stretching in a wide curve around the bay – a tourist *ville* that somehow keeping its distance, does not impinge too obviously on the town itself.

On my *passeggiata*, both for information and entertainment I decided to embark on a brief survey of those whom I met, pretending to be passing through Cyprus with eight hours to spare in Limassol – what should I see, what was there to see?

Not much, said a Swedish couple in their fifties – the castle, of course, and maybe a walk in the old town, they, however, were going to spend the day in Pafos. Not much help there.

Next came a 40 year-old black American, on furlough from Riyadh, who, after spending a year there, expressed shock at the number of scantily dressed women all about. It was, in fact, a breezy, overcast morning and the women I saw were all quite sensibly dressed.

See the castle, he said, hire a car and go somewhere else.

A sprightly man, walking the wall with a newspaper tucked under his arm –

Try the castle, there's also a couple of museums, then have a nice, long, leisurely lunch. A certain appeal in that.

Two Irish girls from Dublin – wait for the sun to come out! Pithy.

The young woman in the information office was more helpful. Castle, mosque, a couple of churches, the covered market, a museum or two and Heroes' Square. We never tell anybody about that one, but as you're writing about Limassol – you see, it's our one and only proper square and ...

What's wrong with it? I asked, curious.

Well, you see, it's in the seedy part of town, full of cabarets and night clubs, kind of, like, you know, like a red light area, but the square itself is pretty. Anyway it's our only one. She showed me how to get there.

Will I be safe?

Of course, she replied, laughing, in the morning everybody is sleeping.

So, off I went – to the castle.

According to Sir David Hunt (*Footprints in Cyprus*, Ch. IX) Byzantine fortifications pre-existed the castle we now see down by the old harbour. An early 14th century construction, the present castle was further improved later that same century by King James I and again, a hundred years later, by the Venetians, who, typically, added the stout walls. With its rectangular exterior it looks more like an artillery fortress or citadel than a castle, though in contemporary descriptions of medieval, military architecture all three words seem interchangeable. It was the Knights Templar who most probably built the lower hall on the foundations of the Byzantine fort. This would have been at the turn of the 14th century, about the same time as they were refurbishing Kolossi. At this time they were still riding high against their brother Crusading order of knights, the Knights of St John. But even then stories were spreading about their religious beliefs and behaviour to the extent that a few years later they were being accused of sorcery and devil worship. It was alleged that they had a secret room in the castle where they communed with a bronze 'talking head', that of the demon Baphomet, who used to appear in the form of a cat, no doubt a black one. All this was taken very seriously by Rome, so much so that the entire leadership was recalled, put on trial, tortured to provide evidence, and eventually burnt at the stake. It's no use looking for the secret chamber as it has long since been blocked up and now we don't even know where it was. They did a good job, however, on the Gothic rib-vaulted roof of the hall; in fact, the whole structure looks solid, compact and, for those times, impregnable. There's a fine view from the parapets though on this particular day access to the battlements was closed – workmen were renewing the stone-stair steps which had become dangerously slippery. All things waste with time.

Though a number of writers nowadays cast doubt on the location, tradition and some historians, too, believe that on the 12 May 1191, Richard the Lionheart and Berengaria of Navarre were married in the small Greek Orthodox chapel of St George (appropriately) that was then part of the Byzantine fort complex. Almost two weeks earlier the ship carrying Berengaria and Richard's sister, Queen Joanna of Spain, on their way to the Holy Land put in at Limassol after surviving a terrifying gale off the coast of Cyprus. The upstart ruler of the island at that time, Isaac Comnenus, rushed to the scene and invited the royal ladies ashore. Afraid of being taken hostage, they refused. Instead they asked permission to re-stock the ship with water and provisions.

He refused. Richard, arriving nearly a week later, was furious and issued threats against Comnenus. At first, Isaac, safe at his base in the Troodos, challenged Richard, then, on second thoughts, decided to parley. He visited Richard's camp, was not impressed, and, when he returned to the Troodos, repudiated the agreement they had reached. Unluckily for Comnenus, however, that very same evening Richard's forces were enhanced by the arrival of several potentates from Palestine, come to greet and welcome him, each bearing in train his own escort of knights. Realising his error of judgement, Isaac hopped about from castle to castle, from Kantara to Buffavento to Kyrenia but was eventually routed in a battle outside Nicosia, himself surrendering, with the sole request that he not be put in irons. He wasn't, being given manacles of silver instead. His wife, an Armenian princess, and only child, a daughter, were attached to the household of Queen Joanna. He, himself, still a captive, died four years later. I suppose it's all a bit remote seeing that the Byzantine fortress no longer exists but we do get pleasure from connections, as Noel Coward knew when he wrote 'I danced with a man, who danced with a girl, who danced with the Prince of Wales.'

The castle is now a Medieval Museum, housed mostly in small cell-like rooms. On display are, appropriately, a great variety of pistols, both flintlocked and muzzle-loaded, rifles, coats of mail, swords and daggers, enough to equip a platoon. There's also a fairly extensive collection of coins and other metal ware, as well as displays of porcelain, pottery and ceramics. Some marble plinths, capitals and statuettes are exhibited in the lower hall. All just enough to give you the Cypriot perspective on Cypriot history and culture.

Before I left, I reflected that the Ottomans had used the castle as a barracks, the British, as a prison. Its present day use as a museum is more peaceful and enlightened. Peaceful? On the day of my visit a whole class of eleven-year-olds, bright as buttons, enthusiastically swarmed to and fro over the small rooms, ferrying isolated pieces of information from their observations on to worksheets. They were perfectly well behaved and it was a pleasure to see how animatedly they consulted their teachers and how eagerly they vied with one another to do the best project.

From that day on, for them as for me, this old castle would be part of their country's history and part, too, of our shared living experience.

I made my way to the Djami' Kebir mosque – the grand mosque – only a hundred metres or so into the old town from the castle. The previous mosque on this site, destroyed by a storm in 1894, incorporated elements of a 14th century church; the new one, bunched between shops, workshops and derelict buildings, is an unappealing mixture of a number of Islamic styles. Notable are the horseshoe shaped arches and the onion windows. A large, circular tank in the forecourt has a number of prosaic looking taps poking out of it for ritual ablutions – a poor substitute for the traditional fountain. Limassol had a significant Muslim population before 1974 and the Djami' Kebir was in the heart of the Turkish quarter. When the twin palm trees are lit up in the evening and the muezzin's call rings out loud and clear from the minaret, as it may still occasionally do, one can feel for a moment the immanence of another culture in this place. There are still Turkish Cypriots in Limassol and if you walk westwards between the grand mosque and another second mosque (the Haji Ibrahim Agha) you will find that the streets still retain a Turkish aura. Indeed, many of them still retain their Turkish names, as well as their Turkish architecture, a characteristic feature of which is the protruding balcony, or oriel, latticed and hanging over the streets from first floor level. The inside of the mosque is unremarkable.

In less than five minutes from the mosque I was at the Katholiki basilica, the principal Greek Orthodox church in Limassol where the bishop also has his residence. I couldn't help but notice the names of the three streets encompassing it, all beginning with E, Eirinis, Ellados and Enosis and it struck me that maybe they delineated the church's (former?) role in Cypriot history as being respectively, pro-peace, pro-Greek, pro-Union with Greece. In quiet and unemotional moments I have heard intelligent and, I'm sure, deeply patriotic Greek Cypriots say that the present political division of the island will become, with appropriate territorial adjustments, the ultimate *status quo* leading to the integration of the TRNC with Turkey and the Greek Cypriot sector, the current 'free areas' with Greece. And all this, peacefully, so that the symbolically named streets will, as it were, be justified. I don't know. But what I do know is that there are many on either side of the Green Line who would consider such a proposition heresy, heresy as rank as that of the Templars and for which they would mete out a similar punishment.

The basilica is relatively new, so new that frescoes are complete only in the dome and the apse, each painting in its liturgical locus. Though three or four women, dressed in traditional black, were cleaning and polishing, the church was peaceful at eleven in the morning with only a few worshippers present, all male. I sat awhile in meditation, immersed in my own thoughts and then was distracted by a well dressed man, possibly in his early forties, standing before the iconostasi, bowing towards it, then falling to his knees, stretching out and kissing the floor, in a gesture reminiscent of the pope when, a younger man, he alighted from planes in countries he was visiting and kissed the tarmac. He raised himself athletically, blessed himself a couple of times, and moving on a little, repeated the same exercise. The man's energetic devotions continued until he had crossed the entire *iconostasi*. I'd never seen such prostrations in a Christian church before and, for a moment, wondered if the man were eclectically religious, attempting in this fashion to combine Orthodoxy with Islam. I left as soon as he did, with the vague aspiration of having a conversation with him, should an opportunity occur. Outside I heard him shout at a policeman writing a pink ticket, *Ela! Ela!* Though I realised any opportunity of conversing with him had gone, I followed him nonetheless, curious and saw just outside the church boundary wall, on a narrow footpath in a narrow street, a new, dark blue Mercedes 300, illegally parked. His. Normally, to park so, does not seem to be a traffic offence in Cyprus but in the case of our devout friend he was also parked on the wrong side of the road on a one-way street. The policeman told him there was nothing he could do as he had already written the ticket. Four pairs of hands gesticulated in the Greek body language equivalent of *c'est la vie*. The devout man pulled an obese wad of notes from his inside pocket, peeled off two in payment of his fine and proffered them to the policeman. There was no ill feeling. I got the impression that they were both embarrassed, that each approved what the other had been doing and that it was a pity it had to turn out this way. Especially in Lent – ah! maybe that explained the prostrations – penitential exercises! The devout man drove off in his Mercedes, the policeman followed as a kind of rear-end escort and I walked east to the municipal market.

The market was a flush with fruit and vegetables, some of which I'd never seen before. There was meat – a couple of butchers' stalls – and, following your nose, fish. Outside, in booths, on stands and tables. was a variety of Cypriot wines, honey, *loukoumi* (sweets) and breads. The scene was colourful and lively. A small number of tourists – it was already past midday – apartment dwellers obviously, were stocking up on sausages, fruit, bread and wine. One woman carried a bouquet of flowers, another stood pointing at a variety of cheeses, selecting some. Her husband, in rearguard attendance, carried half a dozen or more bottles of wine in a box – preparations, perhaps, for a midweek wine and cheese party with a group of friends from home? Certainly if one were interested in eating cheaply and well this would be the place to shop for provisions.

I had some difficulty in finding Heroes' Square and got a few funny looks when I asked directions. It wasn't, in fact, far away, off Andrea Drousiou Street. You can see both the minaret and the Orthodox towers nearby. A pretty square, as the young woman said, in the Italianate style, paved with rather large, off pink tiles instead of cobblestones and public seating under leafy trees. There was a central monument and a kiosk. The two fountain parts of the monument, adjuncts to the north and south sides, had become planters for lack of water but nothing was growing in them. The monument itself, quite large in its total complex, is of cement blocks, raised on a platform of cement blocks and is not impressive, emphasising, as it does, solidity and stark simplicity. On each of the four faces of the plinth there is an embossed wreath and in the centre of each wreath, a single word, or date – Cyprus, Greece, 1821, 1940.

The reference to 1821 is to the Greek War of Liberation and to the executions in Cyprus of those who, formally or informally, supported it. Mid-year, in 1821, the sultan gave his assent to the execution of 486 prominent Christian persons named by the governor. Included among these were three bishops who were beheaded and the reigning archbishop, Kyprianos, who was publicly hanged in front of the Serai on 9 July of that year. Some 30,000 Cypriots are known to have served in the Allied forces during the Second World War. They, too, are remembered. There is a bronze basin on top of the plinth, such as might hold an eternal flame but I could see no flame. There is also a subterranean vault, with steps leading down to it. I peered through the open tiles but could see little as there is a mesh window behind. I thought I saw the outline of a draped sarcophagus – perhaps the tomb of the Unknown Soldier. It should be a revered place.

But the square's night-time activities were all too evident. Every building was either a night club, a cabaret, or a hotel, rejoicing in such names as the Go Go Spot, the Casbah, or the Kit Kat Night Club. There was a Gypsy Rose (of course) and a Playboy with lots of bunny signs. Brazil was eponymously represented. There was a Bulgarian snack bar and a British pub, called the Prince of Wales (what company he keeps!) with darts, snooker and a pub garden. And these places were not cheap. Cyprus champagne was on offer at 60 CP (US$120) a bottle. Whisky and French Champagne tied at 80 CP (US$180) each. The cheapest drink was 4 CP (US$8) a glass and local brandy was going for 40 CP (US$80). Not a place for an impoverished tourist. Surprisingly, considering that Limassol is the centre of the wine industry, no wine appeared on the drinks menu displayed in the window.

There was hardly anybody about, certainly no tourists. An already well-oiled young man was alternatively taking bites of a large Cypriot biscuit and drinking from what was left of a half bottle of brandy. Later, as I was about to leave, two men changed money into Cypriot pounds, using a local 'business man' as a bank. In broken English they also used him as a procurer of 'girls', specifying that they must be either Ukrainian or Russian. I left before a deal was struck. The young woman at the information centre told me that morning that the government intended opening a cultural centre in the square. One derelict building was certainly being renovated. An excellent idea but from my 'noon-day' observations there could be some stiff competition from the 'locals'. I was delighted to read in the *Cyprus Weekly* of January 15-21 1999, that work has already begun on restoring the picturesque square to the more appropriate ambiance of a national shrine. The square itself will be resurfaced with cobblestone; a theatre for 600, the Rialto, is being fully rennovated, as is the memorial itself whose basement will become an exhibition centre. All that remains will be to 'persuade' the underworld to leave and the mayor has the intention of doing just that. It looks as if once again Hero's Square will become a proud feature of the city.

The church of Agia Ekaterini (St Catherine) is on 28 October Street, not far from the municipal gardens and close to where the seafront promenade begins. St Catherine's facade of a triple arched colonnade and twin bell towers fits in well with its 19th century environment. It is a Roman Catholic church under the care of the Franciscan Order, as are most Catholic churches on the island. The followers of 'Il Poveretto di Assisi' first arrived in Cyprus in the 13th century but from the mid-15th they found themselves to be periodically elsewhere and it was not until 1850 that they returned for a definitive tenure. The church was built between 1872-79, to the design of a Franciscan architect, Fra Francesco de Monghidoro, who favoured for the interior a baroque style much in vogue in Europe at that time. Exactly a century after its completion a major renovation was carried out, removing all the baroque, stucco ornamentation and revealing the clean, unadorned stonework of the original building. Six side windows were also added to improve both lighting and ventilation. That is as it is today.

The interior has a nave and two aisles all leading to a single apse, now decorated with modern frescoes in strict Byzantine style by two Romanian artists. From the cupola of the apse, Christ the Pancreator, looks down on the Virgin at prayer, surrounded by a variety of saints representing the Eastern and Western Churches. The lower group, for example, comprises (l. to r.) St Anthony of Padua, St Epiphany, bishop of Amathous, Saints Andrew and Peter, apostles, St Hilarion of Gaza and St Barnabas of Salamis, both native Cypriots, the latter especially honoured by the Greek Orthodox community to this day. This overture to unity between East and West is also reflected in the frequent use here of the Uniate liturgical rite, now almost defunct in its native Romania and Ukraine. The new altar, a single massive slab of stone, rests on a medieval capital.

I liked this church for its unpretentious simplicity and its ecumenical frescoes. If you look up from the street as you leave, you will notice over the chancel of the central arch of the portico, the quartered Red Cross of the Catholic patriarch of Jerusalem, under whose jurisdiction the Catholic Church in Cyprus falls. It is a reminder of the Gothic heraldry of the Crusades and delineates a line that goes back to the Lusignan period.

My last visit of the day was to the Archaeological Museum, with its wide and grandiose entry, north of the municipal gardens and directly opposite the Curium Palace Hotel on Lord Byron Street. It is well appointed and, though not extensive, is definitely worth a visit. Interesting is the display case on your left as you enter the first gallery. It contains the skull and jaw bones of a pigmy hippo and the tusk of a baby elephant, both found by an eleven-year-old schoolboy in 1961, in an Akrotiri cave, not far from Limassol and purportedly dating back to 8000 BC. They certainly look realistic and indicate the earliest evidence of animal life on the island, possibly also of people as there are some beads in the same collection that date from the same time. I was amazed at the quality and size of the jars, of one in particular, large as a small vat that would have contained an enormous amount of liquid. I'm not sure what Cypriots drank in 2300 BC but they certainly liked it. I also noticed a 6th century BC statue of a boy with a bird, found at Kourio. I hope he wasn't going to eat it but the bird, in fact, showed no signs of distress. Customary eating habits can go back a long way.

The enormous statue of Bes in the third gallery also remains with me. He was a dwarf god of the Egyptians and he's intact here from his lower torso up to his huge, flat-nosed, full-bearded head, with no neck worth talking about and two stumpy horns. A kind of buffoon god he was, a Falstaffian figure who, however, had many good attributes, such as being helpful in childbirth and skillful in navigation. For the latter reason he adorned many a ship's prow. What you may find surprising is that he dates from as late as the 3rd century AD when one might suppose that after St Paul's visit in 45 AD and trek across the island in the company of St Barnabas and the great personal influence of St

Lazarus in Larnaka, that Cyprus would have long since converted to Christianity. Not so, for despite the proud boast of Cypriots that their country was the first to have a Christian governor in the person of Sergius Paulus, according to Dr Demetrias Michaelides, in *Footprints in Cyprus*, 'there is little on the island that is indisputably Christian before the mid-4th century AD.'

There is a huge 5th century BC Phoenician sarcophagus in the entry hall, bare of all ornamentation save for the carved female head of the (one time?) occupant. She has her hair waved.

It was evening, the rush hour just beginning. The big, medieval door of the castle would already have been bolted. Church bells were announcing their evening liturgies. Back in the old town the muezzin's call to prayer could be heard in Heroes' Square where the clubs were preparing to open. It was time for me, too, to end my pilgrimage. I had not hired a car, nor had I had a leisurely lunch but I'd enjoyed my day in Limassol and knew there was more yet to see and the Irish girls were right – the sun had been shining all afternoon.

Of Festivals and Wineries

Each day there is an organised tour of the Keo Winery, though so much else is now produced there – beer, spirits, sherry, *and* fruit juice, that I wonder if the name 'winery' is appropriate any more. Keo, though the largest, is only one of four wineries in this capital of viticulture. All are located in the industrial area west of the castle, between it and the new harbour. I didn't visit any of them, not because of an aversion to wine – *tout au contraire* – but because today one winery, with its vast silvery vats of stainless steel and its white-coated contingent of lab workers is very much like any other and I'd seen plenty in New Zealand.

Wine has been made over much of Cyprus for 5,000 years or more but it's traditionally claimed that the best and most extensive vineyards are to be found on the southern slopes of the Troodos Range. On the lower slopes these vineyards are often interspersed with plantations of citrus, apple, cherry, pear and peach. Many villages create their own boutique wines and it's more fun to visit those, which from time to time I have done. The Omodos winepress, for example, known as 'Linos', is one of the most famous on the island. At Kilani, nearby, besides a winery there are examples of traditional, village architecture, some of it recently restored. Vasa, too, which belonged to the grand commandery of the Knights, has a long and prestigious wine-making history. It has been said that 'among the three of them, Omodos, Kilani and Vasa, they produce the best reds in the country'.

Limassol is the Cypriot City of Festivals. Its '*Carnivale*', the best on the island, takes place in February or March, about 10 days before the beginning of Lent, that period of 40 (or, in the Eastern Church, 50) days before Easter when many Christians practice various forms of self-denial. In anticipation, as it were, during the ten days and nights before Green Monday – the beginning of Lent in the Eastern Churches – people make a conspicuous effort to enjoy themselves. They wear colourful costumes, take part in parades, sing and dance in the streets, go to masked balls, marvel at fireworks displays, organise serenading parties and generally 'loosen up' under the baton of King Carnival. Hotels, restaurants, tavernas and discotheques all enter into the spirit of the festival, dressing their hosting areas – and their staff – in appropriate streamers and costumes. In fact, the week is like one long fancy dress party. There's a children's parade, with proud parents cheering them on from the sidelines and, on the final Sunday, there's the traditional grand parade, led by King Carnival and comprising 40 or 50 floats, many of which have been weeks in preparation.

And that's only the *Carnivale*.

In September, when all the toiling in the hot sun is over and all the back-breaking work of grape harvesting, often on rocky slopes, is finished, each village holds its own small wine festival. Then all eyes turn on Limassol, the viticulture capital of Cyprus, where, over twelve days every year, homage is paid to Dionysus, the ancient god of wine. Welcomed by the giant, scarecrow-like figure of a wine producer, in traditional brown skirt and gumboots, long-sleeved white shirt and cross-buttoned red waistcoat, visitors are encouraged – in Greek – 'to drink wine and live longer'. Once you've paid a modest entrance fee all wines of all varieties are offered free of charge. Is it any wonder then that 100,000 visitors consume 30,000 litres of wine during the festival? With wine tastings encouraged at every kiosk and musical groups playing in the background, the convivial atmosphere naturally spills over into singing and dancing. Dionysus is liberally toasted. His ancient festival, while providing all these 'trimmings' also held symposia, provided theatrical performances, set up competitions for group dancing and the reading of poetry. Limassol's Dionysian festival is less structured and, perhaps, less 'cultivated' but it's every bit as merry and carefree. By extolling in a practical way the virtues of wine it thoroughly fulfils its purpose. Should you be in Cyprus during either festival, Limassol is more than ever a place to visit.

Mary Robinson at the beginning of her presidency of Ireland issued an invitation to the world – 'come dance with me in Ireland', the mayor of Limassol, Mr Kontides, who at this year's (1998) carnival celebrations danced with every member of his council and led his fellow revellers in the samba, might do worse than repeat that invitation:

'Come dance with me in Limassol!

23

KOLOSSI – CRUSADER CASTLE

With dark, stone walls 25 m high, 16 m wide and a whopping 3 m thick, the bold, square castle of Kolossi rises stark above the fertile plain of Episkopi, 16 kms west of Limassol. The present structure was built in 1454 but before that there was a previous 13th century, castle-like building on the site, the semi-circular foundations of which are still visible. The courtyard well also belongs to that time.

Initially the lands surrounding Kolossi, including a goodly number of villages, were gifted to the Order of the Knights Templar by King Hugo I (1205-1218) in return for services rendered in battle against the Muslims. After the defeat of the Christians at the battle of Acre in 1291 ownership of the estates was transferred to the Knights Hospitallers, also known as the Knights of St John of Jerusalem. Conflict arose between the two sets of Knights, as often happens in property transfers and the Templars refused to go. They were a tough lot and it wasn't until the pope banned the whole order as heretical in 1308, burnt their leaders and incarcerated their Knights that the Hospitallers of St John were able to take possession. By then the number of vassal villages had risen to 60. The order, in fact, following the example of the Templars, established its own grand commandery at Kolossi and, incidentally, gave the name 'Commandaria' to the full-bodied, red, dessert wine ever since made in that area. It is reputedly the oldest named wine in the world and tastes like port. A good vintage makes an excellent wine for those who enjoy sweet wines. The Knights of St John distrustful of princes, soon preferred to go to Rhodes where they were in sole charge, leaving a commander to look after their many interests in Cyprus.

More than wine, however, was produced around Kolossi. Cane sugar was a popular crop in the area long before the Knights but it was they who set up a sugar factory, adjacent to the castle. In fact, the outbuildings on the east side of the castle, remnants of which are still clearly visible, were used as stores and processing mills. A huge millstone, used to press out the juice from the canes, still also exists, as do the remains of an aqueduct and, near it, the so-called Hall of the Sugar Factory with its aisle-like arches and barrel-vaulted ceiling. It would have provided a reasonably cool and quite secure storage place. When the Ottomans conquered the island in 1571 they continued the lucrative business of the cane sugar industry.

The castle itself is three-storied and had a drawbridge which led up to the first floor. Inside, on the first floor, is the kitchen with an open fireplace and, next to it, a day room with the remnants of Crusader frescoes. A spiral, stone staircase leads to the living rooms on the second floor and thence to the roof from which there is a panoramic view. On the west side of the battlements, over the front door, as it were, there is a machicolation, a kind of projecting turret with channels cut in it, from which stones, or other missiles, could be dropped on unwelcome visitors who managed to get that far. Boiling oil (there were plenty of olive groves in the vicinity) was also used to good effect. Actually it must have been quite a deterrent, not just in its dousing, but also in how difficult it must have made keeping a foothold on the steps. Worse than banana skins. In addition the parapet had numerous, vertical slit-holes, used both for observation and weapons defence. Below the first floor, in the basement, are three vaulted rooms, two of which have wells, making an internal water supply secure. All in all, such castles must have been pretty much impregnable to direct attack.

Some coats of arms and shields are chiselled into the east wall, inside a cruciform frame. Centrepiece, under a crown, is the royal coat, depicting in four sections the emblems of the kingdom of Jerusalem, the Lusignans, and the kingdoms of Cyprus and Armenia. The other shields and coats are those of masters of the Order of St John. Noteworthy, on the lower arm of the cross, is the coat of arms of Louis de Magnac, a grand commander of the order in Cyprus and the person believed to have been responsible for the building of the castle as we see it.

An investiture to the Order of St John took place in the castle in 1959, the first since Crusader times. I imagine it as a truly evocative and romantic occasion. Listen, if you will, to the trumpeters sounding a fanfare from the battlements, watch the great doors slowly opening, see the senior knights of the order, including the commissioner-in-chief and the lord prior, all resplendent in full regalia, walking in solemn procession to the dais, where the colourful insignia are all laid out for the ceremony. It would have been an investiture more alive with ritual and symbolism than the tap of a sword on a kneeling shoulder.

Lania–Village of Artists

Lania is a small village of no more than 250 souls, less than 20 kms inland from Limassol. You can walk round it in 20 minutes and late on a warm Sunday morning in November, when nothing else was stirring we did just that. Even the dogs didn't bark and a lizard basking on a wall disappeared in a blink when I stopped to admire him. We had come to Lania, not because of the attractiveness of its blue-painted doors, gates and window shutters, nor because of the geranium reds in pots and beds outside its charming, neat stone houses, nor yet because of its old-worldly, clean, winding, narrow streets, all admirable in themselves, but because Lania is known as the Artists' Village and, one of them, Michael Owen, was holding an exhibition that day.

Painters, potters, sculptors – they're all here in this tiny village. Four of them at the moment, all ex-pats, but there have been Greek Cypriots, too. And when they hold a sales exhibition it's a social occasion. People come from as far away as Nicosia and Limassol, from the British sovereign bases and, of course, from round and about Larnaka. Glass of good, local wine in one hand and nibble in the other, they greet each other as old friends, which I'm sure many of them are. Owen's spreadeagle house, picturesquely positioned on the outskirts of the village, was as busy-buzzy with the hum of conversation as the rest of the village was silent. The artist himself was there, cheerful, casual, non-mercenary. There was time to talk, ask questions, have a discussion, if you wished.

Unhurried, with a feeling of easeful pleasure, we made our slow way around, walking through three or four rooms full of paintings and prints, admiring in one a bright, yellow burst of crown daisies, surprised in another by a blue, so bold and vibrant of the Mediterranean that you thought the heavens tumbled there, while in yet a third, we were comforted by the warm, dun stolidity of a village church. Sandra bought some prints, Najla, the friend who'd taken us there, commissioned the daisies while I renewed my acquaintance with the lizard outside.

Exhibition or no exhibition, Lania is well worth a visit.

24

THE LIMESTONE CITY
OF KOURIO

My wife's birthday and mine occur within ten days of each other in September so, after our first month in Cyprus, we decided to give each other a weekend away from Nicosia. Where else to go, we thought, than to Pafos, the garden city of Aphrodite. So we borrowed a car and, late on a Friday afternoon, we drove westwards into a blinding sun. Pafos is about 150 kms from the capital so on this occasion we paid only a quick visit to Kourio and looked briefly, as we drove by in the twilight, at the little bay with its several large rocks where Aphrodite is reputed to have metamorphosed from sea foam. We've been to Kourio several times since, once with a group of students who were participating in an archaeological dig. On that occasion we were almost alone among the ruins and had as much time as we wanted.

Kourio (Curium) is situated on a rocky ledge, 70 m above the sea, and about 16 kms west of Limassol. There's a fine view from the ruins, out to sea and over the flat Akrotiri peninsula. Kourio has a history lost in the mists of antiquity. Though the Greek historian, Herodotus, claims that it was founded by Greek immigrants from Argos in 1200 BC, archaeological evidence points to its occupation in even earlier times and excavations have verified that there were settlements in the villages surrounding Kourio as far back as 4500 BC. The ruins we see today, however, date more precisely from Roman and early Christian times. It is quite possible, of course, that another city lies buried somewhere underneath. At its height Kourio was one of the city-kingdoms of Cyprus. Known for its independence despite lying between two powerful neighbours, Amathous and Palea Pafos, Kourio survived by adopting a policy of shifting allegiances, each determined by what was perceived best for Kourio at any particular time. A Machiavellian state long before Machiavelli! In one instance, during the Ionian War (500 BC), it even switched sides in mid-battle! Its last king, true to form, sailed with a fleet from Kourio to help Alexander the Great at the siege of Troy. Fate intervened, however and, after the death of Alexander, when his general, Ptolemy, took over the entire island in 318 BC, Kourio lost its independence for ever. After many centuries of placid living under the Hellenes and the Romans it was destroyed by the enormous earthquake of 365 AD. Rebuilt, it flourished as a centre of Christian worship, until it was plundered to death in one of the Arab raids of the second half of the 7th century AD. In its heyday Kourio had a population estimated at about 25,000, almost as large as that of Pafos today.

Apart from the cult of Apollo whose temple is outside the city walls, about 3 kms down the road, Kourio is justly famous for its ancient and still living theatre. The one we look with wonder on today is the third built on the same site, if you don't count the extensive 1963 restoration. The Hellenistic one (2nd century BC), was a smaller version, cut into the hill in typical Greek fashion. It was enlarged and re-modelled in Nero's time (50-75 AD) – who's to say he hadn't a notion of playing there himself – and a few years later in 77 AD was destroyed by an earthquake. At the very end of the 1st century AD, under Trajan, it was reconstructed and enlarged to the dimensions it has today. It's not, however, at all as large as the theatre at Salamis which had 50 rows of seats and a diameter of 90 m against Kourio's 17 rows with a diameter of only 62 m, but I prefer Kourio's location, facing out, as it does, to the sparkling, blue backdrop of the Mediterranean whilst Salamis has its back to the sea. It could also be called, in Roman terms, a more 'intimate' theatre, seating only 3,500 – but at that time the population of Kourio was only one fifth that of Salamis, which, though no longer the capital, was still the go-ahead commercial centre of the island. It takes money to maintain a theatre and businessmen and entrepreneurs, then as now, make more money than bureaucrats and politicians. The 1963 restoration, possibly for the same reason, does not include the colonnade that used to enclose the auditorium, nor the high backdrop scene building. I'm glad it doesn't. Any further building, it seems to me, would only detract from the purity, simplicity and spirituality of the ambience. The feeling one gets that the drama being performed in the theatre in Kourio is part of the wider but incorporating drama of life and of nature would be diminished.

During the first two centuries of the Christian era theatrical performances were of Greek and Roman comedies and of Greek tragedies adapted for a Roman audience but at the beginning of the 3rd century a crasser kind of entertainment became popular and theatres found themselves transformed into arenas for gladiators and animals. The authorities at Kourio had the bad sense to follow suit but the good sense to remove the two lowest rows of seats and build a protective wall between the competitors and the spectators, the ancient equivalent of the *barrera* in a modern bullfighting stadium. On certain occasions the Romans held special 'performances' in their theatres, whole day (or longer) celebrations. The earlier part of the morning was devoted to animal fights, vicious contests between opposing animals in which both were killed, the interim victor by the sword of the attendant. It was probably considered an act of mercy to slay the surviving animal as both would have been extensively mauled and wounded. Before we shiver at such barbarity we should remember that even in our apparently more civilised time, illegal cock fights take place in many countries and fox hunting is still a sport.

Later in the morning, at Kourio as elsewhere, gladiators fought animals. The former had gone through long years of costly training and were highly skilled professionals. If they survived the contest, they were not condemned to die but were allowed to recover from their wounds to fight again another day. As an appetiser for lunch public executions took place once a month or so. The Romans, not having either a police force, or prisons, dealt summarily with criminals. The late afternoon, however, was reserved for the highlight of the day's entertainment – gladiator against gladiator. *Virtus* – courage becoming a man – was what the Romans appreciated and applauded, so much so that the defeated gladiator was often also honoured, rather like awarding a soldier a posthumous VC. I have recounted elsewhere my unexpected response to a bullfight between a brave bull and a brave man. Apart from being carried along by the pageantry of the ceremony, the arousing spurts of music and the engrossed and cheering fans, I found myself shamefully captivated by the contest itself, even though I knew the outcome was 99 percent certain. Would I, too, have clapped (and booed) the gladiators? In all my saner moments I vigorously say no but despite the vehemence of my denial I wonder ... and I wonder ... But, thankfully, in Kourio, the craze didn't last and by the end of the 3rd century the theatre had reverted to its original use. Unfortunately, the whole complex, as well as the town itself, was destroyed by a massive earthquake that, as has already been said, hit Kourio in 365 AD. When the city was rebuilt it came under Christian influence and the theatre was not reconstructed. Though abandoned and exploited by stone-robbers, the theatre site remained intact and the theatre itself was reconstructed in 1961-63 by the Cyprus Department of Antiquities and now here, as at Salamis, during the summer months visitors can see the classical theatre of Greece and Rome, Shakespeare in the round, and colourful performances of Greek folk dancing. Concerts of classical music are also performed at Kourio.

Almost exactly a year after our first brief visit we were fortunate enough to see a bilingual performance in Kourio of Euripides' *Bacchae* given by the Theatre of Myth, New Jersey. As in the old days, a couple of thousand years ago, the play was timed to catch the setting sun and continue through the soft fall of a semi-tropical twilight. The play was spoken in English and Greek, the latter varying between the classical and the modern. One or two of the monologues were a bit on the long side for those of us who couldn't follow the Greek but there was sufficient English in the script to allow us keep up with the play (if you'll pardon the pun) and we were transported over the parts spoken in the vernacular by the sheer intensity and passion in the voices and actions of the players. Excepting two, all the actors were American, but I was assured by a native speaker that their Greek was equal to that of the locals. The setting (in classical Greek drama there was no scenery) was magnificent, the open stage being variously caught in the ever-changing declension of a splendid, polychrome sunset. The Mediterranean, in front of us, provided a shimmering, dark blue backdrop while the whole surrounding area was graced with the light green of olive groves and the darker green of plantations of carob. The acoustics were perfect. The dance movements, at times formal and stylised, at times rhythmic and seductively fluid, were an integral part of the play telling its story and expressing its emotions in a way that was part classical ballet, part musical gymnastics. Background music was played softly on a lyre throughout the entire play, adding notes of melancholy and poignancy in a kind of gentle commentary on the theme. A truly compelling and artistic performance of great strength and passion in a setting that was out of this world. The citizens of ancient Kourio would have been pleased.

Just above the theatre is the House of Eustolios set on a site with a panoramic view. It, too, was a second or third generation structure, its immediate precursor, also a palatial, private residence, destroyed by the same earthquake which destroyed the theatre. The 'new' house was built toward the end of the 4th century AD by one Eustolios, who, judging by several inscriptions and the symbolic motifs of the mosaics, was a devout Christian, as well as a benefactor of the town. Christianity was recognised as 'lawful' in AD 313 by the Edict of Milan so at this time it could be publicly proclaimed without fear in the decorative elements of the house. Fish, pheasant and falcon, all Christian symbols, appear on both the wall panelling and floor mosaics of the house. Eustolios seems to have been a local lad who made a fortune elsewhere and retired to his home town to live. He provided public baths for the citizens (they would have been in need of such amenities following the earthquake) and also a social gathering room, both attached to his 30-room dwelling. It is tempting to imagine him, full of years, content and respected, sitting outside his house on the hot summer evenings of July and August, catching the soft sea breezes, at peace with his God and his fellow man. The House of Eustolios continued to be used as a communal bathing place and venue for social meetings until, in the middle of the 7th century, in one of those senseless acts of all wars, the Arabs destroyed it in a raid.

The early Christian basilica lies west of the theatre on the road that leads to the city centre. It has a similar history to the House of Eustolios in so far as it was built in the 5th century as a replacement for earlier structures and destroyed in the Arab raids in the mid-7th. The basilica was the cathedral of the local bishop. Clearly visible are the nave and two aisles, with, paralleling these, two annexes, set aside for those converts not yet baptised, the catechumens, who had to leave the church during the more solemn parts of the mass. The floor of the nave was done in mosaic, that of the aisles in coloured marble but the annexes were only flagstoned – benches were, however, provided. You can still see the foundations of four columns in the sanctuary, indicating that there was a *baldacchino* over the altar and it's also obvious that the nave was separated from the aisles by two rows of 12 marble columns. It all must have looked pretty impressive. In addition, protruding from the left as you look towards the sanctuary, was a large baptistery, almost a miniature of the church, with a nave and two aisles. There were also two rooms for the catechumens to undress in prior to baptism, presumably one for men, the other for women. Unattired they were anointed all over with oil (it was expensive – did the bishop pick up the tab?) after which they proceeded to the large cruciform font for their triple immersion. After their baptism the catechumens put on white robes and were led in procession into the church for their first communion. Afterwards there would have been rejoicing and a feast.

Between the bishop's palace, a large two-storey building left of the main entrance, and the atrium or open court area, was the *Diaconikon*, a large rectangular room, consisting of four bays. There the faithful paid their dues to deacons who were responsible for their prudent use. To remind them of 'their duty' the first line of a six-line inscription, which you can see in the middle of the floor in the first bay, read:

Vow and pay unto the Lord, your God.

The munificence of Eustolios evidently did not include the financial support of the church, or its bishop. I have little doubt that some of the Christians, strapped for cash, paid in kind – sugar cane, oil, a kid goat, or a pigeon, wine? To facilitate that kind of transaction the lower storey of the bishop's palace was a storage area and it was quite handy to the *Diaconikon*. A similar alternative still exists in parts of rural Africa, where, at certain times of year, the precincts of some churches resemble a market place.

Close to the basilica, about 30 m to the northeast, is the market place or agora, with its massive colonnaded portico, 65 m in length and 4.5 m wide. You can imagine how imposing the building was by concentrating on the columns, both the ones re-erected on their original bases and the many missing ones whose bases remain. By employing a little arithmetic in measuring the total length of the colonnade and dividing it by the regular four metres between each of the column bases, you will quickly see that there must have been 16 columns and if the colonnade went around on all four sides, 64. It would have looked a spectacularly solid and confident building in the middle of the town but it, too, fell victim to the earthquakes and the Arab raids. Some of the building blocks found their way to the basilica.

Another building ruin worth a quick look is the Nymphaeum, 20 m northwest of the agora. It, too, was built of well hewn limestone blocks – there's an abundance of limestone in the area – and served both as a water supply facility and a kind of leisure complex adorned with flowers, statues and fountains. A tiny Tivoli Gardens, dedicated to the nymphs whose special charge it was to look after the water supply. Although destroyed in the Arab raids, three lime kilns were built on the same location in the 8th century to reduce the blocks, the marble statues and columns to lime. I couldn't find out what was done with the lime. It may have been used as fertiliser.

A few metres from the Nymphaeum is the House of the Gladiators, a typical, Roman-patrician house with the usual peristyle courtyard and baths. The courtyard floor is decorated with multi-coloured mosaics, some of purely geometric design but, more interestingly, two depict gladiatorial contests, whence the name of the house. In these the gladiators are togged out in helmets and what looks like body armour, holding shields in their left hands and daggers in the right. In one mosaic the contestants are named as 'Margarites' and 'Hellenikos' (the Greek?). In the second, which is quite badly damaged, we can still see clearly the referee (Darios) stopping the contest as one gladiator (Lydras) goes in for the kill. These mosaics obviously referred to the fights held in the theatre-arena in the 3rd century AD. It's gratifying to know that the referee stopped the fight. Hand slightly raised, his palm towards Lydras in the traditional gesture of 'that's enough, stop!', he looks quite composed and authoritative.

On the right, two or three kilometres down the road to Pafos, are the final three structures that a visitor to Kourio should see. Nearest the road is the stadium, or athletic park. The 'stadium' was the Greek unit of measure, equal to 186 m which is the actual inside length of the track at Kourio. Its overall length is 217 m. It's U-shaped as was customary and has a seating embankment with seven rows of seats, sustained by massive six metre limestone block walls, to accommodate about 6,000 spectators. Though pentathlon competitions (running, jumping, wrestling, and the throwing of both javelin and discus) were held there, the main billing went to the track races. Two circular holes at one end indicate where stone posts may have been inserted to guarantee a common starting point for eight or more runners. For the most part the competitors ran completely naked, a sight that shocked the good St Barnabas when he dropped in on the games on his way to Pafos. Barnabas was a Jew before his conversion and may have reacted super-sensitively. There is no record of condemnation from the local bishop. In fact, there was another basilica, a much smaller, extra-mural one, about 150 m above the stadium. It had a commanding view, not only of the stadium but of the whole countryside, including Akrotiri salt lake and Episkopi Bay. Almost a complete replica of the cathedral basilica which was the parish church, this one must have been used only on special occasions. One hesitates to suggest that these occasions might have coincided with a track meeting.

Lastly – a must – is a visit to the sanctuary of Apollo only a few hundred metres away. This religious centre would have been in continuous use from the 7th century BC to the 4th century AD – a thousand years or more. For the first two centuries it was dedicated to the worship of some fertility god but from the 5th century BC onwards it became the much frequented sanctuary of Apollo Hylates, Apollo of the Woodlands. Woodlands there are still, a forest of carob and pine trees, wild olive and even wilder native bushes. In fact, thick forest covered much of Cyprus in antiquity so the worship of Apollo Hylates would have been island-wide. Indeed, there is some evidence of this around Pafos and Polis. Apollo, of course, is part of Greek literary tradition and enjoys a litany of attributes and responsibilities – beauty, music, prophecy and archery among them but, as if those weren't enough for one god, he is also named as the protective deity of trees, flocks and herds. Of trees, the laurel, the myrtle and the palm were especially sacred to him, of animals, deer.

The sanctuary covers an area of 15,000 sq. m. Its earliest ruins date back to the 7th century BC though shards of pottery found there go back to the Bronze Age, indicating the possibility of an earlier place of worship. The whole complex was, however, reconstructed and extensively remodelled in the 2nd century AD, following the terribly destructive earthquake of 76-77 AD. The amenities include two rectangular dormitories, one on either side of the Pafos Gate entrance, a bathing establishment, a gym and *palestra*, or ball playing area, a treasury and interestingly, a 'votive pit'. This latter was a well-like hole into which offerings of figurines and statuettes were dumped when they became too numerous and prevented the display of other larger, and probably more munificent, ones. As up to 10,000 figurines were discovered, it's not likely that anybody ever stole one of the cast-asides. Maybe, being human, some wanted to but couldn't risk it as the penalty for just touching the altar of the shrine was, in earlier times, to be cast off the cliffs at Kourio. The baths are still being excavated but are immediately discernible by the blackened bricks of the hypocaust heating system. Once thoroughly cleansed in the baths, pilgrims could approach the temple itself. Weary after their day-long devotions they could then rest in the dormitories provided, hoping for a visitation by Apollo in their sleep. The high priest's residence was on the right of the main, stone-paved street, the Via Sacra, at the northern end of which was the focal point of the entire sanctuary, the Temple of Apollo, with 12 steps leading up to it. The length of the temple is 13.5 m and it's over 8 m wide, the floor area of a medium-sized bungalow. It had an inner and an outer chamber both constructed of local, hewn stone set together without mortar. Trajan it was who added the outer temple in the 2nd century AD with four columns, two of which have been re-erected and today form the distinguishing feature of the temple. They also make an excellent frame for a photograph. Suddenly it was time to rejoin our charges. As I was leaving I couldn't help but think that we in our time could do with another Apollo, Protector of Forests.

Oh, in case you're wondering, the students at the dig found small, human bones, glass and shards of pottery. It was, they said, backbreaking work.

Pafos and Akamas

25

PAFOS – WORLD HERITAGE AREA

When we reached Pafos on that mid-September evening in 1995 it was already dark, not the best time to arrive when you haven't pre-booked accommodation. We had the name of a hotel but couldn't find it and eventually settled for an air-conditioned, moderately priced one not far from the city centre. It was hot. Later we walked through the town's main street which got noisier and more swinging the closer we got to the harbour. Here were restaurants galore, each penned in by wooden posts and heavy rope, all with menus and prices posted, white plastic chairs and tables covered in cotton cloths with plaid patterns, most depending solely on their *al fresco* settings for a common decor, distinguished only by the colours of their awnings and the uniforms of their waiters, the female ones, that is – the males looked all alike, black trousers and white shirts. One of their number, perhaps with the addition of a bow tie, patrolled his section of the street, smiling invitingly, speaking English, soliciting clientele. Sometimes a street looks like one long refectory table and I wondered, for all the ropings-off, how closely related the owners were. Greek music was popular with 'Never on a Sunday' still the all-time favourite. Fish – catch-of-the-day – is, not surprisingly, a frequent item on the menu here, more particularly in harbour-side restaurants and if red mullet are running all the better. But if you only want a drink, a long cool brandy sour (the national drink), accompanied by a bowl of olives, enjoyed at a kerbside taverna while watching the *passeggiata* of visitors intent on showing off as much of their tans as possible, is as good a way as any to spend an hour or two. Delicious fresh, fruit drinks are a wholesome alternative.

This town, once regarded as a sleepy backwater, isolated, by and large, from the rest of the island by the Troodos Mountains (especially before the through road to Limassol) has, over the past twenty years, capitalised on its attraction for tourists. Capitalised also, one must add, on the loss to the regime in the north of the two premier tourists resorts of pre-1974 Cyprus, Kyrenia and

Famagusta. But, in the process, has it begun to sell its soul? Cheeky, large hotels fall over themselves (and over Pafos) in catering to their monied clients. Impertinent, roadside shops sell endless souvenirs that could be recycled among them every other week, so much are they the same from shop to shop. Fast food counters proliferate. Discos blare. Consumerism, a disease brought in by the tourists, is catching. But let us not exaggerate. Pafos is not Honululu, nor even Agia Napa (the brash, new resort, north of Larnaka), but the tinsel is beginning to show and those who control its destiny should reflect that charm, like virginity, once lost, is lost forever. Fortunately, its beach front is small, a factor that must surely slow down, if not halt, future expansion. The tourists that evening were milling about in their thousands, some just arrived, others about to depart (Pafos has an international airport) and, at times, the streets seemed like the streets of Brighton, or Blackpool at the end of an exceptionally fine summer's day. Everybody, it seemed, was speaking English and, away from the throbbing west side, people had a relaxed, abandoned look. Reflecting that Pafos is only 4 hours and a half from London or Manchester I couldn't help recalling with a smile that the first British governor of Cyprus took 10 years to get here – from Nicosia.

Nea (New) Pafos, to distinguish it from Palea (Old) Pafos, 16 kms back on the road to Limassol, is itself very old. It was founded by Nicocles, the last king of the city-kingdom of Palea Pafos toward the end of the 4th century BC. It was a walled city of one square kilometre located around the harbour. Nicocles, unlike the kings of Kourio, had remained aloof from world events until spurred into action by Alexander the Great's determination to conquer the world. He would, he thought, build a Greek city fit to receive him or, as it turned out, his successors. So, on an isolated strip of coast, he built his new city, Nea Pafos, on the Greek model, with a grid of streets, a commercial centre around the agora, a council chamber, or *odeon* and a theatre. It wasn't a lucky move for Nicocles, however, as it happened at the time that two generals of Alexander the Great were, after his death, disputing lordship of Cyprus. Nicocles backed the wrong one, Menelaus, and his people, rather than have him fall into the hands of Ptolemy, the victor, either killed him, or as some would have it, allowed him (and his family) to commit suicide. Either way he met a gloomy end. Ptolemy made Pafos capital of the island in 294 BC and so it remained, even under the Romans (58 BC-395 AD) until it suffered the all too common fate in ancient Cyprus of being destroyed by two devastating earthquakes, one in 332, the other in 342 AD. Thereafter, the capital was moved to Salamis and Pafos fell into a long decline. Its harbour silted up and became a breeding ground for malaria carrying mosquitoes. Even the locals despaired of it and took to the hills.

Pafos had its own theatre dating from the 4th century BC. Plutarch wrote about a fabulous theatre festival organised there in 331 BC to celebrate the return of Alexander the Great from Egypt in that year. The festival was apparently sponsored by the kings of Cyprus who vied with each other in putting on entertaining plays. According to archaeologist John R Green, this event is believed to be the first performance of Greek theatre in foreign lands. Alexander, despite the cost, wanted to provide a taste of home for his troops, in an effort to bond them together by means of their shared culture. In 331 BC this was very important because the Greeks were not yet fully united and consisted of various urban and regional groupings such as Athenians, Arcadians, Thebans, Spartans and so on. The Ptolemies, who made Pafos the capital of the island, were fanatical theatre-goers back home in Alexandria so it's not surprising that they wanted to enjoy the same amenities in Cyprus. The site has been discovered, and excavations by a team from the University of Sydney began in 1995.

When we came down to breakfast the following morning the sun was streaming onto the hotel swimming pool, which was just outside the restaurant's large window-doors, all of which were wide open. Though only 7:30 am it was already hot – hot enough, certainly, for a bevy of pale skinned English girls to be sitting topless round the pool, feet dangling in the water, anointing each other, back and front. Did they even have breakfast? Newly arrived as the visitors were, Aphrodite and the sun were already warming the blood of English *sang-froid*. This 'boobs for breakfast' rubric would, I imagine, be unthinkable at Brighton or Torquay. How many English girls do you know who would, in England, nonchalantly bare their bosoms in full view (apart from the bougainvillaea) of two hundred people eating breakfast? Yet these, in dark glasses and high spirits, seemed singularly unembarrassed. You wondered whether your rather attractive breakfast companion would soon be joining them. 'Pass the marmalade, please' would never sound the same again.

Aphrodite, often called 'The Paphian', goddess of beauty, love and fertility, was formed from the spume of sea-foam around the rocks at Petra tou Romiou, four miles east of Palea Pafos, the latter also, in modern times, called Kouklia. This is where King Nicocles had his capital before transferring it to Nea Pafos. There, at her temple, she was worshiped from the 12th century BC – long before Homer wrote the *Iliad* – until the 4th century of the Christian era when her worship was banned by the Byzantine emperors. According to a usually reliable source, Herodotus, the Father of History, the cult at Kouklia included temple prostitution, a ritual whereby young women sacrificed their virginity, ostensibly to the goddess but, in fact, to whatever pilgrim happened to be passing by. The usual procedure was that on certain festivals, notably the Aphrodisia, celebrating the reunion of Aphrodite with her lover Apollo, who returned from the dead at the beginning of every spring, the young women, wearing special head scarves, went to the temple and stood in line – or sat – waiting to be selected by a man. The man, when he had chosen one, tossed a silver coin into her lap (an offering to the goddess) and off they went for a night of wild passion – according to the same Herodotus. In early antiquity no woman in Cyprus was allowed to marry unless she had first slept with a stranger. In those days Cypriot men considered the deflowering of a virgin a very dangerous enterprise, so the temples of Aphrodite (and there were at least 12 in Cyprus) became full of nubile, young priestesses waiting to be deflowered by strangers. Mostly these strangers were foreign pilgrims. One assumes they rested for a few days before approaching the temple. It is, however, worth noting, though it receives considerably less press, that Aphrodite was also the protectress of vulnerable women, innocent young girls and the sanctity of marriage. In some of her temples the priestesses had to remain virgins and any man who failed to respect their vow, or who wrongly accused them, would have his forehead branded.

It's interesting that in a recent research study Cypriot women were considered the least likely in Europe to have intercourse before marriage. Up to 90 percent claimed they were virgins at marriage. Certainly, if they live in the same town or city as their parents they invariably stay at home until they marry and, as we've seen, frequently enough, after marriage. They say here that, as 'everybody is related to everybody else' secret liaisons would, in any case, be very difficult, if not impossible, to keep secret, especially as traditionally there is also a high incidence of gossip among Cypriots. That same survey, by the way, claimed that Cypriots, both men and women, were the heaviest smokers in Europe, puffing their way through 3,500 cigarettes annually for every man, woman and child on the island. A Cypriot friend, himself a non-smoker, put the puffing down, perhaps jocosely, to 'frustration'. That same friend did not believe the chastity statistics. He did admit, however, that, in one sense, the figure could be accurate, adding that a small number of gynaecologists spent a high proportion of their time doing hymen reconstructions before marriage. Despite some historical precedent his observation seemed rather fanciful to me until I checked in the Yellow Pages of the phone book and found that Cyprus has a far higher number of gynaecologists relative to the size of its population than you'd find in other developed countries. Nicosia, for example, has 38 for a population of 220,000, one for every 5,800 of the total population. In New Zealand the ratio is more like 1 to 8 - 10,000. There could be – and I'm sure there are – many other more valid reasons for such a low doctor-patient ratio in this speciality in Cyprus but in the light of all the lonely young women waiting for pilgrims I thought his comments interesting. What is true is that many Cypriot men have married nordic women. A Finnish woman acquaintance told me that there were about 300 of her co-nationals married and living (principally) in the coastal cities. Nothing singular about that. The Costa Brava is full of Suecas, as they call them, young Swedish women who came down from the north for a holiday and stayed. Whether or not they married Spaniards and many certainly did, their behaviour and influence is accredited with significantly changing Spanish attitudes to sex and marriage. Some would say that a similar change in mores is occurring in Cyprus.

My *akubra* was proving too heavy in temperatures of between 35 and 40 degrees so, on checking out of the hotel, I searched among the side-walk shops and soon found a large, Texan-like straw hat which I bought and continued to wear daily until mid-November to the amusement of some Nicosians who took to calling me 'Cowboy!' In Pafos it looked natural enough. We immediately began our archaeological tour. Such is the wealth of treasure unearthed, and still to be unearthed, in and around Pafos that UNESCO has declared the city and its environs a World Heritage area.

The floor mosaics of Pafos are world renowned and must be accounted one of the highlights of any visit to Cyprus. They range from an early black and white pebble mosaic dating from the 4th century BC to the more sophisticated artistry of the early Byzantine period. Four houses, named for the principal figures represented in the mosaics of each, have been restored. Each house is covered and has platform viewing. Though the mosaics were discovered when a trench was being dug by British soldiers in 1945, work on their excavation only began after independence in the early 60s. Despite being covered in rubble for centuries (some say precisely because of this) they were found in surprisingly good condition and are revealed *in situ originali*. These mosaics are made of small cubes of stone, marble and glass paste and are multi-coloured. Excavation still goes on and new treasures are continually being discovered. We made several subsequent visits to the mosaics and, though each one gave us additional pleasure, certain mosaics continued to delight me. This is an account of some of those.

The House of Dionysos, dating from the end of the 2nd century AD was occupied for almost 200 years before being knocked down in the earthquake of 365 AD. It has an atrium, or inner courtyard from which corridors lead off to all the other rooms of the house. Appropriately, several of its mosaics depict mythical scenes involving the making and drinking of wine. One, adorning the entrance to the dining room, the large room on your left as you enter, details the triumph of Dionysos, god of wine and happiness. He is depicted in a chariot drawn by two wild beasts and crowned with vine leaves. Following him is a satyr carrying an amphora full of wine. Out front a trumpeter leads the way proclaiming the triumphal march past of the discoverer of wine. Pan is there, too, and a woman pouring a libation as well as some other serving members of Dionysos' retinue. It could be a float mounted in a wine festival parade by any leading winery, or hold the second glory spot in a Mardi Gras procession. I like it for its honest celebration of wine. On either side of the Dionysos panel are the two heavenly twins, Castor and Pollux with their horses. These two represent the sacred task of imperial Rome to keep barbarism at bay and hence protect the civilised world. Is there an implication here that wine also is part of the civilising process, or is the artist telling us that the moderate consumption of wine is already itself a mark of civilised intercourse? The conundrum poses itself each time I see that mosaic. St George, on his white horse, killing dragons, was the somewhat mythical descendant of the imperial twins.

Another mosaic on the far side of the horizontal platform that looks down on the dining room, (it's part of the portico panel leading in to the dining room from the courtyard) shows Icarios, king of Athens, who was taught the art of wine-making by Dionysos. The god is offering a bunch of grapes to the nymph, Akme, who is herself sipping wine from a bowl. She was a mixture of oenologist and wine taster whose job it was to supervise the wine until it had reached its acme of perfection which was fairly early in those days as they didn't have corks to stopper the wineskins. Icarios, in the bald head, is seen leading an ox-driven cart full of wineskins. Behind him are two shepherds to whom he has given a skinful. It all ended badly for Icarios because the shepherds, unused to wine and, no doubt, drinking it too fast, found their heads spinning and, thinking they were being poisoned, slew him. The tragic part was omitted from the mosaic but the drunken shepherds are shown reeling about. How they managed to have enough co-ordination to commit regicide I don't know but I'm sure there is a moral there somewhere, one perhaps showing the uncivilising effects of too much wine! It's interesting to note that, though the mosaics were executed in Roman times, the inscriptions are in Greek.

Another graphic mosaic in that same long panel recounts the love tragedy of Thisbe and Pyramus. This couple was forbidden by their parents to marry but in age-old fashion continued to meet secretly. One day Thisbe was chased near their rendezvous by a wild beast and, though injured, escaped. In her flight, however, she dropped a bloodstained veil. When Pyramus arrived at the arranged place he found the veil and, believing Thisbe dead (probably devoured by the wild beast since there was no trace of her) he took his own life. After some time Thisbe, showing great courage, returned to the scene, found her lover dead and, in despair, killed herself. These two 'star-crossed' lovers and their sad story, in part at least, inspired Shakespeare to write his poignant tragedy of *Romeo and Juliet. West Side Story* is its modern equivalent. *A Midsummer Night's Dream* deals with an equivalent theme. *Nihil novi sub sole.*

Other beautiful mosaics tell the stories of Apollo and Daphne, Phaedra and Hippolytos, Ganymede and Zeus, all taken from Greek mythology, all exquisitely executed, all showing that 'the course of true love never does run smooth', that is, if you accept the love of Phaedra for her stepson as 'true' and are not upset at Zeus' homosexual advances even under the guise of an eagle. The Romans were obviously fascinated by these poignant tragedies and, if life reflects art, must have experienced similar sad frustrations in their own love lives. Other mosaics are of hunting scenes (find the moufflon!) and there is a particularly beautiful, small scene depicting a peacock displaying its fan of colourful feathers. It is no wonder that people from all over the world come to Cyprus and to Pafos to see these floor mosaics – nothing quite like them exists elsewhere, certainly not in the Eastern Mediterranean.

In the House of Theseus which has over 100 rooms and was most probably the house of the Roman governor, we find one of the finest mosaics of the Roman world, the slaying of the Minotaur by Theseus in the labyrinth. This mosaic dates from the 3rd century and the central scene is contained within large, patterned panels of concentric circles. The labyrinth is portrayed as an old man while on either side of Theseus' raised club are personifications of Crete and Ariadne whose self-possessed, dark and intent stares belong to a century later when their faces were redone. Their eyes are the eyes you see in most icons. The whole is a wonderful depiction – in the round – showing incredible skill and a tightly controlled imagination. See if you can find the thread which Theseus tied to the lintel at the entrance in order to find his way out. This myth has a melancholic connection with Cyprus. Ariadne, the beautiful daughter of Minos, king of Crete, had fallen in love with Theseus, had shown him the entrance and given him the ball of thread. After he returned they both set sail together, enjoying their 'honeymoon' until a storm drove them towards the shore at Amathous, near Limassol, which seems throughout history and pre-history to have been a favourite place to get shipwrecked. She was heavy with child and stayed ashore while Theseus rejoined the fleet which was blown back out to sea by yet another storm. Ariadne was made welcome and tenderly cared for by the women of Amathous but unfortunately died in childbirth. Her tomb is still pointed out to visitors to Amathous and every year a festival is held in her honour on 2 September. Berengaria! Desdemona! Ariadne! I think if I were a woman caught in a storm off Cyprus I'd take my chances with the storm.

It is surmised that this house was the Roman governor's palace and this room, his audience chamber. Imagine the room lined with marble and the governor sitting on a raised *cathedra* in the apse. St Paul, granted an audience, would have been one of the few not intimidated by the long walk down the chamber to be received by the governor. After all he gloried in the fact that he, too, was a Roman. Also in this house, in a long mosaic in the main hall, you can see the first bath of Achilles immediately after his birth. He looks a big baby. Two other houses, those of Aeon and Orpheus, are also worth visiting, though some of the mosaics are damaged and others are still being restored.

Although it was very hot we continued on our tour and saw vestiges of the theatre and the agora with its many broken columns of granite. Opposite the agora is the restored Odeon, a very impressive monument in the style of the theatres at Kourio and Salamis. Like them it is now also used for productions by professional companies during the summer months. It can accommodate 1,200.

As I intimated above, St Paul, on one of his journeys came to Pafos with Barnabas in 45 AD. At first he was poorly received and a Jew, named Elymas, a practising magus, or magician, is said to have masterminded his flogging near the present 13th century Orthodox church of Agia Kyriaki. The fenced off ruins you see to the right of the church are those of the 4th century basilica of Chrysopolitissa, one of the largest churches of its day in Cyprus with seven aisles. It was repaired in the 6th century, its seven aisles being reduced to five and its earlier triple apse to one. The marble and granite columns and the remaining patches of mosaic floor all belong to this earlier church. It was totally destroyed by Arab raiders in 653 AD. The church of Agia Kyriaki is of typical Byzantine construction and, though it was built by the Catholics, it was handed over to the Orthodox Church after the Ottoman conquest in 1571. In an admirable gesture of ecumenism Roman Catholic and Anglican services are now also held there.

Though the ruins of Chrysopolitissa are still being excavated and studied and the area is, therefore, closed to the public (though you can get in, as I did one Sunday morning) you can see the ruins clearly from the road, among them the broken, conical pillar to which, it is said, St Paul was bound for his flogging. He received 'forty strokes save one', a reference not to the number of strokes but to the kind of whip which was used to administer the flogging. This had 39 stripes, bound together in three groups of 13 and was the typical style of whip used by the Romans and, apparently, by the Jews. Paul makes no specific reference in his writing to his flogging at Pafos but he does note (in 2 Cor. XI, 24) that 'From the Jews five times have I received forty strokes save one.' This could have been one of those times. There's a difficulty about the pillar, however, as it would have been part of the 4th century construction of the church and leaves a gap of 300 years to be filled. Nevertheless it's a long and fast held tradition and one could compromise, I suppose, by imagining that the church was built on the site of the flogging and the pillar incorporated into one of its aisles. A bit farfetched, I suppose, but it depends how credulous you are.

Not unnaturally, especially considering his well-known fiery temperament, Paul was angry with Elymas, and in a fit of anger blinded him, at least temporarily. The Roman governor of Cyprus at the time, Sergius Paulus, lived in Pafos, the capital and most likely, as we have said, in the 100 room mansion, called the House of Theseus, though some archaeologists say in an antecedent house on the same site. Undoubtedly he must have heard about these incidents and, like everybody else, was impressed by the blinding of the Jew. At any rate, he summoned Paul to the palace, listened to him propound his teachings and decided to become a Christian. Quite a catch for Paul and well worth the forty minus one! In the event Sergius also became the first Christian ever to govern a country. Or so Cypriots say. Here, however, I must add a note of caution. If the pro-consul did indeed become a Christian he most probably would have had to resign as pro-consul. The obvious reason for this is, that, had he remained pro-consul, he would have had, *ex officio*, to preside over, or perform certain acts of Roman religious practice, that is, perform pagan rites and ceremonies, something Christians were absolutely forbidden to do. So if, as is the proud boast of Cypriots, Cyprus was the first country ever to be ruled over by a Christian, it can only have been for a very brief period indeed. Once again the answer to a Cyprus 'problem' is yes, maybe and no.

According to ancient tradition cemeteries were always located outside the city walls. Those of Pafos are to the northwest, well signposted on the road from Fabrica Hill out towards the sea. The burial places at the most northern end, the so-called 'Tombs of the Kings', are the most interesting. A friend commented, for obvious reasons, on their proximity to the sea and we wondered whether the Mediterranean was in the same place over 2,000 years ago. In naming these tombs somebody missed the point of death being the 'great leveller' and indulged in a bit of literal upmanship, as no kings at all were ever buried here. Aristocrats, maybe, the wealthy and privileged, certainly. No doubt, the impressive architecture of the tombs with their solid Doric columns (some fluted) contributed to the upgrading. Much of the design, especially that of the open, subterranean chamber with a well in the courtyard, surrounded by a colonnade of columns, was imported from Egypt through the Ptolomies but the style is Greek. The cemetery was used from 300 BC to 300 AD and at times, during the persecutions of the Christians, it functioned also as a refuge, or catacomb. Carved crosses, for example in Tomb 5, confirm this, as do the remnants of paintings with a Christian motif in several of the tombs. Tomb 5, the largest, has 12 rather massive looking, square pilasters instead of Doric columns, and has a depth of 5 metres below the rock surface. It is the only one with its well in the centre of the atrium. Though all the tombs were looted, this one suffered more severe desecration than the others as it was used as a pottery kiln in medieval times and later still served both as a squatters' tenement and an animal shelter. In fact, squatters, during the Middle Ages, occupied nearly all the larger tombs making *ad hoc* alterations (such as tunnelling through to a neighbouring tomb) suited to their own needs.

The tombs and their decorative features are cut out of the soft rock in much the same manner as the famous buildings and tombs at Petra in Jordan, that 'rose-red city, half as old as time', which really has a magnificent series of kingly tombs. There are eight complexes of tombs in all, all numbered. In several there is a stairway (a typical feature of Cypriot tombs) of about a dozen steps down to a peristyle which surrounds an atrium and encloses several open porticoes. There is a well, necessary for ablutions, though it could also have been used to water a small garden, and sometimes a small 'hall' for the holding of ceremonies and the performance of rituals. It was customary at anniversaries and other sacred times to bring out a feast and eat 'with the deceased'. Libations were also poured and I saw one obvious funnel which I presume ran down to the grave beneath. Not the departed, however, but more likely rats and half famished wild cats, benefited from the leftovers.

The *loculi*, or burial places themselves, are cut into the walls of the tombs, some vaulted, others 'chiselled' in precise rectangular form. Though there is a children's section of 5 tombs (out of 20) in this part of the cemetery, one must assume that the small burial niches in the larger tombs were also used for children. Infant mortality would have been distressingly high in those far off times, even as recently as the late 50s when I first went to Africa more than 50 percent of infants born in what was then Tanganyika never saw the light of their fifth birthdays. A truly bewildering statistic. Only two tombs escaped the tomb-robbers. In each the deceased was covered in a linen cloth with a myrtle wreath encircling the head. Two amphorae (from Rhodes) were also found.

On a wet day in late March when we visited the cemetery, cyclamen nodded at us from improbable places on the walls of nearly every tomb. They grow liberally on the surface, too, occasionally falling in elaborate sprays over the open walls, their corms wedged securely in the crevices of rocks. Their pure, long stemmed beauty amid such arid surroundings gives the sobriety of this 'aristocratic' graveyard a melancholy, washed out (dare I say it, romantic) appearance. The tombs are open and you can get the thrill of exploration by going down into them yourself.

For a change of scene we later strolled along the harbour, full of colourful fishing boats and yachts of every description. Fresh in March but if you're lucky you can catch a gentle sea breeze all through the hot summer months. In Roman times, and before, this was a harbour busy with the commerce of coastal shipping and with the sturdier crafts that plied trade between Pafos and a variety of North African ports. Egypt had little or no timber so when the Ptolemies set up their Cyprus headquarters in Pafos there was a continual stream of wood-ferrying ships that plied between there and Alexandria. Even as late as the 1960s, barges brought the produce of the region, carobs, almonds, sultanas and other fruit, to small cargo vessels anchored just off the harbour. These would have brought supplies of building materials and other such goods to Pafos. Now Paphian sea-trade has been eclipsed by the resurgent port at Limassol.

Beyond the tavernas, favoured places for a fish meal, and the bars, there is, at the southern end, a real 'live' medieval castle. This castle, more properly called a fort, built by the Ottomans in 1592, replaced a Lusignan fortress, built by King James toward the end of the 14th century, which itself was a replacement for an earlier one built by the Byzantines and later destroyed. The derelict ruins of the east tower of James' castle can still be seen behind the fort. At the time of the Turkish invasion in 1570, the besieged and embattled Venetians, successors to the Lusignans, again partially destroyed it in an effort to defend themselves. The fort we see today incorporates the west wing and tower of the Lusignan one, completely remodelled, restored and militarily refurbished by the Turks. It's open to the public and within it you can see the Turkish garrison quarters and the adjacent prison cells. The British, in their turn, put the fort to the more peaceful use of storing salt. In September 1996, however, the fort was used both as stage and backdrop for a remarkable open air performance of Verdi's *Otello*.

The original setting for Shakespeare's *Othello* was, of course, Cyprus and there is the well-known Othello Tower in Famagusta but because Famagusta is now 'in occupied territory' the fort in Pafos was chosen to replace it. Again the timing coincided with our birthdays (the following year) so presents in the form of tickets to *Otello* were in order. It was an excellent open air performance on a gloriously balmy evening. Including a snack meal and drinks during the interval, the opera lasted three hours and the tickets were $125 each. It's not, perhaps, a particularly melodious opera but done in the 'right' setting (even the moon shone on the romantic scenes) and with Desdemona sung by the splendid Katia Ricciarelli, who has starred in this role opposite Pavarotti and Domingo, it was an evening to remember. The performance of Carlo Cossutta, who has played the role of Otello in every major opera house in the world, was also memorable. A 95 piece orchestra (the Philarmonia Hungarica) and a 75-strong Cypriot chorus combined effectively. The battlements of the fort were used dramatically as tension-heightening look-outs and as lightning-struck flash-points during the storm. The original moat and drawbridge are still there. The dockside scenes were wonderfully real. The only thing missing was the storm. Instead we heard the gentle lapping of the waves around the fort – and two jets take off and land at the nearby international airport, fortunately at tumultuous times in the drama. One had to make allowances for the clear, star-speckled sky and the very warm, coat-dispensing night. Six performances of *Nabucco*, interspersed with four of *Otello*, were planned for the Otello Cyprus Festival of 97. Organisers had hoped that the festival would become an annual event. So far it hasn't. One hopes it will.

Before we left Pafos we drove up to Ktima, (sometimes, to add further to a profusion of Pafos names, called Pano Pafos or Upper Pafos) which is about two miles from downtown Pafos and sits on a rocky plateau, 150 ft above sea level. Though both towns form one municipality, Ktima is technically the provincial capital of Pafos province and houses all the offices of administration. The town was founded by the inhabitants of Nea Pafos fleeing the Arab raids of the 7th century. Prior to that there is some evidence that Ktima was the necropolis of the lower town while later on, in Byzantine and medieval times it became a much prized location for the wealthy burgers of New Pafos to build their villas. Ownership of land or property up there was at a premium for the soil was good for growing things and the climate more healthy than down below. In fact, the word *ktima* means 'property'. Under the Ottomans it became a Turkish village and even in 1974 before the invasion, 2,500 out of its 3,000 inhabitants were Turkish Cypriots. The unrecognised president of the 'Northern Republic', Rauf Denktash, was born there. Coincidentally, Archbishop Makarios III, the first president of Cyprus, was born in a village not far away. It's a lovely old town to walk through with the narrow streets and laneways of an Italian medieval town. The shops, which have modest window display areas, are said to stock almost anything the resident or the tourist might require. As it was Saturday afternoon when we visited, most shops had closed their shutters for the weekend. This charming place, so contrasting to its lower (*kato*) touristy namesake, has several museums (one, the Byzantine, full of icons) a covered market, a domed mosque, formerly the church of Agia Sophia (15th century) and a *hammam*, or Turkish bathhouse. One captures more of the atmosphere of the real Cyprus walking through Ktima than promenading through the town below.

By late afternoon we were sated with antiquities and decided to drive to the lovely, little beach below Pissouri where we had booked into the only hotel for the night. Just outside Pafos we stopped at the famous pottery establishment of Savvas, which has a high reputation for making traditional Cypriot pottery. Work and display areas are both housed in the same building so, even though it was late on Saturday afternoon, it was possible to see the artists still at work. We bought a few small items.

About 16 kms out of Nea Pafos on the Limassol road, the one we came in on, and about 1 1/2 kms to the left lie the ruins of Palea (Old) Pafos, also called Kouklia, formerly a city-kingdom, famous for its temple to Aphrodite. Nothing now remains standing of the royal capital of Nicocles; its decline probably began when the king moved his capital to Nea Pafos. Signs of habitation date back to 2800 BC but the first sanctuary was built about 1200 BC. Though there are temples to Aphrodite (the Romans called her Venus) all over the ancient world, this one at Palea Pafos was the recognised centre of her worship and, indeed, the most important centre of all religious worship in antiquity. Homer mentions that Agamemnon sent a fine breastplate to the king of Pafos before the Trojan War (1194-1184 BC). The temple site is uphill from where you get your ticket. As you walk up, you will see a number of huge, grey, limestone blocks in an L shape, with holes drilled into them. These belong to the first shrine built here to Aphrodite more than 3,000 years ago. One touches them with a kind of awe. The holes are a mystery. Further on you will come across the ruins of the Roman sanctuary built toward the end of the 1st century AD. Most probably it was built after an earthquake destroyed the previous one and in the same style as the temple to Apollo of the Woods near Kourio. I think you would have to be an archaeologist to find these ruins exciting. It was, at any rate, a tripartite structure with an inner 'holy place', a kind of *sanctum sanctorum*, in which a grey-green-black conical stone, 1.22 m in height was worshiped as the symbol of Aphrodite. Such a stone exists nowhere else in Cyprus and one theory has it that it is of meteoric origin. Only the high priest and the priestesses of love had access to this phallic-shaped stone; the latter anointed it with oil during the four-day festivals and then dried it tenderly and carefully with soft towels. If the one in the nearby museum is really the original stone symbol of Aphrodite it could do with another anointing. I took a picture of Sandra standing by it, her hand rather timidly touching its surface.

Also on the site is an old Catholic church from Lusignan times, with frescoes from the 15th and 16th centuries. The Lusignans were drawn to Kouklia by the attractiveness of the place and the fertility of the soil. Sugar cane was obviously one of their favourite crops as signs of a sugar cane factory have been excavated nearby. The Lusignan Manor House – or Château – though destroyed by the Mamluks in 1426, and rebuilt by the Ottomans (after their conquest of Cyprus in 1571) as a *chiftlik*, or administrative centre for an extensive farm, is now the museum and is well worth a visit. Besides Aphrodite's Stone there are fine displays of various objects found nearby. The finds cover a period from the late Bronze Age to the late Roman and include jewellery, ceramics, sculpture and ivories. The well-known and beautiful mosaic of Leda teasing amorous Zeus, courting her under the guise of a swan, was found just west of the temple in what is called the House of Leda. The original is in the Cyprus Museum, a reproduction, is on the site.

We made one more stop before Pissouri, at Petra tou Romiou, the birthplace of Aphrodite, about 6 kms east of Kouklia. A tunnel under the road, unclean on each occasion I used it, allows access to the beach which is mostly shingle. This spot has been the focus of many a romantic pilgrimage through the ages and is said to be especially appealing at sunset and in moonlight when vows of perpetual love can be pronounced for the first time or renewed. Why isn't there a little Gretna Green bureau here? There is a restaurant but I found prices there rather stiff. People were swimming as we watched (it's a relatively safe beach) and there must be a small challenge to swim out to 'her' rocks, as many were doing so. Nobody was topless – I wondered whether this was out of respect for the goddess, or because people thought it would be simply too corny here. Botticelli, I remembered, in his innocent, seashell painting of her nativity, had presented her nakedness modestly.

Aphrodite is not the only one commemorated around here. Adonis, the handsome son of King Kinyras of Pafos, was madly loved by both Aphrodite and Persephone, a beautiful but devilish god of the underworld. As often in such circumstances the two bewitched lovers quarrelled and fought each other in fits of jealousy. Eventually the gods could stick their continual bickering no longer and decided in council to issue judgement and instructions: Adonis was to spend one third of the year with Aphrodite, one third with Persephone and one third by himself (for recuperation?). Adonis, however, had his preferences and he cheated on Persephone and made her furious. So furious that once when he was out hunting in the forests of Pafos she goaded a wild boar to attack him and he was killed. Aphrodite went hysterical, ran off to the woods and, uncaring about thorns and brambles, cut her legs, making them bleed and it is, according to tradition, this blood which makes the lilies grow in Cyprus. Cyprus, in fact, is famous to this day for its wild flowers in the spring. Rites annually commemorated Adonis' death and, on the following day, his resurrection, to great rejoicing and festivities. You have all the spectrum of human relationships here: love, jealousy, cheating, murder and love again. No wonder the place attracts such crowds!

We, on the other hand, drove quietly on to Pissouri, where we met some friends and went walking on the beach, picking seashells.

26

AKAMAS –
THE LAST HOMERIC LANDSCAPE

On a dark, wet and blustery evening in late March my wife and I met two friends, Kathy and Sean, at Pafos International Airport. They had come from their home in a small village in Bavaria to visit us and quickly overcame our apologies for the weather by describing the snow, sleet, wind and hail to which, at this time of year, they are more routinely accustomed. It had been snowing, they said, in Munich. We drove through sheeted rain, barely acknowledging with a muted *kalispera* the half dozen or so small villages we passed through on the way to Polis, 40 kms north of Pafos. A left turn took us quickly to Prodromi, then it was on to Latsi, where, when for a moment we opened the car window, the tang of the sea enveloped us and we heard the unusual thrash of the waves on the nearby shore. We had caught the Mediterranean in an angry mood but it was only a few minutes farther on to Neo Chorio, aptly called New Village, where we had bookings for three nights in a pleasant, modern and reasonably priced hotel ($36 per night low season rate for a fully appointed two-person unit) with a magnificent view from our private balcony over the whole, wide expanse of Khrysokhou Bay. We were made welcome by our host for the night, Odysseus.

Next morning was bright and mountainy cool. I was wakened by the heehawing of donkeys, still a means of transport in this unspoilt part of Cyprus. They can climb where tractors daren't and, in the grape-harvesting season, are used extensively on the steep, stony slopes. When working, the donkeys are fitted with slatted, wooden frames resting on lightly quilted cushions which cover the entire back of the animal. Deep kreels, like giant tumblers, narrowing from top to bottom and made from woven straw, hang from either side and, besides being used for grape harvesting, also bring home from distant fields and pastures, grass and root crops for animal feed. The donkey is ridden in front of the kreels, especially when empty, often side-straddle.

Cyprus donkeys are widely known for their sturdiness and endurance, not to mention their stubbornness, which seems to be a characteristic of all donkeys. Many were exported for use by the armed services in the Second World War. Many more, up to 2,500 according to reports, at present roaming the Karpas Peninsula, are currently being considered by the authorities in the north, despite protests by environmentalists, for export to Anatolia as working animals. In the south in recent times a number of donkeys have been found uncared for after their working lives have ended, or they have been superseded on some farms by mountain bikes and hill tractors. A 'Friends of the Cyprus Donkey Society' now exists and maintains a sanctuary in the village of Vouni where more than 60 donkeys (with the prospect of adding 100 more) are being looked after by Patrick and Mary Skinner. These two animals lovers are also planning a breeding programme to ensure the preservation of the genetic strain of this hardworking donkey. The idea of the Cyprus donkey, patient as he is, working as a kind of children's ring pony, or on trekking safaris, doesn't exist. A friend of ours had a young niece visit from Australia. Sarah, nine or ten years old, had a great ambition to ride a donkey so our friend, for a modest sum, arranged with a village donkey owner for Sarah to achieve her ambition. She thoroughly enjoyed her ride, as in fact, did the whole village who lined the streets to witness the strange spectacle of a little girl paying to sit on the back of a donkey for pleasure. *Aliae gentes, alii mores.* What is commonplace to some is a wonder to others.

It was the right time of year to see the wild flowers, a miracle that occurs annually in Cyprus. Look in August at the stony, sun-cracked, infertile, scrubland, that covers so much of the island's surface, outside the Mesaoria plain, and you could be forgiven for thinking that this is the most arid and inhospitable land on earth. Nothing, you swear, could ever grow there, yet, come even a sprinkling of winter showers, or sometimes none at all, and by late March, or early April the fields are green and splashed with colour. In the hills, against the dark green of carob trees, or the more delicate green-grey hue of olive groves, you may, as you drive past, catch sight of a field of scarlet poppies, often bobbing their heads in the dazzling yellow company of crown daisies. Kathy was much interested in wild flowers, especially orchids, and, over the two weeks of her sojourn with us, we often followed her on search expeditions through rocky terrain, sprouting meadows and ancient orchards. These wild flowers sprinkle roadside verges and adorn scraggy hillsides as they fall to the road. As often as not they hide and blush unseen, 'wasting their sweetness on the desert air'. But Kathy, with an insider's luck and an uncanny eye, could spot a retiring orchid, no more than 10 or 12 cms tall, from a car travelling at 80 kms an hour. There we would stop, climb and investigate, she, that is, attended by at least one acolyte, usually Sandra. Many's the one she saw and identified and she has roll after roll of film to prove it. I have a memory of her, crouched low in an impossible position on a steep and craggy hillside, hair blowing in the wind, camera carefully angled and miraculously held steady for a close-up of a rare orchid. Besides Kathy, only an experienced goat, I thought, could maintain footing in such an awkward position. Sean was always relieved when, such expeditions over, she was cheerfully back on the road again, pleased as punch. Later that year when staying at their lovely Bavarian home, we had the pleasure of seeing the fruits of such labour displayed in a hundred slides.

What flowers did we see on the Akamas Peninsula, under the pines of Pafos forest and later, on the Troodos Range? Too many to name or remember. Though it was too early in the year for its flowering, we saw prickly oxeye, cousin to the Syrian thistle, with which it will later share a bright yellow colour. There was wild iris, with its clear purplish blue and, not far from it, the white star of Bethlehem. Almost an Israeli flag. Closer to Pafos we saw lots of giant fennel, outlandish tall, each carrying more than a dozen yellow puffballs. Prometheus is reputed to have put the fire stolen from heaven into the pithy stem of this flower. If so, it is quenched for ever. Not a single bright spark remains. There were rock roses in barren places where you'd think no rose should ever be and there was the butter yellow of prickly broom, crusty alongside the delicate, refined pink of convolvulus. Anemones of many hues abounded and we spotted cyclamen growing in crannies.

Cyprus is a must for orchid fans – Kathy must have known that. So far forty-four different species and sub species have been identified and there are undoubtedly many others, like comets in the night sky, waiting to be discovered. Most Cypriot orchids grow also in Anatolia, some in Greece but few in central Europe. Varieties of the insect orchid, so named, not because they eat insects but because their flowers resemble them, are endemic to Cyprus. The pale, purplish flowers of the Anatolian orchid, borne on a loose spike, no more than 20-30 cms tall, look sensitive and dainty; these were the ones I saw most of. Some orchids grew in places so inaccessible as to defeat even the intrepid Kathy. Experts say that orchid lovers who want to see most of what Cyprus has to offer, must pay at least two, and more probably three, visits to the island. In our case, a prospect to look forward to, should Kathy and Sean take up the challenge.

Next day we visited the Baths of Aphrodite, which are only a few kilometres west from Neo Chorio. The road runs out at a pavilion-restaurant below the baths, though there are still well signposted hill trails for the hiker. One, especially beautiful, leads to the Fontana Amorosa, surely in this case a fulfilment of the old adage about travel that 'getting there is more exciting than arriving'.

Despite a disappointing first-look impression, the Baths are definitely more romantic. To bathe where Aphrodite bathed is, according to age-old tradition, to induce erotic love, as well, of course, as its usual concomitant, eternal youth. Unfortunately, you're not allowed to bathe there. In fact, I cannot see any self-respecting nymph disporting herself there for the grotto, besides being surprisingly shallow and small, is fed by an invisible mountain stream and several springs, the combined effect of which might be to cool rather than increase one's ardour. Which, no doubt, is why the Cyprus Tourist Board is taking no chances. The water supply never dries up, a fact, that, of itself, begs a mystic interpretation on arid and drought-stricken Cyprus. The intertwining branches of a gnarled old fig tree suggest a tangle of limbs and there is enough maidenhair to carpet a courtesan's boudoir. Though the fig tree is deciduous and was unleafed at our visit, it is interesting to note the biblical conjunction of fig leaf and maidenhair. Add to all this the continuous drip, drip, drip of water from tendrils of the maidenhair that hang down like stalactites, causing ripples that glint in the water as shafts of sunlight striplight the pool and you have enough of a romantic environment to people the spot with legendary lovers. Not all, however, who came to gaze on, or peep at, Aphrodite's ablutions were acceptable to the goddess and it is said that those who were rejected had to settle for a cold shower from a spring on the east side. Neither is it advisable to drink the water. Perhaps a judicious sprinkling, like the ritual sprinkling with holy water before solemn services in the Catholic Church, would suffice.

There is, however, another pool, that of the incredibly beautiful Adonis, in which you can swim to your heart's content, both literally and metaphorically. This pool is a more recent disc and, as yet, has only a dirt road leading to it. It is set in the scenic village of Kili, 6 kms from Kamares, deep in the Akamas Peninsula and is signposted. I did not go there, as apparently it's a good leap from the rocks into the pool, which in late March would be far too cold anyway, and I, only a very indifferent swimmer, did not wish to be tempted, not for all the favours Adonis could bestow on me. My companions agreed. About a hundred tourists visit these baths each day during the season and, from what one reads, they are even more romantic than those of Aphrodite with lush vegetation all around and the masculine music of a gushing waterfall. There is even a bed, an outcrop of rock, where the couple are supposed to have conceived all of their children, who subsequently peopled Pafos and its environs. Many infertile women stretch out on this rock, even today, in the hope of conceiving, with what success I don't know. It's a bit like kissing the Blarney Stone, I suppose, only with more tangible results, if successful. When Adonis was killed by a boar, Aphrodite was desolate and inconsolable and used all her feminine wiles to persuade the powers that be in Hades to allow Adonis to revisit earth for six months of each year. That his earthly six months covered spring and summer was a convenient arrangement for Adonis, the nature spirit, whose cycle of life and death henceforth corresponded with that of nature. Spring is enchantingly beautiful in these parts and it is not difficult to imagine Aphrodite and Adonis bathing rapturously, undisturbed in the crystal waters of this pool.

Polis is a picturesque village with a population of less than 2,000. Before 1974 it was largely Turkish Cypriot. It has, for the most part, preserved its rustic ambience and has a lovely, old, central 'square', more a small, rectangular mall, really. On the main street there is a post office, a little church, a covered market and a few bars and restaurants. On a Sunday at the end of March restaurants and *cafeneions* had their tables already outside and these were filling up at 10:30 in the morning. Locals, in their dark Sunday suits and ties, sat curious and bemused, basking in the sun, as they watched a scattering of tourists, some already in shorts, take pictures of the scene.

Polis, as is not unusual in Cyprus, had two previous names. It was founded in the 10th century BC by migrant Athenians and called Marion. For centuries the city flourished, maintaining its contact with Athens, and becoming an important commercial centre. It had the advantage of a good harbour through which the 'gold' of copper and some say real gold, too, was exported – hence its full name Polis tis Chrysochou, City of the Golden Land. It had its own coinage, examples of which are in the Cyprus Museum. It became a city of contention between the Ptolomies and Syrians in their efforts to annex the island and, having come under the influence of the Syrians, was razed to the ground by Ptolemy Lagus in 312 BC. When it was re-built in the middle of the 3rd century BC it was called Arsinoe and Arsinoe it remained for over a thousand years until the Lusignans, in a flurry of name-changing, substituted Polis. Nothing of the old kingdom city remains. In fact, it seems that ships, on their return voyages to Asia Minor, having deposited their cargo in the port, were loaded with stone from the old city to use for building back home much as some Americans, in an excess of sentimentality, wanted to do with Blarney Castle, or the Tower of London. I remember how one such singer of the 50s, pretending to be an Irish exile, used to sing the nostalgic lament 'How can I buy Kilarney?' Buy, indeed!

The environs of Polis are renowned for breeding the famous Pafos pony and it is said that Turkish farmers bred a redoubtable stallion here in the Middle Ages.

Most people visiting Polis come up from Pafos on day trips but some, perhaps more discerning, especially those in search of peaceful relaxation, stay in Polis and visit Pafos. Nearby Drousia has a good hotel with a commanding view. Its name, going back to Homeric Greek, means 'cool and fresh' and, apparently, through some accident of topography, by which a cooling breeze is funnelled down on it from the surrounding hills, it is, even in the hot summer months. Latsi is a winsome, fishing village with a long strand and good eating places. With American friends we enjoyed a seemingly endless fish meze there one evening in an old 'reconstituted' stone restaurant. A table of jolly Greek Cypriots celebrating EOKA Day, a national holiday, captured me briefly returning from a nature trip and filled a glass of wine for me. When they found out I wasn't English they filled it again.

The Akamas National Park in the most westerly part of Cyprus, is wilderness country. Named after the mythical son of Theseus, who later founded the nearby city Kingdom of Soli, Akamas is as Akamas left it, rugged, unspoilt, forested and wild. Deep gorges alternate with steep slopes and are the natural habitat of goat herds. Yet other parts have a bare, moorland look, isolated and unfriendly. The low hills are host to pine, carob and olive trees. The Akamas is also a place of military traffic and spent cartridges, as the British army, resident in the extra-territorial sovereign bases, have an agreed right to do their shooting practice and pursue other war exercises there. A number of groups are now beginning to object to this aggressive intrusion into what has been called the last Homeric landscape. The green turtle and other endangered species are threatened. Greenpeace UK is putting pressure on the British government and the Cypriot House of Representatives has requested the Cypriot government to do what is necessary to press its case before the European Parliament and the Council of Europe. An alternative firing range is being sought by the government but nothing has yet been agreed to.

Another kind of intrusion affects the coastline where Greek Cypriot entrepreneurs have begun to build tourist complexes that are not in harmony with the environment and will eventually, if not halted, destroy the very thing that visitors come to see – the primitive, pristine beauty of the place. Several environmental lobby groups are now engaged in protecting the Akamas from this additional danger.

We drove one day from Polis to Pyrgos, passing several villages that seemed to live in another time zone altogether. To our right for great stretches of the road was the Pafos forest, to our left the sea, sometimes with a steep drop of fields falling down to it, other times with only a sharp escarpment that gave to our driving an additional thrill. Several good beaches, some of black sand, others more golden, were visible. These, unoccupied that day (there was a stiff inland breeze), would provide in summer an uncrowded alternative to the crowded ones at Pafos, and Coral Bay. We walked a while on one when the wind blowing in from the open sea began to ease. It was like sharing a secret, unobserved and confidential.

Kato Pyrgos was the end of the line – the Buffer Zone ran nearby. In an undivided island it would not have been far from Nicosia and would certainly provide a more interesting drive to the beach than the road to Larnaka. It's still a sleepy, unspoilt village with cheerful people and rough amenities but one feels a spirit stirring. Massive roadworks were in progress on the day of our visit and it looked as if they were needed. We had a pleasant lunch there in a restaurant overlooking the fishing harbour. That day there was spray on the breakwater.

It was interesting – sad, too – to pass, on the way up, the isolated enclave of Kokkina. It was, apparently, a Turkish village since before the 1963-64 disputes that brought a UN intervention on the island.

Turkish Cypriots in the neighbouring villages were being attacked by General Grivas, the guerrilla commander of EOKA, a secret military organisation fighting for *Enosis*, or union with Greece. One of the first tasks of the UN troops was to round up all the Turks and transfer them to Kokkina which, it is said, they – the Turkish Cypriots – then turned into a supply base for arms 'imported' from Turkey, only a short distance away across the Mediterranean. At the time of the 1974 invasion Turkish troops protected Kokkina, while carpet bombing the surrounding hills and continued to hold it even after hostilities ended and despite the fact that it had no other physical connection with the North of the country, by that time under Turkish control. So today you see the flags of Turkey and its satellite statelet (the TRNC) flying from this isolated promontory completely surrounded by

Southern territory. Three border posts guard it, one Greek, one Turkish, the other a lonely outpost of the UN. If any group were intent on entering Kokkina, whether for a swim, or something more sinister, and took the precaution of cutting the telegraph wires first, one cannot see how even the combined strength of the three outposts could stop them. The inhabitants cannot be supplied except by sea, unless UN transport comes to their aid. Altogether, another one of those tragic stupidities left over from wars everywhere.

Anybody who has ever travelled on Cyprus Airways will have seen, proudly displayed on its planes, the emblem of the airline and the national animal of Cyprus, the moufflon. Handsome and arrogant in posture, sensitive and retiring by nature, the moufflon belongs to the sheep family, though it has a coat of light, brown hair, instead of wool. The horns on the male resemble those of a large ram. Their distinctive curvature actually differentiates the Cypriot moufflon from others of its kind which live in western Asia and southeastern Europe. It's the largest wild animal left in Cyprus and it, too, almost disappeared. Its meat, darker than mutton, is good to eat and was hunted from as far back as Neolithic times when the supply was abundant. It continued to be hunted, by hounds in the Middle Ages and by rifle until as late as the 1930s when the entire stock was reduced to 15. Finally the British government acted and declared the natural habitat of the moufflon, the Pafos forest area, a game reserve. Today, there are, maybe, 1,200 in the wild. They are not easy to come by so about 60 are kept in captivity at Stavros forest station, about 10kms from Kykko Monastery, in the Troodos foothills. Stavros is worth visiting in its own right as it as it lies in the famous Cedar Valley, the only place where cedars, which once covered the island, now grow.

The road to Stavros is not always inviting so a kindly tourist department has set up another enclosure, well signposted, just off the main Kakopetria-Troodos road. One year, in late November, Sandra, Ameeta, a friend who was staying with us at the time, and I drove over to Pafos via the Troodos. We stopped at the moufflon signpost, climbed the steep gradient to an inner enclosure with viewing platforms. A much larger area of hillside was fenced off with strong, tall, wire fencing. We saw nothing, not even moufflon spoor. We were disappointed, especially as Amee and I had been saddened on the way up by the panic beeps and flutterings of a thrush 'glued' to a tree branch. I'd previously heard of this peculiar Cypriot way of catching birds for the table but this was my first eyes-on experience of such cruelty. I'm not certain what substance is used to coat the tree branches but it looked like a dark, sticky mixture of treacle, tar and honey. (Since writing the above I have heard that it is called '*verka*', made from the boiled fruit pods of an oak-like tree) Understandably, Cypriots, at least the ones I've spoken to, are uncomfortable talking about it. Once the bird is caught, it's inevitable that the agitation of its wings in an effort to escape only serves to spread the sticky goo on to the wings themselves, so that, in the unlikely event of its jerking itself free, flight would be impossible. In either case the bird would die a slow and painful death from shock, injury and starvation, unless the 'trappers' came quickly and gave it the coup de grace. With some difficulty Amee released it from the branch and, despite its pounding heart, we tried to clean it as best we could before hiding it in ground cover. I vowed never knowingly to sample such a 'delicacy'.

Trapping birds either by net or 'glue' is illegal in Cyprus but, according to a recent (May 1998) observation by the British High Commissioner, when the armed forces of the British Sovereign Bases agreed, in the interests of conservation, to move their firing range from Akamas to Pyla, near their Dekelia base, they found the range there couldn't be utilised because farmers in the area had planted quick-growing trees which they were then using to net for the pot small birds known as *ambelopoulia*. *Plus ça change* . . .

We decided to walk around the whole of the hillside enclosure and, on the tricky climb down, had almost given up hope of seeing a moufflon when a couple of German tourists announced, with much pointing and a triune raising of fingers, that there were three in the middle distance. The moufflon were slowly walking towards the opposite end of the enclosure so we quickly scrambled down, clinging to the wire and making as little noise as possible. Halfway up the steep steps on the far side we clearly saw the moufflon in two groups, three and two, beneath the tall pine and cedar trees, the stags (one is tempted to call them that because of the magnificence of their horns) standing proudly, broadside to us, heads up, sniffing the air, protective. The females, content to leave guard duties to the males, lay down and almost disappeared from view behind some shrubs. The coats of the moufflon looked a dark, streaky tan and there was a descending curve of a light grey line from their middles down the flanks, reminiscent of the distinctive markings of a Thompson's gazelle widely seen on the African plains. It was remarkable how well they blended with a background of tree trunks and shrubs and a ground strewn with pine needles. We stayed a while looking at them in near silence. They were worth stopping for.

Recently there was an outcry when a cull of several hundred moufflon was proposed, as, so it was claimed, when snow covered their forest feeding grounds they came down and damaged the vineyards of some farmers. Thankfully government has heeded the voice of environmentalists and the problem will now be solved by erecting a fence rather than by executing the moufflon. Could problems arising out of the infringement of human territorial rights be so easily resolved!

Much of what has been written about the Akamas Peninsula and the Pafos forest areas applies equally well to the Troodos mountain area. This whole mountain range, indeed, all of Cyprus, lay at the bottom of a deep ocean 90 million years ago. The two large ranges, the Troodos and the Pentadactylos, surfaced about 20 million years ago, for a long time existing as two islands some 80 kms apart. Submarine eruptions occurring over that immense period of time account for the varying rock formations on Troodos and account, too, for the different vegetation and varied agricultural possibilities of the soil. In fact, the geology of the Troodos is one of the most interesting to scientists all over the world, especially for the research material it offers to students of the earth's crust. No other mountain range has so influenced contemporary geological theories about the expanse of oceans and the movement of tectonic plates. Once, of course, the entire Troodos Range right down to the coast was forested, the dominant tree being the Aleppo pine. Juniper and cedar were also once here in abundance but it is the black pine, in all its different varieties that one particularly associates with the higher reaches (above 1,200m) of the Troodos today. Man's needs, artificial as much as natural, have gobbled up too much of that forest with dire effects on annual rainfall. Even as I write, at the end of the 1998 rainy season, the reservoirs are only 15 percent full and water is rationed. This is the third dry season in a row. Unless the God of the Rains soon be merciful a water crisis is in the offing.

The little service village of Olympos, which takes its name from the mountain peak nearby, is itself 5,500 ft above sea level. Ironically it's the only place in Cyprus where I've seen camels, once a customary form of transport on the island and these most probably were for exotic snow trekking. From January to April – in a good year – the whole area around Olympos is covered with snow and people bring their children up to see it, as it rarely falls in Nicosia and the coastal cities. Whether the snow is skiable or not varies from year to year and from week to week during the colder months. Approximately 15.24 cm (6 in) of snow are required for skiing but in the past four years, prior to 1998, there has not been enough snow. There are 13 ski runs and 4 ski lifts but as there are no free running rivers or streams high in the Troodos, there are no snow making machines. A proposal to pump back up to the ski areas the run off water from melting snow has not so far won government approval. In normal years the ski slopes are heavily patronised by ex-pats from Saudi and the Gulf States. In fact, until the recent warmer winter temperatures, Cyprus was the region's ski Mecca. As part compensation, life on the Troodos slopes is much more salubrious in July and August than life on the plains. This explains the numerous chalets and villas scattered everywhere, as well as the many 'Accommodation' and 'To Let' signs you see in all the picturesque little villages, which for their beauty and relative isolation, remind me forcibly of villages I saw in the foothills of the Alps in northern Italy, or almost anywhere in Bavaria. The same steep-gabled houses, with similar flower-boxed balconies and window-sills, the same steep-sloped hills and sheltering trees back of the village, a church, a gorge where torrents flow in winter (and in Cyprus, only in winter, if then,) a mini-market or two, half a dozen restaurants making the most of their scenic backgrounds, parked cars, people walking, sounds carrying. In all, a few thousand feet closer to heaven.

Streams of cars from Nicosia and the coastal cities of Larnaka and Limassol snake up the mountain every summer weekend and, after 10 August, when Cypriots take their annual holidays, anyone who can escape the oppressive heat down below is' up the mountain'. The president's summer residence, formerly that of the British governor, is near the village of Troodos. Interestingly its main building was constructed in 1880 under the supervision of the then unknown and still youthful French poet, Arthur Rimbaud. I haven't been invited there yet but I did accept, albeit unwittingly, an invitation to the palace in Nicosia. It happened like this. My wife and I were out for a Sunday walk when she suddenly diverted from our nearby park to show me a 'new' one in another part of town. It was tiny when we got there and I grumbled but we saw streams of people, some on foot, some in retro cars and twin cabs, all going through the gates of the presidential palace, seemingly being encouraged by the guards. Police on duty there seemed equally helpful. We rambled over. There was no frisking, no inspection, no demand for documents, no enquiries of any kind.

'Welcome,' said a police officer. 'Please go through. The president's daughter is sharing her marriage with the people of Nicosia.'

Sandra looked at her jeans and bright, white and orange running shoes.

'No way!' she said. I was slightly better attired, in slacks, open-necked shirt, black sports-shoes and light, black, silk jacket.

'At least, let's see the grounds,' I urged, 'it'll make up for the cabbage-plot you took me to.'

We went in. The palace wooded environs looked as dry and 'untidy' as any city park. There were trees and lots of brushwood. Nothing more. When we had got to the top of the hill there was a kind of belvedere to our right, with the low slung palace on our left. My wife was adamant – she was rapt in her new-found admiration for Cypriot bush life and would give me ten minutes. I walked alone – I seemed to be the only one walking alone – over to the entrance where a queue was forming and moving shufflingly forward to where the bridal couple stood. There was a minimum of fuss. I took my place in the queue between an Orthodox priest, who also wore his everyday clothes, toe-length, black cassock and flowerpot black hat, and a rather beautiful mannequin in what was surely an off-the-shelf long, suede coat from a boutique sale. Movement along the reception line was surprisingly fast – how long does it take to shake two hands in rapid succession? When the black wall moved, I saw the groom for the first time and was surprised at how 'settled' he looked. His smile seemed genuine and his warm eyes looked straight at me. His wife, in full automation, looked over my right shoulder and smiled. I swear she never knew that her hand had been shaken by a tall man in an open-necked shirt and a black silk jacket. I was immediately directed to a large, silver coloured, free-standing, cubby hole into which one of the striking, willowy, short-skirted hostesses thrust an arm and brought forth a silver package tied with gold ribbon and presented it to me. She smiled generously and I thanked her, overcoming with great difficulty the impulse to ask her for a second one for my wife who was, I supposed, still diligently admiring the scenery outside.

These gifts of wedding *loukoumia* are offered at every wedding in Cyprus. They are made from a mixture of raisins, almonds and other fruit, rounded into a crumbly biscuit ball, dusted with confectionery sugar, wrapped up in a decorative, little package of shiny waxed paper, tied with a gold or silver ribbon and presented to each guest. Over half a million of these special *loukoumia* are consumed in Cyprus each year, not surprising when you consider that out of 33 countries in a recent survey Cyprus is proportionally second only to Liechtenstein in the number who tie the knot each year. In a survey conducted by Eurostat, the European Union statistics body, Liechtenstein has 13.2 marriages annually per 1,000 of its population, Cyprus 9.9. The European average is 5.1 weddings per 1,000 and the two countries with the lowest average are Sweden (3.2) and Ireland (4.3). Strange bedfellows! Having stowed away the silver packet in the pocket of my jacket, I sidled towards the drinks table where I was offered a glass of bubbly and a canapé. Then the private gardens of the president were mine to wander through. I mixed with several hundred people, speaking only to a small child for whom I retrieved a ball from a pond he'd kicked it into. There were few foreigners there, if any, so I picked up the occasional smile of goodwill and, perhaps, of distant admiration for my eccentricity.

The building itself was small for a palace and unpretentious. There was a rose garden and the roses, I noticed, had been properly pruned but, beyond petunias, there was little at that time of year of floral decoration. There were many grander houses in and about Nicosia but this one had an openness and an unostentatious dignity that marked it as special. Warm and balanced it had a welcoming atmosphere about it, more like Cicero's 'Tusculum' than a senatorial chamber of dark plots and devious machinations. There were few police about. Neither, of course, was the president, who found he had duties to perform elsewhere on the day of his daughter's reception. It all seemed to me both civilised and democratic.

When I came out, my wife, of course, had gone but I did take her home the gift of wedding cake in the silver packet with the gold ribbon wrapping.

Mount Olympus itself, the tallest mountain in Cyprus at 6,433 ft (1916 m.) has a British-controlled radio communication station on its peak, whose purpose is to eavesdrop on what the countries of the Middle East are saying to each other. The station looks like a teed-up golf ball and is visible for miles around. Troodos village is hardly worth a stop unless you want something to eat. I've heard the restaurant there is quite good.

As in Akamas the Cypriot tourist authorities have laid out mountain trails for nature lovers. There are four principal ones, Artemis, Atalante, Persephone and Kaledonia. The latter, at 2 kms, is the shortest and on one occasion Sandra, Amee and I walked down it. The path was very peaceful and shady. It followed the stream which we crossed and recrossed at various points. There were a number of rock descents with a spot hollowed out for your foot, several sharp, angular turns and a few steep declines that, in my view, required the measure of fitness and determination of a hungry goat. There is the occasional resting spot but no rails. I walked down at my own pace.

From a height of about 1580 m the trail drops from the road (near the presidential summer residence) 240 m to the falls. I was two-thirds of the way down when I realised that I would have to return up the same path. I sat on a boulder listening to the river as it rippled busily along and enjoyed the merry sound of birdlife. An enchanting place. Then I heard puffing and shouts in English of male camaraderie. A tall, blond man came into view, followed by about half a dozen others, all intent, focused on the climb, barely looking to right or left. One grunted what I took to be a greeting of sorts. I wanted to ask him how far away I was from the falls but I couldn't break such concentration. Two minutes later an eighth man appeared, somewhat pudgier than the others but whose crew haircut identified him as one of the same group. He seemed glad that I spoke to him.

Far down to the falls?

20 minutes down, 30 minutes back up. British, probably a Liverpudlian.

Worth going on down?

I wouldn't, mate. Couple o 'goats pissin', is all.

You with the group that passed a few minutes ago?

Yeh, tail-end Charlie, that's me.

Hiking club?

In a way. Nah, we're on the Line. Army – we're out for a few days R&R plus trainin'.

Good weather for it. What's the Line like?

Bloody boring, mate but I reckon if we wasn't there they'd be at each other's throats. He picked up a small stone and threw it into the stream.

Be home in a month.

Good for you – just in time for winter, eh?

No worries. He chuckled. Just as long as they don't send me to f----- Northern Ireland. Be seeing ye – wouldn' t go any further if I was you.

I waved. Good luck.

Same to you, mate.

I allowed the silence to envelop me again. A little later, turning over his advice in my mind and reflecting that I'd once seen Niagara, I found myself a tree branch to do duty as a walking stick, and followed him slowly back up the trail. When I got to the top the soldiers were just finishing their cigarettes and about a hundred metres away Sandra and Amee were getting out of a Conservation Department Landrover. I felt cheated. We called to one another and I was surprised the way words carried and then seemed to hang in the silence.

But please, don't let anything I've written here deter you from enjoying the Kaledonia Track. It has all that any nature lover could wish for, all that anyone wanting to be far away from city noises could desire. In December with only a few tourists about, it was uplifting and recuperative and it mattered not at all that I didn't see the waterfall. Indeed, I have an as yet unfulfilled ambition to stay a few days in some quiet Troodos village and walk all four trails. Artemis, goddess of forests, help me!

One knowledgeable commentator, Andreas Demetropoulos, wrote recently, ' it is not just the orchids, the peonies, the cedars and the golden oak, nor the moufflon and the nightingales that make Troodos so enchanting. It is also the silence that reigns in the forest and the aroma of the herbs and that here time stands still.' He spoke wisely and that is enough.

A Day in the Troodos Mountains

27

KYKKOS – THE MOST FAMOUS MONASTERY

Just 18 kms from Mt Olympus stands the 900 year-old monastery of Kykkos, itself at the brisk altitude of 1200 metres. In its full title it has the words 'Royal' and *Stavropegic*, indicating by the former that its foundation and construction was approved and financed by the Byzantine emperor of the day, Alexios Comnenos (1081-1118), and by the latter that it has a cross engraved on its foundation stone, a mark of its self-governing independence.

How it came to be a gift from the emperor and, more significantly, how it acquired the miraculous Holy Icon of the Virgin Mary, painted from life by none other than St Luke the Evangelist, who, of course, knew her, is a story in itself.

It appears that one day in the year 1100 AD or thereabouts, the emperor's representative in Cyprus, one Manuel Voutomitis, went on a hunting expedition in the Troodos forest and got lost. The forest was densely wooded in those days and Voutomitis obviously did not have a compass. After wandering about for a long time, exhausted and dispirited, he, at last, chanced upon a hermit, who, however, by the strict rules he had imposed upon himself, refused even to talk to him. The exalted personage was beside himself. Elation gave way to despair and, in his frustration, the governor of Cyprus, for that, in effect, is who he was, upbraided and maltreated the taciturn hermit. To no avail. Furious, he began again the search for an exit from the forest and eventually, as good fortune would have it, succeeded in finding his way out. He was no sooner back in Nicosia, however, than he fell gravely ill and, despite the efforts of the court physicians, he was at death's door. Though there could have been many other reasons for his illness, Voutomitis blamed it on the rude way he had treated the holy man. God was punishing him for the lack of respect he had shown for the hermit. He, therefore, sent some servants to find him and bring him back to Nicosia, where he humbly and profusely apologised to him and begged his forgiveness. The old man, still holding his peace, bore no grudge. Instead, he prayed mightily for Voutomitis to be cured, which he quickly was. The governor, grateful in the extreme, promised the old monk, Isaiah was his name, that he would give him anything he desired. Always a dangerous commitment, as Herod found out when he made the same offer to dancing Salome of the Seven Veils, daughter of Herodias, his wife. Salome, egged on by her mother, of whom John the Baptist openly disapproved, demanded – and got – the latter's head on a platter. Voutomitis was luckier than Herod for all the holy monk wanted was to get back to his hermitage in the forest but, inspired from on high, he asked for an almost equally impossible favour, the Icon of the Virgin painted by St Luke!

This icon, as everybody knew, was in the possession of the emperor in Constantinople. Voutomitis heard the request with amazement and consternation but, despite his considerable reluctance to undertake such a task, he showed himself a man of his word and took Isaiah with him to Constantinople so they could make the request together. Soon after their arrival they heard that the emperor's daughter was struck down and seriously ill with the same symptoms that the governor had had. None of the treatments of the imperial physicians had any effect. The girl, whom the emperor dearly loved, was in dire danger of losing her life. Knowing of the governor's cure, he had both the governor and the monk brought to court. He besought the monk's intercession and, once again, the monk, praying with all his strength over the girl, interceded with the Lord and God answered his prayers and the girl was thereupon cured. It seemed an opportune moment to present their request to the emperor. He was sympathetic but reluctant. Such a precious treasure should surely stay in Constantinople and not be sent off to one of the furthest outposts of the empire!

But then he, too, caught the disease and was in imminent danger of succumbing to it. An intelligent man, he still had sense enough left to see the hand of God in these successive illnesses and not only handed over the icon but also gave money for the building of a monastery to house it. It is said that the trees of the forest bowed as the icon was carried to the place where the monastery was to be built. At about the same time, by decree of the emperor, the future monastery was declared *stavropegic* (autonomous), which it has remained to this day.

Whatever the authenticity of the legend, the icon of the Virgin Eleousa (the Merciful) of Kykkos is still there, revered not only throughout Cyprus but throughout the whole Orthodox world. Two other icons of the Virgin, one in Athens, the other in Megaspelion in the Peloponnese, are attributed to St Luke and all three are revered as the exemplars on which all subsequent icons of the Virgin are modelled. An interesting fact is that the face of the Virgin, for whatever reason, probably reverence, is now always covered with a cloth and is only uncovered in periods of critical drought, when the icon is carried in procession to the nearby small hill, called Throni, and God is beseeched to send rain. Even then the icon is carried high and no one is permitted to look at the face. Various miracles are attributed to the icon, especially those connected with the ending of prolonged and severe drought. The last time such intercession was made from the hill called Throni was in 1990 but as there has been another creeping drought over the last two or three years another procession may soon have to be made.

Among many testimonies on display, evidencing a successful intercession through the power of the icon, is part of a swordfish, which, when whole and alive, rammed a fishing boat in 1718, making several large holes in its side and almost certainly condemning those who sailed it to certain death by drowning. The sailors prayed, no doubt also promising to be better sailors, and the Virgin of Kykkos came to their assistance. There is no detail that I have come across that tells of the manner of their saving: did they, like the little Dutch boy at the dykes, successfully manage to stop the holes with their fingers and the palms of their hands, or did the spear of the swordfish get jammed in the largest hole after piercing it, leaving only incessant bailing and mopping up operations as a result of the smaller perforations, or were the terrified sailors transported immediately to some safe shore? I cannot answer those questions but, one way or another, they were saved and grateful for it. They must also have caught the fish. Votive offerings of an arm, or a leg, or even of a baby, seem by comparison less dramatic.

The icon is in the centre of the *iconostasi* and, although we can't see it, the figures represented on it as portrayed in paintings and engravings by those who did at one time see it, are those of a young woman, of full face and neck, wearing a red veil, a crown above her head, holding a toddler of perhaps two in her arms. The Infant holds the hem of her veil in his left hand as if for security and protection and in his right, a scroll. The predominant colours are red and gold.

The original buildings, as was natural in the middle of a forest, were made of wood (the name of the monastery is supposed to be derived from the word *koukkos*, the name given to the black wood of the ebony tree) and burnt down twice, once in 1365 and again in 1541, destroying on each occasion the frescoes and other precious adornments of the church. Though re-built in stone the fire saga continued, the first in 1751, the second in 1813; both caused extensive damage and even loss of life. The buildings we see today are, therefore, mostly from the 19th century. A typical Byzantine construction, the church is three aisled and has a dome. A belfry was added in 1882, four years into the British administration. The Ottomans, the previous rulers, didn't like the pealing of bells, at least of Christian bells and forbade them. Of the present six the largest comes from Russia and weighs 1,280 kgs, the combined weight of 15 good-sized men. The magnificent chandeliers in the church also come from Russia and are of exceptional quality. Much building has taken place at the monastery over the last decade and more is still being planned. In fact, there were earth movers and cranes there on the day of our visit. Hostels to accommodate overnight guests (Cypriots free) are among the latest additions. Inside the monastery, too, in the courtyard corridors, both upstairs and down, there has been much rich and rather showy decorative mosaic work. Walls and ceilings everywhere are covered with gold-plate icons, some striking, albeit in the grandiosely still and somewhat posed fashion of Byzantine art. Their colours were for the most part vibrantly bright. It was like entering a modern Sistine Chapel, painted by Picasso in his blue (and gold) period.

The interior of the church is heavily opulent with painted walls, magnificent candelabra, some old, some modern, and rather heavy, ornate furniture. The floor is polished granite. The triple *iconostasi* has to be approached with reverence and some awe. Row upon row of silver lamps and oval pendants hang before it. The icon attributed to St Luke is enclosed in silver, framed in mother of pearl and covered with embroideries. A few weeks before our visit another icon, also of the Virgin and Child, also part of the *iconostasi,* began crying. The tears came from the eyes of both Virgin and Child and the flowing was witnessed not only by the monks but, at various times, by hundreds of the faithful as well. Archbishop Chrysostomos said mass in the church and interpreted the tears as the Virgin weeping over a divided Cyprus, a Cyprus, too, he intimated, that has become more materialistic, perhaps because of events associated with the 1974 invasion as I've tried to explain elsewhere. He called for a spiritual renewal and the substantial donations collected were given to the Defence Fund! The tears had stopped before our visit but I could clearly see the runnels they'd made on the icon's surface. Sceptics, of course, maintain that wood 'cries' periodically and that this was simply one such occasion. Perhaps. A soldier stood guard as the crowds, passing along the platform of the *iconostasi,* devotionally kissed the icon, paying their respects and making their requests. Whatever you make of it, it was touching to see the faith of these people, young as well as old, their lips moving constantly in prayer. A wizened little man rather peremptorily motioned us on.

The connection of the Orthodox Church and, in particular, the Monastery of Kykkos, with the 'national consciousness' is well known. Initially, under the rule of the Lusignans, ecclesiastical works, written by the monks, helped preserve the Greek language and secured for posterity the history of the island. Other cultural activities, such as the copying and illustrating of manuscripts, wood carving and the painting of icons continued the Byzantine tradition and anchored the spiritual, and national, identity of the people. This latter was of the utmost importance during the 300 year long Ottoman rule. As one writer has put it, the Monastery of Kykkos, became the 'breakwater' against islamisation. A pilgrimage to Kykkos by Orthodox Christians became as important and, for many, as hazardous, as the *hajj* was for Muslims. Yet thousands, regularly over that long period of time, overcoming the obstacles, made it, drawing spiritual and emotional strength from their visit, to persevere in the practice of their religion and to resist acculturalisation by the dominant Islamic population.

Cypriots had hoped for a new dawn under the British administration (1878-1960) but sadly found their new 'bosses' almost equally as oppressive as their former ones and just as self-interested. During this period Kykkos became even more identified with the struggle for national liberation. Some of the monks became members of the Legislative Council, an ineffectual kind of parliament established in 1882 and fought there for improved living standards for their people. Others became leaders of the Orthodox Church both at home and abroad. Outstanding among them was Archbishop Makarios III who had been at the monastery from the age of 12. He became a political leader in the struggle for independence, even a leader of the guerrilla EOKA movement, which sought to achieve independence for Cyprus by force of arms. The monastery from its vast resources became a financial contributor to EOKA and also provided places of refuge for its fighters, both within the monastery itself and in the surrounding hills. For three years, 1956-59, the British closed the monastery in punishment for its involvement and participation in the national struggle. Makarios went on, of course, to become the first president of the republic when an 'agreed' constitution was practically imposed on the people of Cyprus in 1960. He is buried in a black marble tomb resting in a natural, open-air cave on the hill at Throni just above the monastery. A little higher up, at the summit, there is a small Byzantine chapel or copula where services are held from time to time, principally to petition rain. On the way down, on your right, there is a prayer tree where pilgrims hang pieces of cloth, a strip torn from a shirt, a handkerchief, or even a strand of hair to remind their favourite saint that a petition has been lodged with him, or her. When – and if – the cloth blows free that is a signal that the petition will be granted. Judging from the number of white cloths (some are pink, or red) fluttering on the tree the saints were having a rest period. On the day of our visit, two soldiers, on guard duty at the shrine were sitting on the wall by their pillbox, smoking and passing comments on those who came to pay their respects at the tomb. One would hope that this kind of casual behaviour is not typical of army discipline. I witnessed another instance of it recently during the election campaign for president when three soldiers, on duty guarding the residence of one of the candidates, spent some of their time, at least, fooling around with their weapons, pretending to use them, aiming them at some local girls who were passing. A friend, also a resident of the area, told me that the previous night a cat, hotly pursued by one of his dachshunds, claimed sanctuary in the pillbox, causing chaos – and flight – among the soldiery. The Turks need have no fear.

In other ways, too, the monastery became a pioneering social and educational institution. It produced well respected scholars, set up a seminary for the training of priests, financed the opening of schools, passed on to the wider community the results of its theoretical and practical research into viticulture, afforestation, horticulture and apiculture. It gave hospitality and provided financial support for thousands of refugees after the 74 invasion. One could be forgiven for thinking that it sometimes operates as a mini social welfare department, providing homes for the elderly, youth recreation centres and facilities for child care. It also finances the purchase of some of the latest medical equipment for state hospitals and assists financially struggling patriarchates in the Middle East.

On 17 May 1998, in the presence of the highest civil and church leaders, a magnificent, new, ecclesiastical museum, built specifically for this purpose, was inaugurated to mark the 900th anniversary of the foundation of the monastery. About six hundred priceless works of art of the Byzantine and post-Byzantine periods, selected from the more than 10,000 that are housed in the monastery's treasury of votive offerings, will henceforth be on permanent display. These offerings, which range from icons and murals to illuminated manuscripts, gospels, patriarchal vestments and embroidered masterpieces, were presented to the monastery over the centuries, not just by pious lay people for favours sought or received but by kings, emperors and church leaders who all had their own needs. This combined display of religious, cultural, artistic and historical wealth is certainly unique to Cyprus and may also be so world-wide, according to Abbot Nikiforos. He also stressed that they form part of the continuing tradition and living day-to-day worship of the monastery. The cost of the buildings, several of which are hexagonal, was 3.5 million Cypriot pounds (US$7m).

But where, I hear you asking, does all the money come from? Obviously not from the agricultural activities, however energetic, of 20 monks, a third of whom are elderly. The monks, however, were not always so few; in 1683, for example, there were 400 and 180 at the beginning of the last century, with the result that much cultivation and expansion of landed property was necessary and occurred gradually over the centuries. There is, as well, the continuous flow of monetary gifts and votive offerings but, most of all, the monastery acquired its wealth from the frequent donations to it of land by farmers and other landowners who sought some relief from the huge tax burdens placed on the Orthodox population at the beginning of the 19th century. The monastery, for example, besides owning large chunks of valuable land in Nicosia, also has property in Asia Minor and Russia. Suffice to say that it has wealth enough to afford beneficence.

Most people know that some of the best drinks in the world are made by monks. Dom Perignon, for example, was first created by a teetotaller holy monk, Dom Pierre Prignon, at the Abbey of Hautvillers in France, Benedictine by monks of the ancient Order of St Benedict and Chartreuse, both yellow and green, by one of the most ascetic of monastic Orders, the Carthusians. Kykkos would not be fulfilling an ancient and respectable monastic tradition if it, too, did not produce a worthwhile and palatable brew. It does, it's very drinkable and it's called *zivania*. Produced now at the winery set up recently by the present abbot, Nikiforos, it is made, as it has been for many centuries, by distilling fermented grapes, adding discrete proportions of cinnamon, cloves and sugar and, also, of course, a secret recipe of herbs collected in the Kykko mountains. *Zivania* comes in three varieties and is marketed under the names of Kykko Monastery Aperitifs (two, both red and rather sweet) and Genevrier, which is white, dry and drunk like vodka. An antiquated law, introduced by the British and still on the books, prevents its being marketed as *zivania*. Although it's quite legal to make and, indeed, most vine growers distill their own, it is absolutely illegal to transport it from one place to another. This law the British introduced to prevent Cypriots from drinking the fiery liquid without first paying taxes on it. Needless to say they didn't succeed and the law is more honoured in its breech than its observance. About 100,000 litres of *zivania* is produced annually and sold under its pseudonyms both at home and abroad, especially to Sweden, Russia and Germany. Some, of course, of the one million visitors who come to the monastery each year take a bottle home with them. We, too, now have our own bottle to compare with the potcheen, illegal to buy or sell in Ireland, that we bought on the island of Lindisfarne, off the Northumbrian coast in northeast England. Both – potcheen and *zivania* – can be bought in secret from rustics whose brew is often well over 65 percent proof.

The abbot's wish in establishing the winery was not only to preserve the tradition of making *zivania* but also to help out the vinegrowers in the villages round and about, some of whom were facing ruin because of a lack of demand for their grapes. About 15,000 bottles of white and red wines are produced annually and are of above average quality. So, a visit to the most famous monastery in Cyprus can provide delight to the palate as well as serenity to the soul.

Though drunk fairly widely throughout the island, *zivania* is not the national drink. Brandy sour is, at least as far as visitors are concerned and two or three of them, long and cool as they are, taken as an aperitif before dinner on hot summer nights, can rob you of your legs. The making of a brandy sour is neither difficult, nor expensive. I've used the following recipe successfully.

Wet the rim of a tall glass and dip in sugar (if you're looking for perfection and have time you can freeze the glass for an hour or so). Next, drop into the glass 3 or 4 cubes of ice, followed by 2 or 3 drops of Angostura Bitters (the Trinidanian variety, preferably). Add a generous tot of local brandy (I used Anglias) augmented by a dash of Filfar, a local liquor, which tastes like Gran Marnier. After adding a little lemon squash, fill up with sparkling soda. *Voilà*, though some might like to garnish with a slice of lemon and/or a sprig of mint. *Eis ugeian*! is as good a toast as any to raise your glass to.

Cheers!

28

OTHER MOUNTAIN
CHURCHES AND VILLAGES

One could spend all one's time in Cyprus visiting churches and monasteries. The island is full of them and yet more churches are being added each year in the ongoing expression of a culture that is innately religious. It was also until recently predominantly rural. Six hundred villages, six hundred churches but many villages have two or more, an old and a new, one small, the other large to accommodate the growth in population since the 13th and 14th centuries. The ones, however, that most interest visitors to Cyprus are the Byzantine ones from the 10th to the 14th centuries. Of these many of the older churches are in remoter areas, or even in places from which a village has disappeared altogether (as is the case at Asinou). As liturgies in such isolated churches take place infrequently, they are usually locked apart from in the high tourist season but the priest in a nearby village will have the key.

In early December one year, Sandra, our friend Amee and I visited what is probably the most famous of all these Byzantine churches at Asinou. You can find it by going out 34 kms on the main Nicosia-Troodos road (B9), then taking a right turn, clearly marked for the village of Nikitari. Asinou church, its short name, is 5 miles above Nikitari and, if the church is locked, there's where you'll have to go to find the local priest who'll have the key. You will most likely have to give him a ride to the church and back. On this clear and sunny morning, however, an alert, elderly gentleman was sitting on a folding chair beside the church's open door. He was the only other person about.

One can see immediately why the real name of the church is Panayia Phorviotissa, Virgin of the Pastures (Our Lady of the Fields) because, though it sits on the edge of a forest, the church is surrounded by orchard and hilly scrub, ideal pasture for goats. Asinou church is one of nine churches with Byzantine frescoes in the Troodos area which have been placed on UNESCO's World

Heritage List. Asinou, *primus inter pares* of all these churches, has often been described as a veritable museum of Byzantine art and is undoubtedly one of the most interesting Byzantine monuments in Cyprus.

The barrel-vaulted stone church, with pitched roof, typical of all the ancient churches on Troodos, was built in 1105/06 by Nicephorus the Strong, a Byzantine official, in memory of his deceased wife. It was originally a small family chapel but a monastery complex was later added in which Nicephorus secluded himself until his death. Nothing of the monastery remains. Towards the end of the 12th century, the narthex, with its two semi-circular apses, was added. But it's the frescoes people come to see. These are of great beauty and date from the 12th to the 14th century. Wondrously in such a small church there are frescoes here from five different periods, relating to four different epochs. The earliest ones, in the sanctuary, dating from the time the church was built, were done by artists from Constantinople and reflect the 'in' style of the capital at that time. Other 12th century frescoes are in the apse and in the west bay of the nave. The galloping St George on his white horse, with red cloak and sky blue shield, is the epitome of the conquering knight, though I thought his features looked more sad than triumphant. This is a 14th century fresco. These frescoes have been cleaned to reveal their true colours and astonish one with the vibrancy of their rich blues and panel reds. Some commentators have 'criticised' the fresco faces in the church proper as being more rustic and coarse than we are accustomed to in the stylised features of Byzantine art. Perhaps. But one could also say that what they lose in spiritual sophistication they make up for in spontaneity and naturalness. These frescoes belong to the mid 14th century.

The paintings in the porch are slightly earlier. I like the majesty of the 'Pancreator' in the dome, surrounded by apostles, looking at His creation (and God saw that all things He had made were good). There is much interesting detail in the 'Last Judgement' and one wonders whether here, too, as Michelangelo did in the Sistine Chapel, the painter features some of his critics and enemies among the denizens of hell. We shall never know. I thought the multitudinous, circular haloes in nearly all of the frescoes had a notable high-lighting effect on what would otherwise have appeared to be crowded 'canvases'. It was nevertheless a bit of a shock in the 'Communion of the Apostles', in the apse, to see that five of them were without haloes. They looked crestfallen. When I asked a question in simple Greek, the caretaker-guide let fly in a torrent that left me speechless and uncomprehending. I thanked him rather effusively which served only to trigger part two of his explanation. With only the slightest encouragement I could have had parts three, four and five as well. Instead I gave him a suitable donation and, as we had already seen all we could absorb, bade him *Kalimera*. There is a booklet available that explains the history and themes of the frescoes.

It is a precious experience to see in this small church in Cyprus, frescoes, intact and vibrant, that pre-date Leonardo and his contemporaries by hundreds of years.

* * *

We drove on to Galata and Kakopetria where there are several other Byzantine churches worth visiting, notably the Panayia Podhitou in Galata, built in the early 16th century and containing some Italo-Byzantine frescoes. We chose instead to visit Agios Nicholaos tis Stegis, off a minor road, just 4kms south of the village of Kakopetria. You can, if you prefer, walk up the Karyotis stream track. With a name like St Nicholas of the Roof we thought it worth a visit and it was.

The church, like that of Asinou, was originally part of a monastery complex which flourished during the Middle Byzantine period and also under the rule of the Franks. At one time, the monastery had many monks and, according to foreign visitors, was revered as equal in standing to that of Kykkos. Its prestige was heightened when the Franks, continuing an old feud between the Christian churches of the East and West, tried to Latinise the Greek Orthodox Church and about 1260 exiled the Greek Orthodox archbishop from Nicosia to St Nicholas. The monastic community continued in existence until the mid-19th century when the church and its environs became the property of the archbishops. During the summer months the area that formerly supported the monastery now plays host to relays of city kids on church sponsored camping holidays.

The small church, dating from 1025, is built in the classic form of cross-in-square surmounted by a dome. About a century later, though some say as late as the end of the 13th century (after the archbishops were rusticated there), a domed porch was added and a second roof, steep-pitched to dislodge snow in winter, and covering the pre-existing roof and dome. The tiles of the earlier roof are clearly visible and contribute to the overall appearance of the church as a barn with a couple of lofts.

A composed and gentle, middle-aged man, who spoke excellent, self-taught English, showed us around the frescoes which date, despite their apparent homogeneity, from the 11th to the 17th century. That span of six centuries in so confined a space allows one to appreciate the extraordinary continuity of Byzantine art. The whole church is covered with frescoes, their locations following the usual pattern of Pantocrator in the dome, Virgin in the apse and Last Judgement in the porch. Our guide, a fountain of knowledge on the history and symbolism of each painting, spoke in soft, reverential tones, almost as if he were afraid that one of the myriad of saints represented might come down and smite him if his commentary were too casual. As he is on permanent duty at the church I won't repeat here any of his comments. Other frescoes that appealed to me are the Raising of Lazarus from the Dead (obligatory, it seems in Cyprus), a solemn 17th century St Nicholas in what looked like chasuble and stole, a procession of saints and martyrs, one of the latter of whom has the interesting name of Bacchus and a panel on the south vault from the mid-14th century, in which Mary, enveloped in what looks like a womb sac is breastfeeding a blond Jesus, while one of the figures on the top, nearest Mary on her left, seems to be about to clap. The ground floor is full of vigorous looking saints, impossible to identify, though the curator-guide seems to know a lot of them. He will certainly show you one of the most famous and cherished frescoes in the church, the Forty Martyrs of Sebaste, which is from the 12th century. The story of the martyrs is popular in Cyprus and was especially dear to the hearts of the Byzantine soldiery. It appears that forty Christian soldiers were persecuted for their beliefs during the late Roman period in Armenia. They were stripped and told to stand in a freezing lake while their former mates lit huge bonfires and made barbecues in a concerted effort to get them to retract. But they all resisted the temptation. Then, when the order was given to stone them, one poor chap decided he had suffered enough and leaped out, only to have his place taken by a Roman soldier-onlooker, impressed by their bravery. In a miraculous acknowledgement of their fortitude and steadfastness forty crowns appeared in the sky, one above the head of each and thus did they all become martyrs. The army liked it because it promoted group solidarity and a doggedness of spirit, with the reward of victory in the end. There is a similar fresco at Asinou.

The composed man was saying goodbye at the door to a couple of other visitors with whom he'd shared his wisdom, Sandra and Amee had gone outside to look at the countryside and I had slipped back in for another look at one of the paintings. Suddenly I heard the massive key turn in the lock. It felt chilly and a little eerie to be left alone in the 'almost dark' of the old church, surrounded on all sides by so many of the holy and vividly dead. But some light did come in through gaps and cracks so I hastened to the great wooden door and pounded out my presence on it somewhat to the consternation of the mild mannered custodian who was already some way down the path. He had never locked anybody in before and thought for a fleeting moment that a judgement was being called down on him. Outside he introduced me to his aunt, a serene-faced, old lady who came to visit him once a week. 'You're lucky you caught me,' he said, 'we go to a quiet place for lunch', as if there were a noisy or rowdy place nearby!

Despite my interest in 12th century frescoes, I, too, felt hungry and went off to look for the others.

* * *

Kakopetria, in the Solea Valley, is a picturesque village about 650 m above sea level, on the main road to Troodos and just short of 60 kms southwest of Nicosia. It is a popular hillside resort and a convenient drive for weekend excursionists from the capital, in search of a cooler environment during the hot summer months, or of freshly caught trout for lunch almost any time. Its name comes from two Greek words, *kakos*, meaning bad, or useless and *petria*, meaning a place of rocks. Put the two together and they indicate the plentiful supply of local rock used for building both villages, the new and the old. Near the bridge at the entrance to the new village and not far from the church, there is a long, egg-shaped rock, encased in cement, around which, hand in hand, the village priest used to lead newly married couples. Three times round the rock, saying the appropriate prayers and their marriage would turn out to be rock solid, or so the story goes. I'm not aware of any historical research on the outcomes but if their homes were built of the same rock, they would certainly last.

There is a magnificent old flour mill not far from the rock, near where the two rivers meet. Solidly built from the 'useless' stone it is at least four storeys tall with a covered, wooden veranda running all the length of the first and third levels. Steps with a slatted, wooden railing, zigzag up to the various floors. Two pagoda-like, wooden structures, on the roof, give the old mill an attractive eastern appearance. Roofing, rails, window lattices and shutters, as well as verandas and other balcony-type projections are all coloured a muted brown which harmonises superbly with the old stone. The flour mill is now a restaurant, called simply 'The Mill' and was being refurbished last time I saw it. I can't think of a more pleasant and atmospheric place to enjoy a good meal, though with all that water about I wonder about mosquitoes in high summer. Perhaps the rivers don't run then.

Kakopetria has a generous supply of restaurants, some first floor, others just off the narrow main street. Round and about a charming, central square, which overlooks thousands of apple trees growing in the Solea, there are several outdoor ones. We chose an off-street one, near the square, where a man, turning a choice of meats on a spit, attracted our attention. We made our way through the restaurant proper to a covered veranda overlooking half a hillside and seemingly suspended in space over a deep drop, steep enough to make you ask yourself– 'what if?' There, fortified by an excellent local beer, we enjoyed a *halloumi* cheese salad, barbecued chicken, *souvla* (lamb roasted on a spit), accompanied by generous helpings of beans and french fries. Not *haute cuisine*, but delicious nonetheless, inexpensive and accompanied by a free frisson every time I looked over the balcony.

A favourite meal in Cyprus is the traditional *meze*, for which a minimum of four people is required. It's a meal that comes to you in waves like the sea, an additional wave or two often catching you unexpectedly when you've thought the tide already full in. Ordering is simple, once you've said *meze* and chosen between 'fish, or fowl', you sit back, relax and let it all happen. Successively your table is covered with a series of dishes, just a few of which would provide a meal in themselves. No two *mezes* are necessarily the same but most will start you off with a saucer or two of olives, of the black and dark green varieties, swimming in a rich garlic sauce accompanied by fresh bread and a lemon dip. Although much depends on the season of the year and the patron's own gusto, there usually follows a Greek salad, with side dishes of *halloumi* (a special cheese made from sheep or goats' milk) and *loundza* (a kind of ham) both often fried together and *kalamari* rings, all accompanied by a variety of garnishes such as *humus*, *tahini* (a sesame paste), *taramasalata* (cod's roe with olive oil pate) and, of course, yoghurt. In all there could be up to fifteen appetisers, varying according to season and the secret is to take a little of each. Each one whets and satisfies the appetite in age-tested, gastronomic sequence. In relays thereafter come the meat dishes, *souvlakia* (grilled meat kebabs), *sheftalia* (a grilled, well flavoured sausage), both beloved of Greeks anywhere and rather delicious. After this it's the turn of marinated pork (*afelia*) and *dolmadhes* (rice and minced lamb, rolled sausage-like in dark green vine leaves). This is when you think the tide is definitely in, but you are soon surprised by either spare ribs or lamb chops with coriander, maybe even a *moussaka* (a baked dish of mince, sliced potatoes and aubergines, familiar to all who enjoy Greek cuisine). All these dishes are accompanied by a variety of vegetables and potatoes. Cypriots who can grow up to three crops of potatoes in a good (adequate rain) year and who export them even to Ireland, or so I'm unreliably told, are expert at cooking them in all ways save in their jackets. No potato, born and bred in Cyprus, bursts when cooked into powdery puffs of white fluff but I do like the small ones, well oiled, garnished with parsley and swimming in butter.

I used sea imagery to introduce the above paragraph on *mezes* so it would be unfair if I didn't mention the fish *meze*. Prawns, *kalamari*, octopus and several varieties of charcoal-grilled, or oil-fried, fish, often imported, make a pleasant change to the traditional meat-dominated *meze*.

Though an island, Cyprus has too shallow a sea shelf for good fishing but you can, of course, get local fish. We once had a fish *meze* in Latsi, a little fishing village about 35 kms out of Pafos and it was delicious. When we'd finished the numerous courses I never saw such a mound of bones in my life – enough to start a piscine cemetery and there were only six of us!

Then there are desserts, pastries, for those who can still stomach them. A favourite seems to be an almond-walnut concoction in a rich, cinnamon flavoured syrup. Fruit and coffee are the concluding items on the *meze* menu. Drinks are extra but one can get an excellent *meze* for about US$12 person. The *meze* is a slow, opulent meal, where the talking is as important as the eating. One should not die without having one.

* * *

The Troodos is full of quaint, traditional villages, all similar but each with its own individual charm, one famous for the growing of a particular fruit, another for the making of a favoured wine, yet a third for its own, village-made handicrafts. Others survive as 'distinguished' because of some cultural, religious or political association with the past.

All these villages become much more enchanting if you visit after the coach loads of tourists have packed up and gone for the day, unless, of course, you happen to be one such tourist yourself – then you'll have enjoyed a different aspect of village life – the camaraderie and commercial enterprise of a village on display.

* * *

Platres is a village we've been to more than once. It sits high in the Troodos at 1,200 m, half-hidden in the pine-wooded hills that surround it like a backdrop curtain. It is cool, fresh as tonic, with a reputation as a health resort and was originally laid out like a hill station in India as a retreat from summer heat for colonial administrators. It is one of the biggest of the hill resort villages and has all the amenities you would expect in such favoured and idyllic surroundings: hotels, apartments, shops, post office and bank, restaurants and now, of course, take-aways. It is a hub from which popular forest walks radiate and, according to its brochure, it's also possible to ride, fish and even shoot, though at what I don't know unless it be at birds. Better a slug than the torture of glue, I suppose. Walk horizontally across the village, looking south towards the distant Mediterranean, as I did late one afternoon after a rather bibulous lunch with friends, and you have the distinct feeling that you are living 'on the edge', so sudden and steep the drop. There is a sensation of being suspended in space. In time, as well, for Platres, with its brick villas, self-possessed high street, healthy, nearby walks and general air of unspoken, contented conformity, is an English village transplanted and still very popular with the English ex-pats.

But others came, as well – rich Israelis, wealthy Alexandrian Greeks and Arab potentates in the years immediately following the Second World War, until they were driven away by the *Enosis* conflict and the armed struggle that accompanied it. Farouk of Egypt once had a villa near Prodromos, 12 kms farther on, the highest village in Cyprus, noted for its apple growing. What kind of Garden of Eden Farouk made of it is not recorded. Depending on how you look at it, Platres may have come down in the world since those days but in the woods you can still hear the nightingales sing.

* * *

Thirty-five kms west of Limassol is, I think, the most beautiful of the wine producing villages on the southern slopes of the Troodos, Omodos. It has a wide and lovely, cobbled square with, at one end, an old Byzantine monastery and now, also, a modern church. The insistent, vocant peeling of the bells as we sat outside a *cafeneion* in the evening sun, was reminiscent for me of similar sounds heard in the hill villages of northern Italy many decades ago, when after a day's hiking in the mountains, our little group found shelter for the night and restored the liquid levels of our dehydrated bodies. Before we had finished our coffees, people, singly or in pairs, were moving towards the church which is said to contain a fragment of the True Cross and some of the hempen rope that bound the hands of Jesus. I have no doubt that the village church in Italy, put to it, could match these relics with some of its own.

While Sandra looked at some of the embroidery for which Omodos is also famous, I visited an old wine press exhibited in a restored old house belonging to a gentleman named Linos. The wine press is also named 'Linos'! He took me down the spiral staircase to the cellar, explaining, as we went, the old methods of production and storage. Basically, no different, except that his press was small, made of wood and manually operated. The house was still occupied too, beds made up, a vine growing, flowers in pots and amphorae standing. There were wines for sale – good reds in unmarked bottles which we drank at home later on. Back in the square Sandra had found a table cloth she liked, French silk thread on Irish linen with a Cypriot motif, brown on ecru, 2.5 m by 1.5. Elsewhere it would have cost a small fortune, in Omodos on that day, only £60 sterling. It had been a long winter and the tour buses had not yet returned. Those tourists who did come stayed down at the coast in the sun and warmth. The lady needed some cash turnover. Sandra was convinced she was getting a bargain. The only problem is that we shall have to buy a much bigger table to fit it and find a house with a much larger dining room to put the table in. I think those might be the very reasons that she bought it in the first place.

Who are the Cypriots?

29

WHO ARE THE CYPRIOTS?

It is not my intention to go deep into the millennia before Christ when human beings first set foot in Cyprus. In 8000 BC there were hunter-gatherers around Limassol whose favourite animal food, judging from the bones discarded in a diner-cave was elephants and hippopotami. They must have eaten the lot.

A thousand years later, the people of the flat heads and round houses turned up at Khirokitia. These we have already met. There is some suggestion that they may have come originally from eastern Anatolia, forced south when land became scarce after the discovery of agriculture but we'll let that one pass. They were an aceramic, Neolithic people, the ruins of whose settlement on the hillside above the Maroni river, continue to haunt the visitor long after he has left the scene.

Next came the pottery users, followed, in three stages (Early, Middle and Late) by the users of bronze. We have visited one of their Late Bronze Age cities at Enkomi. They were a sophisticated, literate and cultured people of whom we shall learn much more when we learn to decipher their Cypro-Minoan script. They wrote a lot and not just bills of lading and IOUs. There were poets among them.

But, as Sir David Hunt observes in his epilogue to *Footprints in Cyprus* it is from the 14th century BC that the continuity of the history and culture of Cyprus really begins, with the coming of the Greeks. These Greeks, alias Mycenaeans, alias Achaeans, were warrior-merchants, not much better than pirates, really (except that they were *Greek* pirates). In Cyprus, in, or about 1200 BC, they razed to the ground and set fire to the Late Bronze Age cities of Enkomi and Kition. The former, we know, they rebuilt – in rectangles. We could, in fact, call them 'the Geometrics', or even 'the Oblongs' as, for all their buildings, the rectangle was their favourite shape.

Though these Greeks (the Oblongs) continued to live in Cyprus and subsequently paid tribute to occupying powers from Assyria,

Persia and Macedonia (the Ptolomies), they remained as Greek as the Greeks of mainland Greece whose own city states suffered equally extensive periods of foreign domination. It is from this time that we are justified in calling the people who lived on this island Greek Cypriots.

The Romans annexed Cyprus in 58 BC and remained until 325 AD, a period 76 years longer than the Ottoman occupation. The biological urge being what it is and the attractiveness of Greek women being also axiomatic, no one should be surprised that there were Roman Cypriots, just as today there are American Cypriots and English Cypriots and Irish Cypriots. These, the progeny, that is, of Roman soldiers and administrators and Greek Cypriot women, would all, however, have spoken Greek. As Sir David Hunt observes in his epilogue, St Paul, when he visited Pafos in 45 AD (almost 100 years after the Roman annexation) would have felt himself as much in Greece as when he was in Corinth. According to Sir David it would not have occurred to him to think he was anywhere else.

When the Roman empire split and Cyprus was ruled from Constantinople, Greek Cypriots would have noticed no change, at least not in their language and culture. They continued to think of themselves as Greek, just as they naturally did, sometimes stubbornly, occasionally defiantly, under the Franks, the Venetians, the Ottomans and the English.

Sometimes, as happens in all such cases, those belonging to the Occupying Powers, having intermarried with the locals, became more Cypriot than the Cypriots themselves, at other times, however, (and I'm thinking here of the governing Franks and Venetians) they treated the locals badly, confiscating their lands and turning their owners into serfs. Their religion, too, Orthodox Christianity, they relegated to the inferior position of a schismatic church. The Latin Church, their Church, took over the four major Dioceses of Nicosia, Famagusta, Limassol and Pafos,at the same time rusticating the four Orthodox prelates to four villages from which they had to administer their dioceses.

When the Ottomans took over Cyprus in 1571, they reversed many of these wrongs, returning their land to the Greek Cypriot serfs and in the process abolishing serfdom itself. They also returned their dioceses to the Orthodox episcopacy. The Catholic churches they either turned into mosques, sold to the Greek Orthodox Church, or converted into warehouses, stores and stables. Catholics were given the option of becoming Greek Orthodox or Muslim; Greek Orthodox, if they wanted to avoid punitive taxes, had the single option of becoming 'believers in the Prophet'. Many, in fact, 'converted'. It is probably true to say that the Catholic Church never recovered from the confiscations it suffered and the penal laws enacted against it at this time. There is, therefore, a real sense in which one could say that the coming of the Ottomans was a liberation for the Greek Cypriots and a persecution for the Latins.

But the Ottomans did one more thing, strikingly similar to what their Turkish descendants are doing today in the northern third of the country – they drafted in thousands of mainlanders and gave them land.

These were widely distributed throughout the country, in a ratio of 1 to 5 of the local population, and became the ancestors of that second ethnic group who are now entitled to call themselves Cypriots, Turkish Cypriots. Over a period of centuries these newcomers established a *modus vivendi* with the Greek Cypriots and, while retaining their own identity, lived more or less harmoniously with them. Unfortunately for some 50 or 60 years now, the differences between them in culture and ethnic allegiance, were exploited by both the occupying colonial power, Britain, and by the two other interested powers, Greece and Turkey. Christopher Hitchens makes this clear in his book *Hostage to History, Cyprus from the Ottomans to Kissinger*. He also details the malign influence of the United States on the Cyprus situation during the critical years before the invasion. After the 1974 war the Turkish Cypriot population moved north in fear for their families' safety in the south and under the imperative of a compulsory ethnic exchange. That is the position today, though one should add that many of those who moved north have now, out of disenchantment with life in the TRNC, moved further afield, principally to Britain. Turkish Cypriots have been part of the landscape of Cyprus for the past 400 years and have as much right to be considered Cypriot as the Scottish settlers, who, under Cromwell, were brought to Ireland, have to be considered Irish, or the Dutch Boers to be considered

South Africans. If I do not write of them specifically in the following pages it is merely because I have not lived among them. Moreover, many of the characteristics I do write about, for example, honesty, patterns of family behaviour and so on, are equally applicable to all Cypriots.

So, what manner of people are these Cypriots, anyway? The people of Cyprus, like the people of Goa, have always been admired for their honesty. I'm not quite certain whether this stems from adherence to a moral imperative, or is the consequence of a natural – and inherited – reluctance to steal from one's own family. For the family in Cyprus is island-wide. Here, as the saying goes, everyone is related to everyone else, within the same ethnic grouping, of course – there is little miscegenation. So, it's not surprising if Panos from Pafos does not steal from Loucas in Larnaka; they're either cousins, or cousins of cousins and if Panos needs something that Loucas has, he'll ask for it and, more than likely, get it. Or, to be more accurate, that's the way it used to be. Nowadays things are changing. The uncertainty with which people have lived – and are living – since the war of 74, when a third of the Greek Cypriot population was rendered homeless almost overnight, has had two apparently opposite effects. The first is that an attachment to material possessions is seen as senseless: you could lose the lot tomorrow 'if the Turks come down', as they were on the verge of doing recently when Greece and Turkey almost went to war over a little island in the eastern Aegean, called Imia, really an outcrop of rock that wouldn't feed a goat. The second, seemingly contradictory attitude, is actually a corollary of the first: 'spend up large and enjoy the good life now because you know what happened 25 years ago.' So, today Loucas from Larnaka is less likely to have anything in reserve to help out his cousin from Pafos and anyway, they're probably both deeply in debt to the bank and driving expensive cars, bought on hire purchase. Who wants to throw the first stone?

Still, the village and the village virtues die slowly. There is hardly a Greek Cypriot alive today who does not relate with nostalgia to his own, or his parents' village, who does not visit it at every opportunity, taking sustenance from its ancient mores and gladness from its homely *joie de vivre*. Among those village virtues honesty was – and is – paramount; nothing can hurt the harmonious functioning of village life more than its harbouring a thief.

It was the Greeks who first used the word ostracise to mean the secret, consensual agreement to remove from any social grouping an unacceptable member. Not unlike our peculiar custom of blackballing applicants from membership of a club or association because of some perceived, unacceptable trait (how often in the past merely on the grounds of race!). Shells, or ball bearings- what's the difference – somebody, for whatever reason, is being excluded from the group. The Inuit of Northern Canada and the Eskimo of Arctic regions follow a similar custom and manage to do without courts and police and prisons. I doubt, however, if being cast out to walk the Mesaoria of Cyprus would have the same capital effect as being turned loose to tramp the endless tundra of the Arctic but the message would have been the same: leave us, you are no longer worthy to be a member of our community and, in both cases, the victims would have seen the justice of it. Shame, the shame brought by miscreants on their families and villages, helps to keep many Cypriots on the straight and narrow. And not only Cypriots, of course. Here, however, because of the number of villages (600) and the closeness of families, this common enough human sentiment has the force of a new commandment in a Cypriot endecalogue: thou shalt not shame thy family or thy village.

I have a friend, an Irishman, who wanted to build a house in a beautiful, coastal village in Cyprus. All his documents were in order but still nothing happened. No permit. Then on a Sunday morning some time later, he and his wife were invited to a local taverna to meet the *mukhtar*, the village headman, representative of all the village elders. They met, had a drink together and talked about this, that and the other. Nothing serious, mind you. Nothing about the building. A few days later he got his permit. Without knowing it, he had passed the test and been approved for membership of the village community. Without the *mukhtar's* approval, however, despite all the legal documents being in order, he would not have been allowed to build in that village.

And it nearly didn't happen. My genial friend, unfamiliar at the time with local custom and ignorant of Greek, somehow misconstrued his invitation, conveyed by phone in English, to go down to the village restaurant at noon for a drink and to meet the *mukhtar*. Oh, the vagaries of inter-language communication! He thought he was being hospitably invited to have a drink at noon and eat the *mukhtar* in the local taverna. Understandably he concluded that the *mukhtar* was a local delicacy, one he'd not yet had the pleasure of tasting. It was a warm, lazy Sunday morning and my friend took his time – the delicacy wouldn't melt, would it? At about 12.20 pm he got an urgent call from his bank manager – would he please hurry up as the *mukhtar* was waiting! He needed to ask only one question, then quickly turning to his wife, he said, 'the bloody *mukhtar* isn't grub at all, it's the village headman – we've insulted him – let's go'. My friend apologised to the *mukhtar* and told the story against himself. They all enjoyed it (he tells a story well) and the ice was broken. So it was that, without benefit of blackballing, the vetting took place and my friend's chemistry was judged congenial to that of the village.

Despite the feeling of impermanence with which they now live, despite, too, a sometimes arrogant and ostentatious front, the Greek Cypriot today still respects the norms of the village community. These he took with him when he settled in the city and one continually hears evidence of it. In Cyprus you need never count your change.

One man told me that, though he himself was unaware of it, he had been unwittingly short-changed at a neighbourhood supermarket. It so happened that he was then out of Cyprus (off-island, as the Cypriots say) for a while and didn't return to that particular supermarket for some time. When he eventually did, to his great surprise, the manager greeted him like a lost brother: 'thank God you came back,' he said, 'I've been looking everywhere for you, all over the neighbourhood, without ever finding you.' Had he won a raffle, my friend wondered, or was he being rewarded for being the millionth customer of the supermarket to buy a slab of *halloumi*? 'Our apologies,' the manager said, 'we are very sorry but the last time you were here you were overcharged – three Cypriot pounds and 20 cents,' (about US$7) and he shook hands with him. At the same time he instructed the cashier to deduct that amount from my friend's bill and presented him with a bottle of wine. In a world of Watergates and Whitewatergates that manager's simple act of restitution strikes one as particularly wholesome.

Another friend told me that once when he had briefly used the telephone he left his almost unused ten pound ($20) card in the slot. Back home he discovered his mistake and naturally assumed it was gone, gratefully pocketed by the next customer and by now responsible for a surprise call to a loved one in Moscow, Calcutta, or Timbuktu. But he was wrong. On retracing his steps he found that it had been removed from the slot and carefully placed on top of the card-call box, waiting for him to retrieve it. In other parts of the world, in Italy, for example (and Italians have 'explained' this to me on numerous occasions) if you drop something unawares, or leave it behind you on a table or desktop through forgetfulness, there is a ready, unspoken assumption that you have done this deliberately and have no further use for the article concerned, whether it be your hat, your umbrella or your wallet. Here in Cyprus the expectation is that you'll return to collect it and it's kept safe for you.

My neighbour recently had the experience of dropping on the footpath of a busy street a large sum of money – hundreds of pounds in notes, which he had tucked into an envelope for a specific purchase. As soon as he returned to his apartment he missed it and threw up his hands in horror and despair. He besought the gods to flail him for his carelessness. On recovering his composure, however, he decided to retrace his steps, clinging to a hope engendered by many visits to Cyprus over the years that the envelope would have been handed in to a nearby shop. He asked in several but nothing had been handed in. He was about to admit reluctantly that, at last, as was probably inevitable, Cypriots had succumbed to moral laxity when he found the envelope – empty. And, a little farther on, the entire sum of money lying on the footpath still in its roll, undisturbed. Somebody must have kicked it out of the envelope and then knowingly, or unknowingly left it to its fate. This incident confirmed the decision of my friend to make his permanent home in Cyprus. I, being sceptical, advised him to tempt the gods no more.

My own experience is very limited. Once I arrived at the check-out of a supermarket at a busy time of day with my loaded trolley.

Half way through her spiralling logarithms the checkout girl noticed what she thought was a higher than normal price on my beer cans. She excused herself, gave a cheery, placating wave to the queue behind me and disappeared 'back stage' to consult with some know-all oracle. 'Too much,' she said with a grin on her return, 'they put the wrong stickers on it' and contentedly punched in the lower price on her abacus. I felt that, despite the inconvenience, the queue was on her side. The error, by the way, would not have cost me more than 50 cents.

There is petty crime in Cyprus. Of course, there is – perpetrated mostly by 15 to 17 year-old school boys who look for excitement during the school holidays. With virtually full employment the incentive to steal simply isn't there. Much of the more serious crime, drugs and prostitution, for example, is imported, mainly, it appears, from Russia and countries of the former communist block, more specifically, in the case of Cyprus, from Bulgaria and Romania. One hears talk of a Russian mafia which has taken over the small-time, local variety, especially in the coastal towns. One politician recently made the comment that the biggest statistical increase in employment in Cyprus is in ballet dancing! He wasn't referring to an increase in the number of children taking classical ballet lessons but to the recruitment by the local cabaret industry of large numbers of 'ballet dancers' from Eastern Europe. He went on to say that this signifies nothing less than 'an alarming expansion of prostitution', which, he allowed, goes hand in hand with the spread of drug abuse. A total of 1,108 artistes were working in cabarets and night clubs in Cyprus according to a reported statement of the police immigration superintendent in March 1998 while the police chief speaking of the growth of prostitution called it 'the new fruit of our society, imported from abroad'. 'Crime free' is no longer a description that we can unreservedly apply to Cyprus. Organised crime, protection rackets, murder vendettas and drug-related offences are all on the increase and it is hardly a matter for complacency that their incidence is still so much lower than elsewhere. The minister of justice himself has revealed the staggering statistic for Cyprus that one third of the 15-16 year olds on the island had indulged in addictive substances, especially alcohol. Youthful experimentation? Possibly – there is still no widespread real drug culture among the young in Cyprus.

But there is some local white collar crime. Not a lot, but some. Take cars, for example. Cars matter to Cypriots, not just as means of transport but, perhaps more importantly, as status symbols. Whether owned by the banks or not, one sees proportionally more BMWs, Mercedes, Volvos, Golf GTIs and Cruisers of the 4-door, 4-wheel drive varieties in Cyprus than in other countries. They are almost attachments to the person and just as the English say 'hurt my dog, hurt me', Cypriots say 'damage my car, damage me'. And they do. Out of fits of pique, revenge, or jealousy they blow them up. They're not interested in blowing up people, mind you, but bombing cars seems quite a pastime.

Despite all this increase in crime, a judge told me the other day that 70 percent of a lawyer's time in Cyprus is taken up with financial matters, now that Cyprus has taken over from Lebanon as the financial capital of the Middle East. Offshore companies with their offices in Cyprus spring up like mushrooms and banks are more common than petrol stations. Of the banks there are 8 domestic and 26 foreign owned with several more being built for a population in the 'free areas' in 1995 of 645,000. Since 1974, 22,216 offshore companies have been registered, most of which are 'brass plate' companies only, taking advantage of the low 4.5 percent tax on off-shore sector profits. Fully fledged off-shore companies numbered 1,168 in 1995, employing a staff of 6,440, about two-thirds of whom are foreigners. This sector alone brought approximately $355m. into the local economy in 1995, a tidy little sum that, spread out, would give every man, woman and child in the country a sparrow's nest egg of $550 ($2,750 for a little aviary of five, enough for a family holiday in the mountains!). The total number of off-shore companies in 1997 was 31,739 and these contributed 3.8 percent (or CP168.8m) to the country's GNP. Apart from the recalcitrant problem of the occupation of Northern Cyprus, it's a good time to be alive and well in the Greek administered part of the island.

One hears as well of another contrary effect of the island's close network of family relationships. The police, it is said, working within the wide and intricate web of the clan as they do, often refrain from pressing charges, especially in cases of the smaller, statutory offences, though instances of 'corruption' at higher level also surface from time to time. Blood, one woman told me, in a variant on the English idiom, is more sticky than water. And it's certainly true that you can get a much better bargain when buying an item of furniture or a piece of electrical equipment, if you have a local Greek Cypriot do the bargaining for you. But they know that, too, and have the good grace to laugh at it. Cypriots live too close to the Middle East not to have absorbed the rituals of deal-making.

A corollary of the family network is nepotism. One hears continual griping about the lack of fair treatment on merit for all; 59 percent believe there is either none, or very little. Significantly, a bill promoting meritocracy was introduced to parliament in 1993, but it still lingers there, too much of a hot potato to handle. The minister of justice was demoted in a cabinet reshuffle in April 1997 because, he said, he would not bow to pressure and use his influence at the request of a colleague to effect certain promotions within the police. 'I have failed in my bid', he said 'to stop nepotism'. One man told me that he had spent six years in the US studying business management and economics, ending up with a master's degree. Shortly after his return he applied for a position in a government department. He had more than the minimum qualifications required and was eventually called for an interview which, he thought, went off successfully. He wasn't appointed and naturally thought that a better qualified or more experienced applicant had got the job. Two months later he found out that a cousin of the manager, with only two years post-secondary education had been appointed. He was furious. Jobs in the civil service are well paid, have good superannuation terms and carry a cachet of prestige. Stress is less than in the private sector.

George Lanitis, an entertaining feature writer for the *Cyprus Weekly*, experienced a good deal of trouble trying to contact an 'officer in the civil service'. He tells this story – the story of the billy-goat of Athalassa – which I hope he won't mind my repeating. It appears that some years back, senior civil servants from the ministry of agriculture discovered in a village not far from Nicosia a billy-goat belonging to a local farmer. They greatly admired how this billy-goat worked tirelessly at his task of impregnating nanny goats and were so impressed with his performance that they offered his master a considerable amount of money from the Republicís treasury and bought the animal to work for the government at an agricultural farm. There, George continues, the billy-goat ate well, washed regularly, slept softly but, after the first day, when he truly performed magnificently, he only serviced one goat before eleven in the morning and thereafter lay in the sun scratching his rather enormous private parts. The civil servants who bought him were chagrined and disappointed and drove him back out to the farm belonging to his former owner. The farmer, on hearing the sad tale, remonstrated with the billy-goat:

'You have brought shame on me and my family. You lack energy and are lazy. Now these gentlemen want their money back. Whatever happened to you?'

The billy-goat raised his horns, sighed deeply and said:

'Boss, when I worked for you I was working for my keep and earning through my abilities, good money for you. Now I am a civil servant and like the rest of them, I work a little, eat a little, rest a little in the sun and scratch myself and whatever happens, I get my fat cheque at the end of each and every month, plus a pension at the end of my meritorious service.' The response of the men from the ministry of agriculture is not recorded. A story that I'm sure is told, tongue in cheek, about civil servants everywhere.

In Cyprus, however, more than elsewhere, it's who you know that counts in seeking employment. There is widespread support for the idea of helping your own, whether 'your own' be family or village, this, even when other things are not quite equal. Again that 'stickiness' of blood. A brother helped by a brother is like a strong city.

Having said all that, unemployment in Cyprus is low at 3.1 percent in 1996, a figure that any country in the European Union would be happy to have. But it has been lower, below 2 percent, and the labour minister blames the increase on the slow rate of growth in the economy and the influx of foreign workers. There is a conundrum here as a large proportion of the legal, and illegal, foreign workers take the jobs that the Cypriots do not want to do. Of a total of approximately 26,000 legal foreign workers on the island, 10,800 work in the construction industry, agriculture and tourism. A further 6,500, mostly Filipinos and Sri Lankans, work as house help. Targeting foreign workers may not, of itself, reduce the unemployment percentage.

Cypriots are often accused – indeed they often accuse themselves – of another kind of targeting, that of racism, the principal victims of which are immigrant workers. A propensity to equate the worth and dignity of the person with the work status of that person seems to be at the root of it. Not, by any means, an exclusively Cypriot attitude but one, perhaps, that they should be more than ordinarily sensitive to, for, in a historical role reversal, it is precisely how Cypriots themselves were treated in the immediate post-war decades when many of them emigrated to Britain, Australia and elsewhere in search of a new and better life. They, too, then, in their adopted countries performed the menial jobs and suffered consequent humiliations. There is also, too often, an unworthy tendency to generalise, as for example, when all Russians, Romanians or whoever, are categorised by one lower denominator. It was heartening recently to see something being done at official level to counteract these base attitudes. Toward the end of May 1998 the Nicosia Municipal Council organised a ten-day festival to celebrate ethnic diversity in Cyprus, surely an innovative and even courageous step in the right direction.

A large number of Cypriots, however, also work in tourism, especially in senior staffing and on the managerial side: in fact, up to 25 percent of the country's total work force, either directly or indirectly, is employed in the industry, which grosses 21 percent of the country's GNP. About 2,000,000 visitors come to the island each year, 40 percent of whom are from Britain and most of the rest from countries in the European Community, especially Greece and Germany. The aim is to make it 2.7 million by the turn of the century, – pretty dense saturation, you might think, for a country whose 'free area' is no more than 4,734 sq. kms. There has been a significant drop in hotel occupancy in 1996 for which more than one factor is probably to blame. One unpredictable factor is the change over time of the mass popularity of tourist destinations. Once it was the French Riviera, then Spain's Costa Brava, over more recent times Cyprus became a favoured destination, now the star of Turkey is in the ascendant, a bitter pill for Cypriots to swallow. But there are some things that Cyprus can do to retain its share of the market and these have been identified by the Cyprus Tourist Organisation as a return to the ways of traditional hospitality, a greater care for the environment and the packaging of Cyprus in all its diverse attractiveness as a tourist destination. The 'island in the sun' cliché has been worked too hard in promoting Cyprus abroad. Sun, sea and sand, with, in several resorts, the addition of some spicy night-life, is no longer enough. According to the Board a better attempt must be made to mix the ubiquitous and attractive hedonism of lolling about in shorts on sandy beaches day after day – whether in France, Spain, Cyprus, or Morocco, it hardly matters – with an experience of the culture of its multi-layered past that Cyprus has to offer. A serious and prolonged decline in the number of tourists, for whatever reason, would have disastrous effects on the economy.

What kind of person is the young Cypriot, man or woman under 30? From my own observation and from studying several surveys it would seem that they are conservative, rather than radical or liberal. A recent (1995) fairly comprehensive survey reported in the *Cyprus Weekly* found that they were, in general, well educated, live with their parents, eschew political parties, are lonely and look forward to a marriage based on love, despite the fact that 13 per cent of marriages here are still arranged. Overwhelmingly they believe in God and the institution of the family. Homosexuality is not acceptable to the majority (63 percent), nor has it been legal here until very recently (May 1998), and their major concerns, besides 'the Cyprus problem', are drugs, road deaths and, surprisingly, Aids, which has a very low incidence here. 70 percent no longer believe in a marriage dowry and, as you'd expect, nearly 100 percent would like to get to know and have a relationship with the person they're going to marry – three-quarters of the males but less than half of the females would like this relationship to include sex. Whether they succeed or not (and presumably well over half don't) more than 50 percent are dissatisfied with their social lives. Their spare time they spend watching TV, listening to music, attending sports events (and sometimes playing sports, too) as well as going to discos and bars. All the ones I've met have been serious, cheerful and friendly and none ever thought of themselves as a statistic!

Over 90 percent of Cypriots are strongly attached to their native land and over 70 percent to their village or town. It's true that those who can manage it like to live elsewhere for a while. This was, in any case, inevitable until four years go, for those who sought a university education, as, until then, Cyprus did not have its own university. *Enosis* (union with Greece) seems a dead issue with only a fifth of the population expressing a strong attachment to Greece. I have, however, seen a few *Enosis* offices both in Nicosia and elsewhere but I doubt if they are much more than social clubs for those who fought in the EOKA underground in the 50s. Cypriots are passionately patriotic and the young men willingly spend 30 months in compulsory military service and report for exercise duty at regular intervals thereafter. They know that there is a Turkish army of 35,000 in the North and that, apart from the US, Turkey has the largest standing army among NATO countries yet they are not dispirited and neither do they cringe.

Divorce? There were 164 divorces in 1980 but this figure had climbed to 757 in 1995, representing a breakdown in 15 percent of marriages, an increase that is lamented by most Cypriots. A total of about 2,000 children are affected by divorce in Cyprus and another 2,000 have parents who are separated. Gender discrimination in the citizenship status of children of mixed marriages is legal. The child of a Cypriot male married to a non-Cypriot female becomes automatically a Cypriot citizen, not so if the mother is Cypriot and the father not. So too, a non-Cypriot male married to a Cypriot woman can apply for citizenship after one year's residence but if a non-Cypriot female is married to a Cypriot male she has to wait five years for the same privilege. Presumably a change in all such discriminatory legislation will have to take place before Cyprus joins the European Union.An ammendment to the citizenship law under which both male and female spouses of Cypriot citizens can apply for citizenship after two years of marriage was finally passed into law on December 10th 1998. Because divorce in any numbers is new to the country, the government has been slow to get involved administratively in helping single parent families. In 1991 (more recent statistics are not always available) 21 percent of single parent households headed by a woman were deemed 'poor', that is, on an annual income in 1991 of approximately $3,392 per annum but a much smaller percentage only 6.6, actually lived in poverty, owing to the strong tradition of family support. One has to bear in mind, too, that Cyprus was one of the least expensive countries in Europe to live in then and, if you additionally take into consideration that accommodation was nearly always provided by the parents of the woman, the income figure was not as bad as at first it seems. There is one reckoning that says, whether divorced or not, about 4 people in every 100 are today living below the poverty line. Although that calculation may be accurate one sees little or no evidence of it and I have never yet been approached by a beggar, or other indigent person. No doubt there are some but pride, dignity and self-respect tend to mask what poverty there is.

Non-Cypriots, who have lived in Cyprus longer than I, tell me that I will never understand Cyprus and the Cypriots if I look at their culture as 'Western' – by this they mean belonging to northern Europe. The culture here, they say, is a mix of Middle Eastern and Mediterranean and, to buttress their argument, they point to the lesser role of women in public life, the influence of the family, the importance of religion and religious feast days, the subtle and personal ways people have of doing business, the institution of 'pay-back' for favours received and the exaggerated role of men in public and domestic life. What can I say? Whilst it's true that all countries are to some extent prisoners of their geography, it is, nevertheless, not wholly convincing that countries which pride themselves on their Greco-Roman heritage, should find their cultures now so different from those of either Greece or Rome. In the end, all countries are excitingly different and delightfully themselves. Cyprus, too, is the sum of all its parts.

AFTERWORD

Another book could be written about all the places in Cyprus
I haven't been to – yet. A more comprehensive book, certainly,
a better book, maybe. I make no claim that what I have written
is more than a record of some of my own experiences, my
personal encounter with Cyprus. My hope is that others may
be enticed by it to extend their own encounters with this ancient
and pleasant land. There is so much to enjoy. So, for the
moment, I bid farewell to,

Cyprus, island of the sun, shining for 340 days a year,
to Cyprus, island of love, smiling for all 365 of them,
enchanting land, dedicated to Aphrodite and Barnabas,
both born here, uniting the profane and the holy,
seductive lanof a lover's gift from Julius Caesar to Cleopatra
and, after him, from Anthony, to the same 'serpent of Old Nile',
land of scintillating light and scorched earth,
land of golden beaches and no lakes or rivers worth talking about,
bewitching land of ancient shrines and ancient theatres still in use,
stark land of the tragedy of Desdemona and Othello,
happy land of the marriage of Richard and Berengaria,
divided land, welcoming land, land of two cultures,
gaunt, unfinished land of a thousand half-built buildings,
contrasting land of white high-rise structures
and small, dilapidated, brown houses,
land of disastrous earthquakes and burnt, stony plains,
fruitful land of the orchard and vine,
land of the 21st century and any other century you may wish to
name,

often cheek by jowl, the one with the other,
land of the ghosts of its many pasts,
Egyptian and Mycenaean, Byzantine and Roman,
Venetian, Turkish and British,
Phoenix land that again and again has risen up
from the smouldering ashes of spent empires,
proud land, sad land,
third largest island of the Mediterranean,
it's been good to be here.

SELECTED BIBLIOGRAPHY

a) General – history, politics and travel:

David Hunt (ed.), *Footprints in Cyprus – An illustrated History,* 1990.

Christopher Hitchens, *Hostage to History – Cyprus from the Ottomans to Kissinger*, 1997 (updated edition).

Lawrence Durrell, *Bitter Lemons*, London, 1957.

Colin Thubron, *Journey into Cyprus*, London, 1975.

Dr. Stavros Panteli, *The Making of Modern Cyprus from Obscurity to Statehood*, Interworld Publications Ltd, London 1990

The Cyprus Problem, published by Press and Information Office, Nicosia 1997.

The Republic of Cyprus, An Overview, published by Press and Information Office, Nicosia 1998.

b) General guides:

Barnaby Rogerson, *Cyprus (Cadogan Island Guides)*, 1994. Excellent text. No pictures.

Cyprus (Inside guides). Concise text. Beautiful pictures.

Kevork Keshishian, *Romantic Cyprus*, 1987.

Robert Bulmer, *Days Out in Cyprus*, 1988.

Cyprus Tourist Organisation, *Cyprus – 9000 Years of History and Civilisation*. Brief text with pictures.

George Karouzis and Christina G. Karouzis, Touring Guide of Cyprus, published by SELAS 1997

c) Specific guides:

Vassos Karageorghis, *The Cyprus Museum*

Paphos, Land of Aphrodite, fully illustrated by Renos G Lavithis, revised edition, 1994.

Maria Hadjisavva, *The Tomb of the Kings*. A colour guide.

Demos Christou, *Kourion: a Complete Guide to its Monuments and Local Museum,* 1994.

E Rizopoulou-Egoumenidou, T*he House of the Dragoman of Cyprus,*

1991.

Harvey Ayerst, *Bellapais Abbey*, 1994.

Handbook of Kykkos Monastery, 1995.

Bernard P Robinson, *St Paul's Visit to Cyprus*, Paroecia Latina, Paphos.

d) Nature guides:

Donald brown, *Walking in Cyprus – Cicesone Press Milnthaspe, Cumbria, 1995.*

William MacFarlane, *Cyprus Walks – Kyriakou Books, Limassol, Cyprus, 1994.*

Christos Georgiades, *Nature of Cyprus, Environment, Flora, Fauna – author*

Christos Georgiades, *Flowers of Cyprus, Plants of Medicine*, vols, I and II *– by author Nicosia, 1992.*

George Sfikas, *Wild Flowers of Cyprus – by Ejstathiadis Group S.A. '94.*

George Sfikas, *Birds and Mammals of Cyprus – by Ejstathiadis Group S.A. '96.*

G Elliot and R Dutton, *Know Your Rocks – An Introduction to Geology in Cyprus – by authors 1963 MAM, Nicosia, Cyprus.*